Images Out of Africa

The Virginia Garner Diaries of the Africa Motion Picture Project

Edited with an Introduction by Glenn Reynolds

Foreword by J. M. Burns

Photos by Virginia and Ray Garner

UNIVERSITY PRESS OF AMERICA, ® INC.
Lanham • Boulder • New York • Toronto • Plymouth, UK

Copyright © 2011 by
University Press of America,® Inc.
4501 Forbes Boulevard
Suite 200
Lanham, Maryland 20706
UPA Acquisitions Department (301) 459-3366

Estover Road
Plymouth PL6 7PY
United Kingdom

Library of Congress Control Number: 2010935142
ISBN: 978-0-7618-5380-0 (clothbound : alk. paper)
ISBN: 978-0-7618-5381-7 (paperback : alk. paper)
eISBN: 978-0-7618-5382-4

Contents

Foreword

Americans get their ideas about Africa from the movies. From the earliest silent pictures to contemporary Hollywood blockbusters, film has provided the prism through which we have come to view the continent's people and history. Early silent films like *Tarzan* (1918) depicted Africans in crudely racist caricatures. More recently Hollywood has traded its simple racism for subtler stereotypes. Yet Hollywood is only one source of the images that have shaped public attitudes about Africa over the last century. Before the age of new media many Americans first saw Africa in short films screened in schools and churches. These shows were intended to enlighten audiences about life in the 'real' Africa. Their educational agenda invested them with an authority which was absent in the serials and features screened at Saturday matinees.

The diaries published here cast light on one genre of these films, the missionary documentary. Before the Second World War missionaries were a crucial source of information about Africa for many Americans. The visiting missionary was a familiar figure to Christian congregations all over the country. Their sermons painted vivid tales of 'primitive' Africa, and invariably concluded with an appeal for donations. Missionaries were among the most diligent film-makers in the colonies because motion pictures helped their fund-raising. Their shows were often quite effective. Churches provided a viewing context that was different from that of the cinema-house. Missionaries had been to Africa, and could vouch for the authenticity of the images in the movies they presented. But while the missionaries' role in Africa has been widely recognized, until now scholars have known relatively little about their foray into film production.

Virginia Garner's diaries cast light on the making of these films. They reveal that working in Africa produced immense challenges for her generation of film-makers. She and her husband labored under arduous conditions. Travel was difficult. Creating sets, recruiting actors, and writing scenes were all done on an *ad hoc* basis. To these idealistic young Americans, the Africans seemed uncomprehending and often uninterested in their efforts. Disease, poor weather, and set-backs plagued their journey. Yet throughout the narrative Virginia maintains an unflappable enthusiasm for their work and a confidence in their mission.

The diaries also provide invaluable insight into the preconceptions and expectations of these film-makers. Virginia's voice is plucky, indefatigable, and optimistic. Yet at times she invokes crude prejudices when describing Africans, and the diaries contain candid observations about race, religion, and politics that one suspects would have been edited by a contemporary publisher. Such views informed a generation of film-makers in Africa, and indeed, most of white America in the first half of the 20th century.

Garner's diaries are particularly valuable because they contribute a woman's voice into the dialogue about early colonial film-making. Before the Second World War film production was a man's preserve. But the exigencies of working in Africa opened up a space for a handful of Western women to collaborate in the creative process. Filming in Africa meant being away from home for months, sometimes years, which encouraged some western couples to travel together. Thus Garner's diary joins a short list of books by women film-makers working in Africa from this era. Perhaps the most famous was Osa Johnson, whose memoir *I Married Adventure*[1] recounts her adventures filming wildlife in East Africa with her husband Martin during the 1920s. Osa became a minor film-star in the silent era through her appearances in several nature documentaries she produced with her husband. In the 1930s Natalie Barkas published *Thirty Thousand Miles for the Films,*[2] which recollects her experiences shooting on location in Africa with her photographer husband Geoffrey Barkas. But while Garner was not the only woman film-maker in Africa, her diary reveals that she played a greater role in the production of the movies than any of her contemporaries.

Glenn Reynolds has done the academic community a great service by bringing these journals to light. But Garner's diaries should appeal to an audience beyond academia. Her narrative provides a snapshot of one American's worldview at the cusp of the 'American century'. It exudes a self-confidence in herself, her culture, and the colonial project which would soon be swept away by the World War. Mission work in Africa would continue, and film-making on the continent would gather momentum in the post-war era. But the colonial film-making project would never again enjoy the self-assurance revealed in these diaries.

J.M. Burns
May 2010
Clemson University

NOTES

1. Osa Johnson, *I Married Adventure: The Lives and Adventures of Martin and Osa Johnson* (New York: J.B. Lippincott Co., 1940).

2. Natalie Barkas, *Thirty Thousand Miles for the Film: The Story of the Filming of "Soldiers Three" and "Rhodes of Africa"* (London: Blackie & Son, 1937).

Acknowledgments

For every published text there are a host of people who made such a daunting project possible. I would like to extend my appreciation to Brooke Bascietto, editor of University Press of America, who first expressed interest in the topic and ably guided this project from conception to completion. Mount Saint Mary College generously provided a research summer grant in 2009, while the *Journal of Social History* kindly allowed republication of material from the introduction that previously appeared in a group of collected papers entitled *Arts in Place.*

Images Out of Africa evolved out of my years of research into the introduction of film into Africa south of the Sahara. My deepest gratitude goes out to three families who were involved in the process, although in very different ways. As a child, my mother and father always provided me with unqualified support for my varied interests. Not surprisingly, my father's own personal involvement in, and love for, film, as both hobby and occupation, spilled over to the next generation. My siblings and I worked hard in the 1970s filming our own Super 8 masterpieces, more often than not exhibiting a strong and perhaps morbid fascination for the Hollywood horror genre.

Many years later in graduate school and beyond, I shifted from my dubious role as amateur producer, director and actor, to researcher of African history and colonial filmmaking. And during this time I was blessed with a family of my own. My beautiful wife Melissa has remained by my side during the often laborious process of research and writing, and the arrival of my daughters Miranda and Amelia changed my life in ways I would never have thought possible. For all three of them I am eternally grateful.

In researching this project, a third family entered the picture. Years after initially procuring copies of the Africa Motion Picture Project films, I was fortunate to track down Gay Mackintosh, daughter of Virginia Garner. Gay provided critical assistance in publishing her mother's diaries, including transcribing the originals, proofreading, and organizing Virginia's photographs. I am gratified that when I began this project with Gay, her mother gave us the green light to proceed. I thank Gay and her husband for graciously welcoming a stranger into their home and entrusting me with their family's cherished memories.

Introduction

THE AFRICA MOTION PICTURE PROJECT

The lights in the church flashed back on as the final credits brought the film to a close. "It [was] better than a dozen missionary addresses," one pastor declared enthusiastically, while another pontificated, "it ought to be shown in every church in America!"[1] The film in question was *The Story of Bamba*, a collaborative result of eight Protestant mission boards that came together in 1937 under the auspices of the recently formed Africa Committee of the Foreign Missions Conference of North America.[2] The Africa Committee, spearheaded by famous Disciples of Christ missionary Emory Ross, was responsible for organizing the "Africa Motion Picture Project" (AMPP) primarily to expand funding and recruitment in American churches for foreign mission boards.[3] The recently discovered diaries that make up this book, written by Virginia Garner while filming for the AMPP in Central Africa with her husband, Ray Garner, in 1938–39, provide a unique look into the quotidian interactions and negotiations between African villagers and film crew during the production phase of this hitherto overlooked film project.

This two-year experiment in producing missionary films in Africa—primarily in the Belgian Congo—on the eve of World War II broke new ground for its technical quality and provided a rare look into the life-world of the BaKuba and other African communities, in many instances where motion pictures were being produced for the first time. Movies had first been introduced into the continent, however unevenly, during the latter part of the frenzy of European colonization referred to by historians as the 'Scramble for Africa.' By the onset of the Great War, scattered missionaries were augmenting their lantern slide shows for indigenous people with religious films produced in the United States, and thus were responsible for opening new

1

social space for film in Africa, a process circumscribed, of course, by their desire to entrench the power of the Christian gospel in African communities.

In some ways this book is part of an expanding genre in African Studies. In the past several years, the number of scholarly works analyzing the role of film in African cultural life has grown exponentially, filling a gap in our understanding of how a particular form of media closely identified with the West—motion pictures—has been consumed, co-opted and contested throughout the continent. Yet in one crucial aspect, this study serves as a departure from the existing genre, for a closer look at the spate of recent books on the subject reflects the fact that, overwhelmingly, these studies are restricted almost entirely to the post-World War II period, and the heroic attempts by Africans themselves to create a post-colonial, independent cinema produced and distributed under rather strict budgetary constraints against overwhelming odds. What has been noticeably absent in the genre to date is an adequate exploration of how, and under what conditions, film—either for production or consumption—was first introduced into the continent as a whole, and into areas south of the Sahara in particular, during the colonial period.

Following on the heels of earlier, scattered essays on the topic, J.M. Burns' path-breaking book *Flickering Shadows: Cinema and Identity in Colonial Zimbabwe* (2002) was one of the first full-length studies to examine how cinema was used by a colonial power, in this case Britain, to sell the colonial project to its African subjects by both producing and exhibiting instructional and propaganda films in Southern Rhodesia (now Zimbabwe). *Images Out of Africa* charts a different course in three ways. First, whereas Burns looked at what scholars refer to as 'colonial cinema' (making films in Africa for African consumption during the colonial era), this book traces a film project made in Africa for American viewers. Second, the AMPP was a pre-World War II phenomenon, completing its work just prior to Nazi Germany's assault on Poland. Third, rather than focusing on a film project developed by British colonial officials to foster development initiatives and strengthen colonial rule, this study highlights the determination of a variety of Protestant denominations in the United States to harness the medium for rather different ends.

This project began in 2001, when I first discovered copies of the AMPP films in the National Archives in Washington, DC, coupled with production files relating to the project. On the heels of this initial find I uncovered some of the original reels resting on the shelves of the Disciples of Christ main archive building in Nashville, Tennessee, where for years they have lain dormant, slowly decaying in small cardboard boxes. Although these particular reels are probably unusable now, upon its dissolution the Harmon Foundation in New York, which served as a key sponsor of the project, submitted its copies of the films to the National Archives where they patiently awaited the critical gaze of the historian. Armed with material from both locations for several years, I still hesitated to publish on the topic, sensing that there was more to the story. My hunch paid dividends. A few years ago I was fortunate to track down Gay Mackintosh, daughter of Ray and Virginia Garner, the principal filmmakers hired for the project during the Great Depression. Gay was gracious enough to allow me privileged access to her family's diaries, scrapbooks, still photos and other files relating to the Africa Motion Picture Project, and continued to play an instrumental role in this project by transcribing her mother's diaries for editing and publication.

IMAGES AND EVANGELISM

The material provided by Virginia Garner's family helped to answer key questions concerning the vagaries of making movies in Africa during the colonial period, including the everyday cultural transactions, negotiations and confusions that attended the film shoots. With the full complement of the AMPP films, production files, newly discovered diaries, scrapbooks and even an unpublished memoir of the principal filmmakers, we now have a wealth of material through which to analyze the Western missionary construction of 'Africa' in the interwar world, reflecting the shift in European and American interventions in the sub-Sahara from shooting Africans and animals in the era of late nineteenth century conquest, to shooting images in the era of twentieth century colonial consolidation.[4] Emory Ross's film crew—the newlyweds Ray and Virginia Garner—produced approximately ten films in less than two years.[5] Shooting in Central African villages under trying climatic conditions, the project sought to reinvigorate missionary endeavors and to establish a more secure footing for Protestants in the Belgian Congo, especially in the face of the general hostility of Catholic missions and the Belgian colonial state to Protestant attempts to engage African subjects.

Although strengthening the missionary presence in Central Africa was the explicit aim of the AMPP, it is important to recognize the pivotal role played by the deployment of a new technologically-based, consumer-driven art form—motion pictures—in achieving that goal. This is particularly important due to the fact that many standard narratives of the first half century of cinema portray the Christian establishment as struggling mightily against the film industry to either censor films outright or impose rigid moral codes for filmmaking through vigorous support for regulatory bodies on both the local and national level. We often hear about the clamor of Protestant church groups in the wake of the Fatty Arbuckle debacle, for instance. Following the comedian's arrest for the rape and murder of Virginia Rappe, Hollywood elites responded to public pressure by hiring church elder William Hays to clean up the industry, a move which eventually culminated in a wave of new censorship after the implementation of the Hays Code of 1930.

This book serves as something of a revisionist interpretation to accounts of cinema's early years that imply a narrow-minded, unyielding opposition to film by the American Christian establishment. Too much emphasis on the link between the moral dictates of the church and various restrictions on film production and distribution makes it imperative that a submerged counter-history of the intersection of religion and cinema be explored more fully. In fact, the use of projected religious images within the Christian tradition has a long history, and helped to facilitate new aesthetic forms in the emerging visual culture of the West. In order to appreciate the scope of the AMPP and the role film would play in fostering interdenominational cooperation, we need to understand that religious groups played a role not just as outside critics of film, but also as entities that often actively produced films in their own sphere, and thereby served as a major social force in promoting moving images among their parishioners and the broader public at large.

As early as the 1680s, Catholics enjoyed the visual pleasures of the *laterna magica*, a simple device consisting of a lens, an oil lamp, and a series of images painted on small glass plates projected onto a wall or white sheet.[6] Even in the Protestant world, despite early Calvinistic opposition to graven images, the magic lantern proved enormously popular, especially following the 1850 Langenheim Brothers patent for transferring photographic images onto glass slides. And lantern slides with religious themes were increasingly deemed beneficial for foreign mission work where other forms of verbal communication proved problematic for lack of adequate translators. Indeed, by the 1890s more than a few Protestant missionaries around the globe had begun to utilize them regularly as a supplement to standard Biblical sermons.

By the turn of the century the stereopticon—essentially a magic lantern utilizing two lenses—had made its debut within religious circles. This early version of 3-D pictures combined the basic magic lantern projection beam with the advances of Euclidean binocular vision, creating an exhilarating sense of depth and reality for the spectator. Lantern slides made from black and white photographs were often hand tinted, creating a vibrant visual effect through a broad range of colors and hues. Through 'tours' of Palestine and other iconic sacred sites, repackaged as part of an emerging twentieth century commercialized visual culture, many Christians in America were able to foster a new-found identification with scenes from the Bible by experiencing their 'actual settings' without the tedium or expense of travel.[7] It was through a variety of mass produced arts at the dawn of the twentieth century, then, that 'place' became something (or 'somewhere') often perceived or experienced less as a geographically unique locale than as a set of images and discursive formulations in mass distribution, a process that merged almost seamlessly with the pre-existing stereotypes regarding 'the Dark Continent'.

Protestants began to exploit other didactic visual tools during this period: flannelgraphs—framed felt backgrounds to which fabric characters could be attached—became popular in Sunday school classrooms in America and mission stations abroad; and filmstrips, composed of 35mm still images projected in a series, also came into heavy usage domestically and in the mission field in the 1920s due to low production and exhibition costs.[8]

Despite the openness of many in the Christian community to experimenting with new forms of visual technology, the wisdom of using cinema as an adjunct to religious sermons and missionary work remained a subject of heated debate following the American nickelodeon craze of 1905–6. Many ministers frankly doubted that film could be rehabilitated from its perceived role as purveyor of cheap sensationalism and commercial exploitation, especially in large metropolitan areas where cinema was quickly refashioning the leisure patterns of millions of urban residents. The ambiguities that greeted the use of images in these early years of the spectacle were evident in the campaign begun in 1910 by Congregational minister Herbert Jump of New Britain, Connecticut, to include films with 'religious and moralistic themes' as part of Sunday evening services. Although the church's Standing Committee rejected his initial plan because of concerns about the medium, just a few months later this same body approved the use of a stereopticon slide show entitled 'The Christian Conquest of the World' in its evening services for the congregation.[9] Despite his early rejection, by the early 1910s Jump, through a series of lectures and published essays, was emerging as a forceful advocate for exploring the possibilities of visualizing Christian topics through cinema. In particular, the perceived immorality of the nickelodeon, for Jump, was merely an aberration that could be resolved by co-opting the medium for more noble purposes. Furthermore, as might be expected, he was also a vocal proponent of using films in mission work abroad.

It was during the 1920s that broad-based African film spectatorship in many areas south of the Sahara began—Anglophone Africa in particular—as film began its ascendancy as an icon of twentieth century Western culture and marched into peripheral markets in colonized areas around the globe. In those African regions where cinema in its earliest days was consumed exclusively by white settlers and colonial officials, the pressure for market expansion and the efforts of missionaries to provide cinematic portrayals of biblical themes for colonial subjects led to a tectonic shift in the global demographics of film-viewing. For instance, in 1920, black spectatorship in southern Africa expanded exponentially through the efforts of Congregational missionary Ray Phillips, who sought to 'moralize the leisure time' of a quarter million black mineworkers in South Africa through the Mines' Compound Cinema Circuit, a program that would soon come to include mining areas in Southern and Northern Rhodesia.[10]

At the same time, black spectators in Nigeria were learning about the dangers of plague through the newly-introduced medium of moving pictures. And in the Congo, which had recently been 'sold' to the Belgian state by King Leopold II following the embarrassments of the rubber scandal (described in further detail below), Catholic missionaries who had been showing films to urban Congolese in Leopoldville as early as 1910 soon extended the privilege to black residents of Stanleyville and Elisabethville.[11] Although opinion among whites as to the wisdom of allowing Africans to view films was divided in the Belgian Congo (as late as 1945, for instance, colonial legislation was enacted specifically to restrict native Congolese from seeing commercial films, most of which were American imports), the AMPP of the late 1930s must be seen within the context of an emerging consensus among many missionaries and colonial officials that cinema might, in a variety of ways, play a positive role in dramatically transforming the life of indigenous people.[12]

READING BETWEEN THE FRAMES

Film scholar Peter Davis, in his seminal analysis of commercial movies with South African themes, argues that the "invention of the movie camera began a second conquest of Africa," a theme re-articulated by Paul Landau who reminds us of the very real parallel between the technology involved in shooting ammunition and shooting images.[13] But the medium in a colonial context must be understood as more than simply another 'tool of empire' designed to distort an existing African reality. Rather, I argue that that 'reality' had in part to be created in the first place. We must remember that the Western imaginary of a greater 'European' community had itself been constructed rather late in the game, evolving largely out of the Columbian Exchange, slave trading, and the articulation and reaffirmation of a common racial heritage (ie. 'whiteness'), and refined through such pivotal political events as the Treaty of Westphalia, the Concert of Europe and the Berlin Conference. Similarly, the conceptualization of 'Africa'—despite its long history of indigenous kingdoms, cultures and communities, and despite its short history of African welfare societies and proto-nationalist organizations in the years after World War I—also congealed initially on a conceptual plane largely within Europe itself, and was largely framed in contradistinction to the notion of the 'civilized' accomplishments of the European community.[14]

The films of the Africa Motion Picture Project, in keeping with the discourse of missionary and Belgian paternalism and borrowing from the new languages of cinema deployed so effectively by Soviet propagandists and British documentary filmmakers, were conceived in part as technologies of truth providing ethnographic portrayals of 'vanishing cultures,' from a Western perspective. And yet the films also explicitly promoted the 'civilizing' effects of proselytization and industrialization in Central African communities, lauding the efforts of various missionary groups to build mission schools and alleviate physical suffering on the continent through development initiatives.[15]

Looking at the particular social imaginings of the AMPP, the films might loosely be placed into three categories: *ethnographic* (showing scenes of 'native' life), *missionary* (comprising medical and educational topics) and *colonial* (explaining the everyday functions of the colonial bureaucracy). And yet, ultimately all the films worked in concert to construct an overarching image of an Africa in need of Christian missionary beneficence. There were, of course, 'real' African communities that served as referents for the AMPP films, but the mission-oriented productions explored here were a critical part of a broader, evolving symbolic universe on which were grafted Western constructions, or at least Western understandings, of African realities. As Kevin Dunn has noted in his study of the policy repercussions of racial stereotyping in Central Africa, "the Congo has become overly textualized; it has been a discursive space onto which numerous actors—internally and externally—have projected characteristics, images, and meanings in their attempt to define and delineate the identity of the Congo."[16] Thus, there was no stable, single identity for the Belgian Congo, or for a broader Africa for that matter: in the case of cinematic constructions of Africa in particular, the global proliferation of the medium, requiring the rapid movement of filmmakers, screenplays and images back and forth across the Atlantic world and beyond, suggests that there were multiple discourses worked and reworked according to different agendas at different times.

Given the preponderance of stereotypes of Africa, an obvious question then arises: have Africans been entirely disempowered in this modern era of image-making, mere victims of European cultural representations over which they had no control? While it is certainly true that studies of colonial African political life have been actively uncovering and recuperating both quotidian and 'heroic' forms of contestation on the part of indigenous communities opposing European intrusion, the same can hardly be said of research examining early images of the so-called 'Dark Continent,' which focus overwhelmingly on the ready storehouse of denigrating stereotypes which putatively lord over the discursive universe(s) known as 'Africa': Africa as a land of Wild Animals, Primitives, Cannibals, Noble Savages, and so on.

Perhaps, though, it is time to call into question the seemingly pervasive effects of Western stereotyping generated through mass produced image-making, a de-centering made possible through a greater emphasis on the point of production in the field, and a greater appreciation of the quotidian cultural negotiations involved in the on-site construction of those very representations. It is precisely here, then, that Virginia Garner's 1938–39 diaries emerge as an important new source allowing for a sharper analytical focus. Admittedly, we still lack the 'authentic voice' of the Africans starring in the films, yet Garner's diaries move us far beyond the stated goals of the project that we find in the Harmon Foundation production files. She reports how, and why, Africans served as actors, their expectations for remuneration, the subtle attempts to retain some vestige of African resistance to, and control over, the image-making process, and other unexpected problems and cultural confusions that plagued the small film crew as it moved from village to village. In fact, without the benefit of Garner's daily reportage, critical analysis of the project would be forced to rely merely on the declared aims of the producers, and the films themselves; in essence, we would be left with initial proposals and final product, but little sense of process, as we try to read between the lines—or 'between the frames'—of the Africa Motion Picture Project.

A poignant example in a similar context highlights the importance of both process and 'place' in unpacking the relations of power inherent in artistic production, and reflects the limitations of analyzing images as mere 'free floating signifiers.' During the filming of the epic *De Voortrekkers* (1916) in South Africa, colonial officials had fretted about the possible downside of arming a large contingent of 'Zulus' (in fact they were black mineworkers of varying ethnic backgrounds hired as extras) as they tried to recreate the famous Battle of Blood River, a key event in the originary myth of the Afrikaner nation and the Great Trek. The result was that while the 'invading' Africans were armed only with collapsible assegais (spears), white Afrikaner film extras had their own ideas about art reproducing reality, and were rumored to have secreted live ammunition into the laager for the 'shooting.' Although it is unclear whether Africans or Afrikaners initiated the ensuing fracas, there is no dispute that director Harold Shaw quickly lost control of the situation: "While the natives were charging the laager, the Europeans within had fired shots . . . The natives charged the laager furiously; but instead of recoiling and falling 'dead' [as the script required to reflect the actual events of 1838], continued into the laager itself where blows with Europeans were exchanged. Mounted police . . . were forced to intervene to prevent the natives from attacking the laager in earnest."[17] Not surprisingly, the scene had to be filmed again later under increased security.

This event throws into stark relief the way in which artistic production not only 'reproduces' reality through image dissemination, but has the potential to remake and redefine (and potentially, to contest) that very reality itself as it is being (re)constructed in a particular place at a particular time. Some scholars have suggested that *De Voortrekkers* was the South African equivalent of *The Birth of a Nation*, the W.D. Griffith film released only a year before in the United States that contributed to the further marginalization and degradation of the African American population. But as we saw in the example above, the filming of *De Voortrekkers* ironically opened up a new space, however briefly and however circumscribed, for African extras to attempt to avenge their loss in one of South Africa's most historic conflicts. Clearly, for the actors in *De Voortrekkers* (both black and white) the very physicality of the filmmaking process extended far beyond a narrow academic exercise in artistic representation. This tells us that images and representations are not mere static, inert reflections of a past reality, but can themselves be dynamic and fluid processes of creation and cultural negotiation.

Thus, while I will engage in a necessary textual analysis of the films in this introduction, I move beyond the limitations of framing the AMPP films as mere 'ideological fronts' justifying European hegemony (and working in tandem with other artistic forms referencing the 'primitive' in magazine stories, travel accounts, postcards, museum dioramas, colonial exhibits, and the like), through a greater appreciation of the often convoluted and *ad hoc* process by which a particular Africa was created in a particular place and time. Greater focus on the point of production—in the case of the AMPP, the very real difficulties of filming in Central Africa, the negotiations required for access to villages, villagers, ritual artifacts, and so on—serve to highlight the uneasy tension between the imagined Africa(s) of the West and the alternative social imaginings of indigenous people that could never be fully reconciled to the constraints of colonial rule. Moreover, the response of chiefs who sanctioned the filmmaking process, as well as the rank and file of the colonized who served as actors, displays an indigenous appreciation for the power of representation as a mediating force between imperial rule and local governance, and gives voice to those who are generally rendered mute in most scholarly critiques of 'white-over-black' systems of representation.

Virginia Garner also emerges in this story as an important if overlooked figure during the interwar period for an entirely different reason. For several centuries, Africa was considered the 'white man's grave' due to the high risk of tropical disease and/or armed resistance on the part of local communities. Throughout the long nightmare of the Trans-Atlantic Slave Trade, relatively few European visitors ventured inland, least of all women (although there were, of course, Boer settler families who did just that in search of farming land). Moreover, European slaving vessels that plied the West African shoreline were staffed with male captains, officers, and crew. Slave trading was finally curtailed in the nineteenth century in favor of so-called 'legitimate commerce,' but a new generation of European visitors during this period generally comprised, with relatively few exceptions, male merchants, missionaries and explorers. As numerous observers have noted before, the latter was a particularly male domain, as virile white men struggled to 'penetrate' the continent and 'open up' Africa. In addition, the ensuing late nineteenth century process of continental colonization (the 'Scramble for Africa') was similarly the prerogative of white males, although by the early twentieth century wives of colonial officers in some areas were often sent over to reduce the number of embarrassing liaisons between white male colonial officials and African women.

Seen from this perspective, Virginia Garner was the exception to the rule: she was a rare example of a white woman traveling to the heart of the continent prior to World War II, especially as she was neither a missionary (although her employers were of the faith) nor the spouse of a colonial bureaucrat. As such, her journalistic impressions are relatively unencumbered by the ideological baggage that we would be likely to find in other circumstances; her accounts of the project are vivid and display an honest appreciation of, and interest in, cultural worlds alien to her as she traveled from village to village.

Virginia Garner's black and white photographs also provide us with a unique portrait of the project and the villagers who starred in the films. Hired by Harmon as still photographer (explained in greater detail below), Virginia was able to capture a variety of rich images during her travels through the central region of the continent. Many of these have ethnographic interest in their portrayal of local customs and handicrafts, while others show the actual film production process, including shots of her husband Ray as he prepares to shoot a scene. While a few of these photos accompanied articles in leading magazines of the day describing the project, most of the photos included in this collection are being shown for the first time.

AFRICA IN FAST FORWARD:
EMORY ROSS AND THE AMPP

European influence throughout the vast realm of the Congo Free State (renamed the 'Belgian Congo' after 1908) emanated through three primary institutions: the Church, the colonial government, and the host of companies serving as the Western world's catalyst for capitalist development in the interior.[18] Scholars have long recognized the crucial role of missionaries as capillary representatives of imperial power. Indeed, Marvin Markowitz makes the claim that "[t]he history of European colonization in Africa is to a large degree a story of Christian missionary penetration."[19] But if "political imperialism was inextricably bound up with the kingdom of God"—to borrow Jean Comaroff's phrase[20]—in fact this arrangement was often an uneasy one beset by the many tensions embedded within the daily realities of colonial life itself.

The Congo Free State, for instance, provided a particularly poignant example of conflicting ideals as missionaries as early as the 1890s worked to expose the Red Rubber atrocities of King Leopold's private fiefdom, an effort which caused a scandal of worldwide proportions.[21] But the resulting uproar over the humanitarian crisis in the Congo evolved largely along pre-existing religious rivalries and divisions within the colony. While Catholic missionaries from Belgium generally remained silent in the face of abuses for fear of antagonizing their chief sponsors, American Protestant missionaries critiqued Leopold through a number of damaging articles that publicized the plight of local Congolese pressed into service as forced labor for the rubber regime.

In the ensuing few decades, the two Christian communities would engage in an escalating struggle to expand their relative zones of influence in the vast territory of Central Africa. By the 1930s, Protestants were complaining that the colonial state provided preferential treatment for Catholic educational institutions at the expense of Protestant mission schools. In January 1933, Joseph Oldham of the International Missionary Council (IMC) warned that unresolved disputes in the colony had resulted in an unparalleled "crisis in the history of Protestant missions."[22] The Congo Protestant Council (CPC) and the denominational boards of the IMC determined that the time had come for a more forceful presentation of their case, and drafted a petition to the colonial minister complaining of unfair discrimination. In June, Henri Anet of Belgium's Bureau des Missions Protestantes du Congo Belge, went one step further and spoke with King Leopold III himself. While Anet applauded the fact that "gross abuses" had recently been curtailed, he complained about government subsidies for Roman Catholic village schools, which gave them a *de facto* state monopoly on education in the colony.[23]

For the Protestant community in the Congo, education was a critical issue. One of the primary goals for the Belgian Congo devised by Disciple of Christ missionary Emory Ross was the expansion of religious education along Protestant lines, made possible through the formation of an indigenous Christian church to assist the colonized in acculturating to the Western world and preventing what the *Congo Mission News* termed "absolute spiritual and physical disaster."[24] The impetus for the Africa Motion Picture Project, then, came from two sources. First, a committee of the Missionary Education Movement in the United States came to the conclusion that while many missionary boards had independently produced a number of short movies on Africa, there was as yet little ecumenical cooperation allowing for the production of longer films of better quality for interdenominational use.[25] Second, in the Congo itself, the ongoing hostility of Catholics and the colonial state served to strengthen the resolve of Protestants who began to close ranks across denominational lines to seek new ways to strengthen their cause. Cooperation was first formalized through the creation of the Church of Christ in Congo[26] (CCC)—a central administration for the colony's 'native churches'—which would soon serve an important role as cultural mediator for the AMPP film crew traveling between villages and mission stations.

It was Ross who took the next step and conceived *Africa Joins the World* as a film that would bring Africa within the purview of American church-goers, in the hopes of expanding awareness and funding for the evangelization of the continent. Unlike the AMPP productions to follow, this preliminary venture was primarily made with pre-existing footage, and produced in three parts: "What Africa Is," "How Africa Lives," and "From Fetishes to Faith." In 1936 the Africa Committee had issued a general call for footage suitable for inclusion in *Africa Joins the World*. Selecting from over a hundred reels, including contributions from numerous missionaries, the Legation of South Africa and commercial filmmaker Martin Johnson (producer and/or director of *Simba: The King of the Beasts* [1928], *Wonders of the Congo* [1931], and *Congorilla* [1932])[27], Ross and missionary William Rogers produced the first segment, "What Africa Is," as a general primer introducing Western audiences to such topics as sub-Saharan fauna, tribal political structures, and African arts.

While Ross and Rogers had a voluminous amount of material to choose from, these varying representations of Africa were all products of the white world, whether they derived from colonial, missionary, philanthropic, or commercial sources. In the film's opening segment, Africa is portrayed as a simplified totality, combining village scenes with a few charts and a rudimentary map of the continent. The Africa constructed here, though, no longer functioned merely in the classic mode of ideological distortion (although there is that), wherein the image distorts a pre-existing reality; rather it is a copy of a copy—what Jean Baudrillard refers to as a simulacrum to the second power (in this case, a film of a map of a 'reality'). Moreover, the map is notable not for its plenitude, but rather its dearth: it consists only of a crude white outline of Africa on a black background, with a white line drawing of a monkey and an elephant in the middle.

Complementing this image of Africa as a place filled first and foremost with exotic, wild animals is Johnson's footage of members of the Maasai tribe in their traditional setting in Kenya.

The film's second reel, "How Africa Lives," opens with a more detailed look at African social life and physical culture, including various shots of indigenous architecture, clothing and ornamentation, culinary preferences, and traditional work rhythms. The film then illustrates, in the words of Rogers, "the conquest of Africa by the white man with ensuing industrialization; the wealth of Africa's natural resources; and some of the effects of industrialization upon the native African."[28] "From Fetishes to Faith," the film's third and final reel, builds upon the previous segments by examining the missionary engagement with pagan Africa and the struggle to build self-sustaining Christian communities in local villages. Notably, while the first two reels were essentially descriptive in scope, "From Fetishes to Faith" takes a more programmatic approach and looks toward transforming Africa's future by raising funds and awareness in American churches for foreign mission work.

Africa Joins the World brought into focus two key elements of Ross's thinking in the mid-1930s: the use of film for religious purposes in Africa, and that continent's perceived place in the modern world. Ross had actually followed Ray Phillips' 1920s Mines' Compound Cinema Circuit with great interest, and had conversed with Phillips concerning the positive role the medium could play in Africa. He clearly believed that film could have a 'civilizing' effect in that corner of the world that seemingly had been 'left out' of history, a reiteration of the common Western notion of Africa as a site of arrested progress.[29]

In *Africa Joins the World*, as well as an article similarly entitled "The Last Continent to Join the World," Ross suggests that Africa is both the oldest and newest member of the world community. Through the herculean efforts of Henry Morton Stanley (a "hard" but not "cruel" man[30]), who succeeded where others had failed in opening up the Congo to modern commerce and industry, Africa as "the largest primary society still in existence" offered up its bountiful natural resources needed so desperately by the highly industrialized West, and in return was to be guided by both the secular and spiritual forces of the modern world.[31] Ross was a confirmed devotee of the trusteeship doctrine, acknowledging the excesses of African partition (when the continent, in his terms, became the "territorial grab-bag of Europe"), yet concluding that the Scramble was merely an episodic side effect of the more noble project of conveying rapid social and economic development to Africa: "First-generation descendants of witch doctors and medicine men," he intoned, "[now] sit with trained and knowing eyes at the latest high-powered microscopes in scores of hospitals and laboratories, picking trypanosomes out of blood smears and determining which of a score of long-named intestinal parasites is troubling the patient."[32] The success of *Africa Joins the World*— measured primarily by the willingness of a number of denominational boards to purchase copies—led Ross and the Africa Committee to launch the much more ambitious project of sending their own film crew across the Atlantic.[33] The AMPP was soon officially launched with primary sponsorship from the Harmon Foundation's Division of Visual Experiment, which agreed to attach its name to the project. Through its first quarter century the foundation had evolved through several stages. In 1911, William E. Harmon had originally established his charitable institution to assist small American communities in establishing parks, playgrounds and other community services, but in the 1920s the foundation shifted gears and began offering substantial fiscal support to struggling black artists during the Harlem Renaissance by organizing exhibits of African American art, and serving more generally as a booster for local black painters and sculptors.

In the late 1930s the foundation expanded its mission to include a greater emphasis on Africa itself. In addition to offering funding for the AMPP, it provided new sources of patronage explicitly for African artists who had recently arrived from across the Atlantic. Despite the existing literature on the Harmon Foundation, which has explored in some detail its earlier philanthropic connection with the black New York art world, there has been no recognition of its role as a primary sponsor of the AMPP. While on the surface this support for missionary filmmaking would seem consistent with the foundation's other philanthropic endeavors, there was a key difference: unlike its earlier exhibits of distinguished African American art in the 1920s, Harmon's Division of Visual Experiment, as well as key members of the AMPP like Ross and Rogers, attempted to control virtually all aspects of filmic representation from conception to realization, including storylines, scripts, and image-making in Africa.[34] Their Africa was largely conceived in New York.

GARNER AND GARNER IN AFRICA

With Emory Ross as executive director of the new Africa Motion Picture Project, William Rogers was given the task of overseeing production, drafting potential scenarios for the films, and acting as liaison to the Africa Committee, while Kenneth Space was appointed editor. In addition to the crucial charitable support provided by the (secular) Harmon Foundation, further sponsorship came from the American Mission to Lepers (of which Ross was also secretary) and eight mission boards.

Given the dire effects of the Great Depression, the Harmon Foundation had little problem attracting potential filmmakers for the AMPP. It was the Christmas season of 1937, and Ray Garner of Brooklyn was one among many desperate for work. Mary Brady, director of the foundation, was already in the process of interviewing a line of prospective filmmakers willing to travel to Africa. By the time Garner arrived, there were already twenty-nine applicants, but she nevertheless told Garner to come back to meet with Rogers. In what Garner referred to jokingly as the "first step in my indoctrination" during his subsequent interview, Rogers showed him a religious film and asked for an honest critique. "It stinks," replied Garner, who continued to "point out the many reasons why it failed to carry off its story, and of how its obvious amateurism would make it unacceptable to any audience."[35]

Despite the embarrassing fact that Rogers himself had actually produced the film, he and Brady were both impressed with Garner and offered him the position. Garner was exhilarated and quickly accepted, but began to plot how he could involve 'Jinny,' his fiancée, in the project. He soon returned to Harmon's headquarters in Lower Manhattan with Virginia and suggested that the foundation hire her as official still photographer for the project. Although in truth Virginia had little experience taking pictures, she had hurriedly purchased a camera and put together an impressive portfolio. Rogers approved of the idea, but because of budgetary constraints the foundation only agreed once a private donor offered to cover the extra expense of a two-person crew. Virginia, it would turn out, became indispensable in seeing the project through to completion, serving a far more crucial role than her official position suggested by helping to secure actors and working as a light technician, assistant cinematographer and so on.

Six weeks before they set sail Ray and Virginia gave their vows and prepared for their 'honeymoon' in Central Africa. In May 1938, with ten screenplays prepared by Rogers and his script-writing team, and four cameras in tow (two 35mm and two 16mm), the Garners arrived in Matadi, on the mouth of the Congo River. Their first inland destination was Sona Bata—a Baptist mission station near the town of Mboko that they reached by way of an old steam engine.

THE MISSIONARY IMAGINATION
IN CENTRAL AFRICA

The 'Africas' depicted in the AMPP films evolved as faith-based representations of an African referent, constructed by missionaries and professional scriptwriters, some of whom had never visited the continent. It should be noted that the Garners' employers mandated that the film crew follow faith-fully the general contours of the storylines and scripts prepared in the United States, although occasionally the film crew was forced due to unforeseen circumstances to interpret these rather liberally. In the remainder of the intro-duction, I provide a fuller description and critique of the 'Africa' constructed in the AMPP films, followed by an analysis of Virginia's diaries, which in many ways open the doors to yet another 'Africa'; in fact, her daily rumina-tions on location undermine the hegemonic pretensions of the project by exposing the complex social interactions between film crew and villagers, including everyday forms of contestation and other tensions arising during the production process.

The Story of Bamba was the first film shot in Africa by the AMPP crew. Based in Sona Bata, the plot is, in essence, a medical missionary morality tale. At the beginning of the film, we see Bamba, a BaKongo boy, training to be a 'witchdoctor' (traditional healer) under his uncle. Following the on-set of an epidemic, from which Bamba and others suffer, the uncle accuses newly arriving missionaries of being evil spirits and relocates his village to a 'luckier' location. The missionaries, meanwhile, find Bamba in the fast-emptying town and take him to their field station where he soon recovers. He grows up under their protective wing, becomes a medical missionary, and returns to his village as an adult after receiving his diploma. Although he opens a clinic to minister to his people, his uncle initially curses him. In the final scenes, however, the aging witchdoctor falls ill but fortunately is cured by his nephew, after which the medicine man belatedly acknowledges the 'deficiencies' of African healing practices and embraces Christianity (and, by extension, Western medicine).

In addition to being a medical morality tale, *The Story of Bamba* can also be seen as a dramatized documentary that employs a variant of the Mr. Wise and Mr. Foolish morality trope so common to colonial filmmaking through-out the sub-Sahara through the 1950s.[36] Initiated by William Sellers in Ni-geria in his plague-fighting film, and later deployed by colonial filmmakers throughout much of Africa, this narrative device has been described by histo-rian J.M. Burns as delineating "a contrast between the hero, who is rewarded for embracing the modernizing project of colonialism, and the villain, whose intransigent traditionalism inevitably brings suffering and hardship to himself and his family."[37] William Rogers recast the traits of foolishness and wisdom in generational terms: Bamba symbolizes the younger, mission-educated Af-rican population putatively more sympathetic to the introduction of Western mores, while his uncle remains mired in the debilitating traditions of African superstition until his life-changing epiphany in the final scenes, and his aban-donment of witchcraft.

James Sweet has noted that what was broadly conceived by representatives of the West as 'witchcraft' in Central Africa, "was just one component of what might better be understood as a bundle of hidden religious powers" that served to restore a degree of social harmony to tribal communities. Furthermore, Sweet argues that the use of occult powers by African communities in the colonial world should be understood in part as a response to modern pressures and intruding malevolent forces, such as the Trans-Atlantic Slave Trade, rather than mere atavistic forms of 'tribal' superstition.[38] Seen through this prism, the decision at the beginning of the film by Bamba's uncle to relocate villagers beyond the reach of missionary influence is quite revealing. In this key scene, the actions of the witchdoctor must be seen as an attempt by the uncle to re-establish tribal harmony by escaping and countering the malevolent influence of colonial power, which he explicitly associates with 'evil spirits.' But it is at this juncture, tellingly, that Rogers' script introduces a double healing and thereby re-imposes Western dominance, for the tireless work of medical missionaries applauded by the AMPP serves to heal the rupture between Africans and outsiders by healing the sick, and through this process exposing the weakness of African medicinal practices.

The Story of Bamba's morality tale of evangelical bio-medical success is even more prominent in *Song After Sorrow*, an AMPP film designed to elicit support for Presbyterian missionary Eugene Roland Kellersberger's efforts to eradicate leprosy from the Congo. The film crew arrived at the Bibanga leper colony at a propitious time. Kellersberger, it turned out, was preparing to move his wards to a newer location nearby, and the Garners were able to capture riveting shots of the 'homeless lepers' *en route*: "We showed the whole procession in sihouette [*sic*] on their way. The ones without feet rode in carts, the women carried baskets on their heads, and the crippled hobbled along with sticks to help them walk. It really was quite a scene and should be very effective."[39]

Colonial leprosaria in Africa functioned as a particular type of social engineering—institutions promoting what Megan Vaughan describes as "new African communities, isolated from, and expunged of, all those features of African society which they saw as impeding the development of Christianity."[40] The Bibanga camp depicted in *Song After Sorrow* thus falls within the category of what Vaughan calls a "colony within a colony," in which sufferers of Hansen's disease are treated by Kellersberger with Chaulmoogra oil, learn the practical skills necessary to construct their own village segregated from outside 'tribal' communities, and imbibe a heavy dose of Christian moralizing from both white missionaries and 'native ministers.' Ironically, while details on the transmission and genetics of the disease were insufficiently understood in the 1930s, recent research by the Pasteur Institute in Paris revealingly suggests that the explanation for the high incidence and spread of the malady in the sub-Sahara and the Caribbean can in fact be traced to the earlier migratory patterns of slave coffles and the intercontinental transportation of human cargo during the tragic years of the Trans-Atlantic Slave Trade.[41]

Rogers' screenplays display his determination to give viewers a sense of 'traditional' African life devoid of sensationalistic excess, as well as showing the experiences of new missionaries working in Africa for the first time. *A Day in an African Village*, for instance, offers little explicit instruction to the potential missionary recruit, but rather provides an empathetic snapshot of Africans during the course of an 'average' day. Shot in the Belgian Congo and French Cameroons, the film shows a number of villagers warming themselves by firelight in the morning; men weave straw, spear fish, gather palm nuts, and burn brush for community gardens; women, on the other hand, plant, cook palm nuts, and prepare manioc for dinner. American viewers unfamiliar with the history of the Congo under colonial rule, of course, had no way of judging the veracity of such a bucolic milieu without prior knowledge of the atrocities visited upon the general population by the agents of King Leopold's concessionaires some thirty to forty years earlier.

Despite its rather simplistic depiction of 'African' life, the film compares favorably not only with the embarrassments and misrepresentations of *Tarzan* (which erroneously depicted a tiger, not native to the continent, running wild in the 'African jungle'), for instance, but also with the crude sensationalism of pseudo ethno-documentaries made just a few years before the AMPP films by explorer Paul Hoefler and others. *Africa Speaks!*, for instance, Hoefler's 1930 "true life adventure," touted Africa as "a land of savagery and dangerous adventure . . . where nature is without mercy . . . and deadly beasts of the jungle are supreme."[42] Hoefler played upon, and helped fuel, familiar interwar stereotypes of African culture that reverberated throughout the United States and Europe. Indeed, the popularity of *Africa Speaks!* spawned a burst of similar shorts, including *Africa Shrieks*, *Africa Squawks*, and *Africa Speaks English*.[43] Despite their popularity, though, the ideological construction of African savagery driving Hoefler's films was becoming somewhat archaic in the interwar period. By the 1930s, as Jan Pieterse has argued, the 'Others' were being transformed from the 'savages' of the late nineteenth-century conquest of Africa to the primitive 'children' of the era of colonial consolidation.[44] In both cases, however, Africans and other colonized populations around the globe were generally represented as de-individualized visual objects—or put another way, turned into docile and nameless subjects subservient to the reigning colonial order.

Thus, one might argue that there was a degree of ambiguity embedded within the AMPP film *Children of Africa*. While explicitly referencing the daily activities of African youngsters, one senses that all the men, women and children of the village featured in the film were collectively, and equally, perceived as 'the children of Africa' in a land virtually devoid of nation states or meaningful historical development: a mother stirs the porridge with the help of her daughter, while a boy assists his father in the construction of a new thatch roof; boys engage in a game called 'foot matching' as their female counterparts take part in a dance called Kebo, which entails dancing and clapping in rhythm.[45]

Children of Africa, A Day in an African Village, as well as many scenes in other AMPP films, purported to show Africans 'as they really are'—as harmless, nameless and primitive subjects living outside historical time and ruled by an imperial order of which they know little. This careful construction of an ahistorical Africa in the scripts of Rogers, though, conveniently suppressed the realities of colonial rule following the 1884–85 Berlin Conference. Just a half century before the inauguration of the AMPP, the Congo, 'owned' and ruled solely by Belgium's King Leopold II as the Congo Free State, became the staging ground for one of the most ruthlessly exploitative regimes in the sordid history of African partition. Beginning with the extraction of ivory, followed in the 1890s by the intense exploitation of wild rubber to satisfy escalating demand in the industrial world, Congolese who resisted the grueling dictates of forced labor were kidnapped, mutilated and often killed.[46]

While Ray Garner recognized the excesses of Leopold briefly in his private notes, it is this very history—one loaded with significance for indigenous subjects in the Congo—which one looks for in vain even in the one AMPP film that references the 'realities' of colonial rule explicitly. *How an African Tribe is Ruled Under Colonial Government* is worth looking at in some detail, for ironically it is remarkable both for its denial of—and frank acceptance of—European interventions in African life. The hastily-typed notes for Harmon's 'Program Material' describe the film as something of a departure for the AMPP: "Other films in the series produced by the Africa Motion Picture Project show mission influences in eliminating that fear and subjstituing gaith [*sic*] and courage, in preparing Africans to accept hygienic methods and scientitifci [*sic*] cures for their deiseases [*sic*] and in throwing away their fetishes and incantation; in educating Africans; life in a typical African village; child life in Africa; the missionary at work, and in training; leprosy controls." *How an African Tribe is Ruled*, while reiterating the debilitating effects of African "fear and superstition" represented in other films, goes further in showing "government methods in action, men and women as they fit into the colonial system; indistrial [*sic*] and raw material occupations; the westernization of Africans as far as training goes."[47]

The film, of course, makes no mention of the depredations of Henry Morton Stanley, or the subjugation of African communities during the period of late nineteenth century conquest. Yet it does present some stark aspects of day-to-day life in the Congo under later colonial rule, including the celebration of

Belgian holidays, with the Force Publique (an African military/police force[48])
marching for the entertainment of Belgian colonial officials; the ubiquity of
medal chiefs; the collection of taxes; the registration of workers; public works
programs such as brush clearance; and finally, a long, dramatized segment
contrasting European and African systems of justice. Although the intent of
the film was to show the 'civilizing' benefits of Belgian rule in Central Africa, read through a postcolonial lens it now reads more like a laundry list of
grievances on the part of the subject population. In fact, during the 1930s the
Force Publique was considered by many Congolese to be little more than an
occupying force, medal chiefs were often viewed as puppets for the colonial regime, and onerous taxes provided justification for localized popular uprisings.
Moreover, the registration of workers elicited similar complaints, as did forced
labor requirements for clearing roads. While conscription for compulsory road
construction could be justified as an improvement over the reliance on 'native
porterage,' the work was nevertheless grueling, often exposing African males
to malaria-infested conditions and resulting in more direct colonial control over
rural areas due to improved transportation.

   How an African Tribe is Ruled concludes with a long dramatized segment
comparing the merits of 'native' and European justice. Following a death at-
tributed to witchcraft, the life of a young woman whose family is (unfairly?)
accused of the deed is demanded by the victim's family as payment. Following several trials in native courts, the case is finally brought before a tribunal
headed by a Belgian colonial officer, and the young woman is promptly released. While the story highlights the 'objectivity' and fairness of European
judicial decisions, it unwittingly exposes the fact that rulings in indigenous
courts could be overturned at will by lowly colonial officials.

CREATING 'AFRICA' IN AFRICA

Left alone with the Africa constructed in (and for) these films, viewers may
wonder how the AMPP managed to procure any actors at all. Were Africans coerced, or were they unaware of the ideological slant of the films? In
fact, as the diaries in this book show, Ray and Virginia Garner were held in
high esteem by many local villagers, and the film shoots were quite popular
events which brought out the multitudes as the cameras were being set up.[49]
Yet the diaries and scrapbooks of the filmmakers also expose the ambiguities involved in creating a reel Africa; in contrast to the Harmon Foundation
archives stored at the National Archives, Virginia Garner's reflections offer a
rare, thick description of the social realities and power relationships involved
in producing images in Africa. Unlike the AMPP films, which were con-

ceived in New York through a moralizing, missionary lens, the diaries supply a relatively unfiltered, secular account of the vicissitudes of filmmaking, in which we find fascinating stories of weather delays, technical difficulties, cultural confusions, and most importantly, quotidian forms of resistance on the part of some African villagers, chiefs, and even actors.

Although not as dramatic as the violence that erupted during the filming of *De Voortrekkers* in South Africa, the Garners did encounter a number of obstacles during production. One ongoing problem was climatic. The Harmon Foundation estimated that the project would take six months to complete, but constant cloud cover and other unexpected weather constraints in Central Africa stalled the shooting endlessly, leading to months of frustration and a shooting schedule that ballooned to three times the expected length. Weather concerns, mixed with extensive tree cover, often forced the crew to improvise for lack of light, which then led to other problems: for one film, Ray Garner found it impossible to shoot in a local graveyard, a problem he remedied by having villagers build a temporary one in a location of his own choosing. The day of the shooting, however, he decided the grave markings did not look 'African' enough, leading him to construct rather hurriedly a number of his own African fetishes for a more 'authentic' look. In addition, some villagers had concerns that Garner had ulterior motives for having the graves dug, fearing they might become victims in some diabolical plan devised by the film crew.

We also learn through the diaries that the Garners succeeded only in recruiting mission-educated Africans to star in the films after discovering that other villagers seemed 'sullen and withdrawn' and refused to participate. While the Garners perceived the intransigence of unwilling locals as reflecting an isolated traditionalism, it is more likely that their antipathy was due not so much to a lack of contact with the West, but rather because of it: while as late as the 1890s the BaKuba still jealously guarded their seclusion with some success, in 1900 Congo Free State forces invaded Mushenge to bring the kingdom under the sway of Leopold's government. The Kuba kingdom, however, remained defiant and revolted in 1904, a conflict which saw the nearby Luba and Lulua ally with the colonial state. The following year, the kingdom was invaded again, this time decisively, forcing a reluctant King Kot aPe to sign a treaty transferring political authority over to the Congo Free State.

It is not surprising then that significant lingering resentments required that the Garners draw primarily upon the mission-schooled population to act in their films. The role of Bamba (as child and adult), for instance, was played by two brothers—Minsoto and his older brother Bafiba, a fifth year student in the Ecole Prostestante des Assistants Médicaux au Congo. While working with the mission-educated elite enabled the films to be made, Virginia Garner fretted that this led to some unexpected problems as the film crew was forced to re-impose a measure of 'primitivity' on their actors:

> We had a hard time with the villagers as they didn't want to wear loin cloths. The Chief got after them though. Then the women wouldn't take off their blouses. Some of them wear grass skirts here but they look silly with a blouse on top. We were told we could never get the villagers again and we just had to finish then. Africans are sure terrible when it comes to taking pictures. Half of them ran off in the middle of the morning because they said 'we're tired.' We had to chase them up and promise to pay them in order to get them back.[50]

As African historian Roger Anstey observed decades ago in his seminal work on the Belgian Congo, missionary "impact was usually restricted to individuals and fragments of tribes" during the colonial period.[51] Thus, the Garners' access to certain areas was restricted, and permission to film in most local villages had to be carefully negotiated with local chiefs, as the BaKuba were known for their attachment to the surviving remnants of traditional power. Even when formal permission was granted, for several films the Garners found filming the secret idols of the Kuba difficult: the keeper of the artifacts (which generally remained out of sight when not in use for special ceremonial purposes) remained reluctant to produce them for the films, and quickly returned them to storage after shooting every scene, frustrating the crew that often required a second or third shot.[52]

The Garners' films successfully convey a natural, documentary feel to the viewer, as one sees Africans going about their daily business in villages and towns. But as Virginia Garner noted above, the crew often had to promise financial remuneration to convince villagers to play their parts and to stay on location given the endless hours of preparation for shooting, a policy which only initiated new problems:

> While I was working like a demon Ray and Dr. Freas paid off the people. We planned with Mfienge to give the faithful women each 8 francs and the others a little less to equal the cloths we gave the men in the beginning . . . First the women bellyached about the 8 francs. Freas paid 21 of them, many of whom came once or twice and others appeared at ten o'clock instead of eight. The men then began hollering for pay even though they already had had more than the women—10 francs of cloth. Then Mfienge, who is supposedly fair but always over generous to Bokoites because his daughter is marrying the Chief's son, said to give the men each 5 francs. This they flatly refused! They demanded 10 and Freas immediately gave it to them with no argument. One man objected to this because he was a 'Kapita' in the village even though he did no more than the others. Freas gave him an extra 5 then after more bellyaching another 5.[53]

If Africans were seemingly being put on ethnographic display, they never-theless attempted to exert a measure of control over the process of represen-tation. In Sona Bata the chief "tried to call the people for a meeting but they just wouldn't come. They went right on with their work and some even went off to the gardens."[54] The next day their translator confirmed the dilemma. "Erickson finally arrived and started out with very bad news. The villagers all went off to their gardens this morning and obviously won't cooperate at all in the making of this picture. It doesn't speak very well for this mission—we just can't find a single village with enough Christians to help. We can't blame the Catholics, Salvation Armyists, and heathens for not being interested."[55]

In another setting, King Lukengo of the Kuba warned the Garners: "Show our likenesses only to a few people."[56] Yet surely the king was being somewhat coy. In fact, for one scene in which he was going to appear, he kept the crew waiting endlessly as he tried on twenty different costumes before coming to a decision as to which one he would wear for the shoot. Whether the king was being vain, or whether he was simply sending out a not-so-subtle message that he, and not the Garners, would control the pace of the project, is difficult to say. But what made the situation even more unbearable for the film crew was that the king was entirely paralyzed (except for the use of one hand), and the film crew watched helplessly hour after hour as the king's tribesmen assisted him in trying on his entire wardrobe before allowing the cameras to roll. "With all his fancy clothes to choose from," complained Virginia, "he had to keep us cooling our heels for so long that the sun went in." In fact, the day was a total loss, and the Garners had to wait until the following day to try again.[57]

The BaKuba clearly appreciated and understood the power of visual rep-resentation, and the king was, no doubt, thrilled that moving images of the kingdom were making it out to the broader world for the first time. For some decades, in fact, the Kuba had enjoyed a reputation as one of Central Africa's most 'famous' tribes with a proud heritage of sculpture-making and raffia cloth weaving. Worldwide recognition of the Kuba dates back to the Red Rubber period, when African American missionary William Henry Shep-pard struggled to advertise the exploitation of the Kuba tribe to the outside world. The BaKuba, many of them children, agreed to be photographed with their bodies wrapped in white sheets, providing a stark contrast to their dark-skinned, mutilated hands exposed in the foreground. The strategy paid divi-dends: the photographs were shown in 'atrocity meetings' in British churches and elsewhere, and activists throughout the Atlantic world began applying pressure on Leopold II to reform the Congo Free State.

The BaKuba had other opportunities to pose for the outside world during this period. Twenty years after the Red Rubber depredations, Casimir Zagourski was allowed unparalleled access to BaKuba villagers and produced an impressive number of ethnographic photographs that today remain virtually unparalleled in the field. And just a few years after the Garners' departure, another European photographer, Eliot Elisofon, was allowed into the kingdom to shoot a set of black and white images for *Time* magazine (including the cover photo), a spread which cemented the kingdom's reputation as a 'noble' and creative one, if still primitive, in the Western world. These examples show that while many Africans were opposed to any contact with the Western world, there were factions in the community that were fairly savvy when it came to advertising the kingdom through visual means, and who sought to capitalize on the opportunity for having their images distributed to the outside world.

CONCLUSION

The AMPP films and the diaries and scrapbooks of the Garners demonstrate that Central Africa was not simply a *tabula rasa* for American missionary endeavors, but rather a site for complex cultural engagements between representatives of the West, mission-educated villagers, and chiefs who attempted to salvage a measure of control over the production process. Africans who took part in the Africa Motion Picture Project, of course, ultimately had little control over how the celluloid Africas would be exhibited and distributed, a process controlled primarily by the Africa Committee and the Harmon Foundation. Moreover, to my knowledge, the films have never been shown in Africa.

The Africas of the AMPP were initially textualized in New York through script-writing and re-contextualized in Africa during the production phase. Finally, they were reframed yet again in the United States during the process of post-production and distribution, for it was Emory Ross and other missionaries who largely set the prism through which the films would be edited and exhibited in American churches and schools. For instance, these missionaries envisioned that *A Day in an African Village* would help stimulate discussion of parallels that "might be drawn between these people and the Indians on our own continent, with special considerations to customs in common, primitive attributes of each and how they differ, and the civilizations or extent of culture to which they have attained."[58]

The film was to be much more than a simple ethnographic display viewed by each spectator in isolation, for it was to be accompanied by Christian hymns, sung by the audience to piano and victrola, such as "Sheltering Wing" (by Joseph Barney), and "Tidings" (by James Walch), followed by a group reading of Psalms 53:2: "God looked down from Heaven upon the Children of Men, to see if there were any that did understand, that did seek God." According to the Harmon suggestions for exhibition, viewers should "consider this statement in the light of the good and bad to be found in the life of *A Day in an African Village*. Or do you see evil in this primitive state? Is it entirely good? Why and how have men aspired beyond it, both in material things and in religion?" In closing each exhibition, a prayer was to be read that framed the film squarely within the tradition of Christian proselytization in Central Africa:

> O God, may we see in this picture today the goodness which abides in the simple life of these people in an African village; and may we, through the courage which comes from our strong faith, avoid the pitfalls of their superstitutions [*sic*]; and the childlike quality which at times leads them to cruelty and ignorance; may we aid in carrying to them the Christian message of faith and love among all men; and so learn to take our place in that larger world of a whole globe, to whose eventual organization in the spirit of Christian values we look ever forward with faith in Jesus Christ.[59]

This prayer exposes the weighty effects of appropriation in the dissemination of cultural images beyond the arena of their initial production, and must be understood as a type of cultural theft, wherein forms of signification are extracted, distilled and disseminated through a particular ideological lens. Despite this fact, however, the diaries that comprise this book suggest that subjects of empire, while living far from the centers of power that sponsored and distributed such images, were both aware of the importance of cultural representations and sought to exert a measure of control over the conditions under which they were produced in the field. Kings and chiefs forced the film crew to negotiate for permission to shoot, and sometimes delayed shooting on a regular basis. While many villagers refused to act in the films at all, even mission-educated Africans wandered off, demanded payment for their services, dickered over pay scales, and contested the construction of 'primitivity' that the film scripts dictated.

In order to form a deeper understanding of the impact of the images on disparate cultures and individuals, and especially to heed for the first time the voices of the unheard, we need a fuller appreciation not just of the larger global structures which dictated the flow of images in their final form, but an appreciation of the micro-politics of the production process. Although a textual analysis of the films is vital to that understanding, refocusing our analytical lens to include the site of their physical fabrication—in this case through the help of a unique set of diaries—is vital for comprehending the micro-negotiations involved in their creation, enabling us to visualize a hitherto-obscured measure of agency on the part of the colonized. What this tells us ultimately is that the production of images is not just an aesthetic/intellectual process engaged in by an individualized subject, but rather is a profoundly social act that cannot be divorced from the historical conditions which led to its creation in the first place.

Virginia Garner's diaries help us to understand that several competing Africas were struggling for ascendancy during the interwar period. Missionaries imagined an Africa in need of profound spiritual and physical regeneration in the context of a burgeoning Christian consciousness; colonial officials sought to pull a profit in the context of an Africa that required the civilizing effects of Western culture in order to modernize; and, finally, indigenous communities attempted to construct an Africa that retained a degree of local, autonomous control, even while accepting many of the dictates of both missionaries and white colonial elites.

Of course, there are many other treasures to be discovered in Virginia Garner's diaries. Some readers will be particularly interested in her trip to the diamond compounds of Tshikapa in the Belgian Congo's Kasai region, in which Congolese worked by the thousands with shaved heads and underwent rigorous daily examinations to prevent smuggling. Others will be fascinated by the role of women in the diaries, including Virginia's own duties as photographer as well as her description of the unappreciated political position of women in the Kuba kingdom, particularly her ruminations on the role of the king's mother in the affairs of state. What is certain is that we are all richer for Virginia's attention to detail and her determination to keep a record of her travels for posterity.

NOTES

1. Cited in Howard M. Freas, M.D, "Real Life and Reel Life in African Jungles," *African Missions Through the Camera's Eye* (1939?): 2. Emory Ross papers, Union Theological Seminary (UTS), NY.

2. William L. Rogers, "New Moving Pictures of African Missions," *Missionary Review of the World* 60 (1937): 251. Rogers states that ten mission boards contributed to the project. However, AMPP filmmakers Virginia and Ray Garner, in a magazine article a few years later, make mention of eight contributing organizations. Virginia and Ray Garner, "African Expedients," *Movie Makers* (Feb 1940): Virginia Garner scrapbook of the AMPP, author's possession. The article "Dramatizing Missions: Work of Converting Africans Filmed by Foundation," *Newsweek* (Oct. 17, 1938), also in Garner's scrapbook, reaffirms that eight boards were affiliated with the AMPP: North Presbyterian, South Presbyterian, Methodist Episcopal, Southern Methodist, Northern Baptist, Disciples of Christ, Seventh Day Adventist, and Brethren.

3. Emory Ross served in the Congo as general secretary of the Congo Protestant Council (CPC) and editor of the *Congo Mission News*. After his return to the U.S., he became executive secretary of the Africa Committee. For biographical overview, see "Dr. Emory Ross, Noted Missionary to Africa, Dies," *The Washington Post*, Sunday Mar. 18, 1973: B6.

4. This is not to deny that Western representations of Africa always played a foundational role in Europe's engagement with the continent. Indeed, a key premise of this paper is precisely that the symbolic universe of "Africa" itself up until the mid-twentieth century was largely a creation of the West.

5. The original reels, in poor condition, are located at the Disciples of Christ (hereafter DOC) headquarters in Nashville, TN. Copies can be found in the Harmon Foundation archives, United States National Archives and Records Administration (NARA), Washington, D.C.

6. Barry Bowen, "A History of Christian Film," http://www.christianheadlines .com/filmhistory.html (accessed July 17, 2007).

7. The rise of a visual Christianity through postcards, films, illuminated Bibles and the like has engaged many scholars in recent years. See Burke O. Long, *Imagining the Holy Land: Maps, Models and Fantasy Travels* (Bloomington: Indiana University Press, 2002); David Morgan, "Protestant Visual Culture and the Challenges of Urban American during the Progressive Era," in *Faith in the Market: Religion and the Rise of Urban Culture Commercial*, edited by John M. Giggie and Diane Weston (New Brunswick: Rutgers University Press, 2002): 37–56; Paul Gutjahr, "American Protestant Bible Illustration from Copper Plates to Computers," in *The Visual Culture of American Religions*, edited by David Morgan and Sally M. Promrey (Berkeley: University of California Press, 2001), 267–85.

8. William Hockman, *Projected Visual Aids in the Church* (Boston: The Pilgrim Press, 1947), 22–3.

9. Oliver M. Wiard, *History: South Congregational Church* (n.p., n.d.: privately published church history), 7. Jump continued to promote motion pictures with religious themes in a privately published pamphlet. See Herbert Jump, *The Religious Possibilities of the Motion Picture* (n.p., n.d. [1911?]). See also Herbert Jump, "The Social Influence of the Motion Picture." *The Playground* V, no. 3 (June 1911):74–84.

10. Glenn Reynolds, "Image and Empire: Cinema, Race and the Rise of Mass Black Spectatorship in Southern Africa, 1920–40" (Phd diss., SUNY Stony Brook, 2005). Bhekizizwe Peterson, "The Politics of Leisure during the Early Days of South African Cinema," in *To Change Reels: Film and Film Culture in South Africa*, edited by Isabel Balseiro and Ntongela Masilela (Detroit: Wayne State University, 2003), 31–46. In his programs, Phillips interspersed religious films with travel shorts, topical shorts, comedies and other films. The program soon expanded to mining areas in Southern and Northern Rhodesia.

Emory Ross of the AMPP was no stranger to the Mines' Compound Cinema Circuit. In his missionary treatise *Out of Africa*, he applauded Phillips' efforts to provide for the recreational needs of Africans in the "congested labor concentrations of the Rand." Emory Ross, *Out of Africa* (New York: Friendship Press, 1936), 115.

11. Philip Mosley, *Split Screen: Belgian Cinema and Cultural Identity* (Albany: State University of New York Press, 2001), 34.

12. Ordonnance Législative No. 12/Inf. du 12 Janvier 1945: "Il est interdit d'admettre à des représentations cinématographiques, ouvertes ou non au public, des personnes outres que de race européenne ou de race asiatique ("It is forbidden to admit to cinema exhibitions, whether open to the public or not, persons other than members

of the European or Asiatic race"). L. van Bever, *Le Cinéma Pour Africains* (Brussels: G. van Campenhout, 1952), 55. Notably, the Belgian Congo soon revised its position and enthusiastically embraced the production of didactic films tailored specifically for black audiences within the colony. During the political turmoil of 1959, a new commission implemented general censorship for all films in the colony, irrespective of the racial makeup of audiences. Georges Brausch, *Belgian Administration in the Congo* (London: Oxford University Press, 1961), 26. See also L.Van Bever, "The Cinema in the Belgian Congo," *The Colonial Review* (Sept 1952): 210–11.

13. Peter Davis, *In Darkest Hollywood* (Cape Town: Ravan Press, 1996), 2. Paul Landau, "Empires of the Visual: Photography and Colonial Administration in Africa," in *Images and Empires: Visuality in Colonial and Postcolonial Africa*, edited by Paul Landau and Deborah Kaspin (Berkeley: University of California Press, 2002), 147–49.

14. For a slightly different treatment of this concept, within the black diaspora, see James Sidbury, *Becoming African in America* (New York: Oxford University Press, 2007). This notion of a constructed Africa is sure to find disfavor in the Afrocentric community, which posits an essentialized Black community in contradistinction to an essentialized White community. In fact, though, only in the late nineteenth century, in response to European constructions of the Dark Continent, did activists within Africa and the Diaspora begin formulating a Pan-African awareness—an awareness that, in the late twentieth century, was expressed in the political/economic sphere through the African Union and similar organizations.

15. For the British tradition, see John Grierson, "First Principles of Documentary," in *Nonfiction Film, Theory and Criticism*, edited by Richard Meran Barsam (New York: E.P. Dutton & Co., 1976), 19–30.

16. Kevin C. Dunn, *Imagining the Congo: The International Relations of Identity* (New York: Palgrave Macmillan, 2003), 8.

17. Thelma Gutsche, *The History and Social Significance of Motion Pictures in South Africa, 1895–1940* (Cape Town: Howard Timmins, 1972), 314, n. 24. See also Davis, *In Darkest Hollywood*: 128–35. For an interpretation that suggests the film was more a validation of British imperialism than Afrikaner hegemony, see Keyan G. Tomaselli, *Encountering Modernity: Twentieth Century South African Cinemas* (Amsterdam: UNISA Press, 2006), 129.

18. Ruth Slade, *The Belgian Congo* (London: Oxford University Press, 1961), 2.

19. Marvin D. Markowitz, "The Missions and Political Development in the Congo," *Africa: Journal of the International African Institute* 40, 3 (July 1970): 234.

20. Jean Comaroff, *Body of Power, Spirit of Resistance* (Chicago: University of Chicago Press, 1985), 31.

21. King Leopold II of Belgium maneuvered successfully at the 1884–5 Berlin Conference to have other European powers recognize him as the sole 'owner' of the vast Congo in Central Africa, after which his regime became notorious for its brutal methods of labor mobilization and the resource extraction (primarily ivory and rubber). Stanley Shaloff, *Reform in Leopold's Congo* (Richmond: John Knox Press, 1970), Ch. 6. Adam Hochschild, *King Leopold's Ghost* (Boston: Mariner Books, 1999): Ch. 11–15. Pagan Kennedy, *Black Livingstone: A True Tale of Adventure in the Nineteenth Century Congo* (New York: Penguin, 2002). In contrast, most Catho-

lic missionaries tacitly or openly supported Leopold. See Markowitz, "Missions:" 235–7; René Lemarchand, *Political Awakening in the Belgian Congo* (Berkeley: University of California Press, 1964):122–3. Catherine Ann Cline, "The Church and the Movement for Congo Reform," *Church History* 32, 1 (Mar, 1963): 46–56.

22. IMC/CBMS, BH2003, Box 293, #139, Anet to Oldham, 14 Oct. 1932; IMC/CBMS, BH2003, Box 293, #140, Oldham to Anet, 4 Jan. 1933.

23. IMC/CBMS, BH2003, Box 293, #142.

24. "Twenty Eventful Years," *Congo Mission News* (Oct 1932): 3.

25. Rogers, "New Moving Pictures:" 250–1.

26. In French, the organization is known as Église du Christ au Congo (ECC), and is currently a union of 62 Protestant denominations. In the Congo it is commonly referred to simply as 'The Protestant Church.'

27. Kenneth M. Cameron, *Africa on Film: Beyond Black and White* (New York: Continuum, 1994), 94–5. Osa and Martin Johnson were among the most prolific filmmakers in East and Central Africa in the 1920–30s, until the latter's death from an airline accident in early 1937 soon after submitting footage to Ross. *Simba* was later remade and updated for the Mau Mau emergency. See David M. Anderson, "Mau Mau at the Movies: Contemporary Representations of an Anti-Colonial War," *South African Historical Journal* 48 (2003): 71–89.

28. Rogers, "New Moving Pictures": 250–1.

29. Sidbury, *Becoming African in America*, 6.

30. Emory Ross, *Out of Africa*, 9. Ross speaks in decidedly Eurocentric terms of the tremendous changes overcoming the continent: "And in the Congo we have the amazing, the unique spectacle of the very sons and grandsons of the men who repeatedly ambushed Stanley and more than once carried off the dripping flesh of his followers to their waiting villages . . . aiding in one of the swiftest and most lucrative of economic penetrations the world has ever seen." Ross, *Out of Africa*, 10–1.

31. Emory Ross, "The Last Continent to Join the World," *Missions Magazine* (May 1952): 278.

32. Ross, *Out of Africa*, 11.

33. Ray and Virginia Garner, *1972 Manuscript* (unpublished joint memoir in author's possession), 113.

34. For the early efforts of the foundation, see "Lebanon Trust: An Experiment in Small Parks for Small Cities," *Survey* 40 (Feb. 1, 1913), 749–753. The Harmon Foundation also funded playground construction in black neighborhoods and provided scholarships to black students. For a detailed look at the programs offered by Mary Beattie of the Harmon Foundation, see Gary A. Reynolds and Beryl J. Wright, *Against the Odds: African-American Artists and the Harmon Foundation* (Newark: The Newark Museum, 1989). For Harmon's shift in emphasis to African artists, see John C. Walter, "The Harmon Foundation and the Sponsorship of Contemporary African Artists, 1947–67," *Contours: A Journal of the African Diaspora*, http://www.press.uillinois.edu/journals/contours/1.2/walter.html. (accessed Jan. 15, 2008)

35. This account is taken from Garner and Garner, *1972 Manuscript*, 82–7.

36. The standard formula contrasts the wise African, who benefits from his decision to conform to Western culture, with the foolish African who suffers from his

irrational refusal to abandon tradition. See Glenn Reynolds, "'From Red Blanket to Civilization': Propaganda and Recruitment Films for South Africa's Gold Mines, 1920–1940," *Journal of Southern African Studies*, Vol. 33, issue 1 (March 2007). J.M. Burns, *Flickering Shadows: Cinema and Identity in Colonial Zimbabwe* (Athens: Ohio University Press, 2002), 79–80.

37. Burns, *Flickering Shadows,* 79.

38. James Sweet, *Recreating Africa: Culture, Kinship and Religion in the Africa-Portuguese World, 1441–1770* (Chapel Hill, University of North Carolina Press, 2003), 161. Sweet gives acknowledgement to the research of Peter Geschiere, *The Modernity of Witchcraft: Politics and the Occult in Postcolonial Africa* (Charlottesville: University Press of Virginia, 1997).

39. Virginia Garner, *Africa Diary*: August 23, 1938.

40. Megan Vaughan, *Curing Their Ills: Colonial Power and African Illness* (Stanford: Stanford University Press, 1991), 79.

41. Cited in "Slave Trade Key to Leprosy Spread," BBC News (May 13, 2005), http://news.bbc.co.uk/1/hi/health/4540461.stm. (accessed April 14, 2008)

42. Paul Hoefler (Dir.), *Africa Speaks!* (1930), distributed by The Incredibly Strange Filmworks, Inc., Jamestown, MO. Curiously, the poster displayed on this VHS edition is a painting of a grizzled Paul Hoefler pointing to a map of South America.

43. Cameron, *Africa On Film,* 51.

44. Jan Nederveen Pieterse, "The Parade of the Vanquished," *African Societies*, http://www.africansocieties.org/n4/eng/pieterse.htm. (accessed July 1, 2008)

45. NARA, Harmon Foundation, *Children of Africa,* Program Material, 2. The Program Notes for the AMPP confirms this interpretation, as American viewers were encouraged to perceive African beliefs as the 'superstitions of children' which needed to be eradicated.

46. See Kevin Grant, *A Civilised Savagery: Britain and the New Slaveries in Africa, 1884–1926* (New York: Routledge, 2005). See also Hochschild, *King Leopold's Ghost.*

47. NARA, Harmon Foundation, *How An African Tribe is Ruled Under Colonial Government*, Program Material, 4.

48. Military shots of soldiers marching in lockstep were a common theme in the late 1930s, proliferating both in the United States and in Fascist Europe.

49. Local villagers in the Congo, for instance, presented the Garners with a number of artifacts to take back home to America.

50. Garner, *Africa Diary*: June 10, 1939.

51. Roger Anstey, *King Leopold's Legacy* (London: Oxford University Press, 1966), 35.

52. Garner and Garner, *1972 Manuscript*, 118.

53. Garner, *Africa Diary*: April 29, 1939.

54. Ibid: February 8, 1939.

55. Ibid: February 9, 1939.

56. Garner and Garner, *1972 Manuscript*, 116–19.

57. Garner, *Africa Diary*: October 21, 1938.

58. NARA, Harmon Foundation, *A Day in an African Village*, Program Material, 3.

59. Ibid.

Africa Diary:
1938

[Editor's Note: Virginia Garner made detailed entries in her diaries every day from April 8, 1938, when she and her new husband, Ray Garner, embarked for Africa, through their return home on September 5, 1939. The following excerpts highlight their adventures, with particular focus on the Africa Motion Picture Project. Virginia's mostly typewritten entries are transcribed as written, retaining the original spelling and punctuation errors. Handwritten notes added by Virginia or Ray are shown in brackets. Editor's notes are shown in brackets and italics.]

Friday Night, April 8 ["SS Konigstein": New York Harbor—Rotterdam—Antwerp]

We're off! It has really come true and we are going to a big country to do a big job in a big way.

It is raining and foggy so we can see very little of New York. The air is so fresh and invigorating that we have been out on deck a long time. Ray sang me a new song which was very lovely and just for me. We are so happy together and thank God for this work we have been given.

Saturday, April 9

Our first day at sea and what a glorious feeling to have nothing but sky and water on every side. The day is rather stormy and every once in a while the boat does some real rocking. We have not been seriously affected however.

What a night! The clouds are blowing away and the moon and lots of stars are shining. Tremendous waves go up and up till they're level with the boat and just as we are about to be swept overboard the boat lifts us high into the sky. There's so *much* water!

31

Sunday, April 10

I kept skidding back and forth in my bunk all night. I didn't feel sick but would just drop off to sleep when I'd skid from the wall right to the edge of the bed where I clung till I slammed against the wall again. I couldn't get much sleep and finally crawled in with Ray. He slept like a log all night. For once I wish I weighed 165 pounds!

We feel wonderful today and are getting some work done besides lots of games. We have a schedule and are enjoying it enormously. It got very stormy during dinner and one of the girls tipped over and sprawled on the floor. It was very windy and snowing a bit. The cold air makes you feel glorious.

Monday, April 11

A clear, cold day. Perfect for pictures but too cold to stay out long. Shot a roll of panatomic with my new filter. Spent a long time chasing the sea gulls that follow the ship. They are lovely shimmering in the sunlight.

Spent a long time going over equipment and typing lists. We shall soon have a complete list in each case and a duplicate in the file. We also have a long list of things to buy during our two days in Belgium. It looks like a weeks worth of shopping.

Tuesday, April 12

Saw "Silent Barriers" tonight. It was good but we were a little disappointed not to see more mountain climbing.

Wednesday, April 13

Have finished working on our equipment. We find we are short 7-100 foot rolls of movie film. We had a Bavarian party tonight. Our band dressed up and we all got silly hats. They had hot dogs & sauerkraut but we had gone to bed.

Thursday, April 14

Developed a roll of my negatives. Some of them look very good. Practiced typing a long while. Was cold and rainy so we couldn't stay out long. Played hearts and rummy.

Saw "Double or Nothing" tonight which was real funny. We wish there were lots more movies.

Saturday, April 16

Ray went and took a few pictures of the masquerade with my new Kalart Flash. He held me & sang so I'd sleep.

Sunday, April 17

Awake at 9 A.M. with my darling singing 'Happy Easter.' It will be a happy one I'm sure. Our first since our wedding. I wish we might see into the Congo today. Easter time there must surely be an inspiration. Those people have so much faith I'm told.

Monday, April 18

Got some sewing done and took a number of pictures. Developed 2 rolls myself.

Tuesday, April 19

Brr! Is it cold! Went out on deck and found the sun just coming up through a mass of clouds. Took a few pictures. We should have color film to preserve the beauty of such a moment the way it really is. When the sun was well up we went back to bed to get warm and slept till 11:50!!

At 1:30 we sighted land! Far off in the distance—Scilly Islands. Our first view of foreign land and what a thrill it is. Ray was so excited he got out the Special and frantically took pictures for an hour.

Worked in our cabin all evening washing & developing. Bed at midnight.

Wednesday, April 20

Got up at 8 A.M. & found five sailors washing the smokestack. Took a number of pictures which I developed after breakfast.

Thursday, April 21 [Rotterdam]

Got up at 6 AM because everyone else on board seemed to be up. Had breakfast at 7 and then dashed off the boat to see Rotterdam.

The city is a maze of canals and everybody rides on bicycles. They all seemed to be going to work and really it was hard to ride in a car there were so many. They put out their hands when turning and look so silly.

The streets are marked with pictures showing what vehicles can use them. Some have only bicycles and others a regular gallery of pictures.

We took a few pictures and then our taxi driver took us shopping. Ray got some Dutch Kill-Me-Quicks that would kill anyone! The salesgirls got a big kick out of us. We went to a camera stone and tried to get an orange filter. They only use yellow ones here though. We found a leather goods store nearby so got a fibre case thing for our shoes. Ray took the other one for the stationary equipment as soon as we got out of New York.

Friday, April 22 ["SS Anversville": Antwerp—Lobito—Matadi]

Got up at 6:30 to find a wet and cold day awaiting us. We got ashore with our baggage and had to get a truck to move it to the pier where the "Anversville" docks. Then we chased all over Antwerp trying to get the customs straightened out. We even had to type new lists of equipment and evaluate everything in francs. Finally after hours of waiting we got our films & cameras in OK and paid duty on our personal belongings, typewriter, and the flares & bulbs that we will use and discard in the Congo. It took us till 2:30 to get all straightened out and get our things on board. We have an extra inside cabin for our luggage. M. Pigeolet said he hasn't had so much trouble in six years and he meets all the missionaries, some of them having a ton or two of equipment.

We managed to stop and buy our cork helmets. Mine is a white-woven straw and Ray's a Khaki material. His is just like a London Bobby's but he says he looks like Livingstone.

Antwerp is a rather dull and dirty looking city. The buildings are mostly very old and the customs building positively ancient and just black inside. It hasn't been washed or painted for twenty or thirty years.

What a laugh I got when we got our tickets and found Reverend Raymond Garner on it! And its on our cabin door as well! Ray is having a fit. He's sure they'll ask him to lead the Sunday Services or Something. It proved helpful in one respect however. We were put at the table with the other missionaries and reverends on board which is so much nicer than French or Belgium people we can't talk with.

There are three Swedish Missionaries, Mr & Mrs. Stielstrom and Miss Palmesten, and an American couple with their two little boys 6 and 3 years old. They are very nice and are going to help make the voyage interesting for us.

Sunday, April 24

At ten A.M. Mr. Sprunger had a service in the Salon. It had been announced the evening before but no one came other than the Swedish Missionaries. The sermon was the "Constitution of Christianity" and Ray told Mr. Sprunger that it was the best he ever heard. The three of us got into an involved discussion which lasted till dinner time. We can not quite agree with him that all are lost who do not know Jesus, even those who never have a chance to hear of Him. Mr. Sprunger is grand to talk to—he is so young and outspoken. We like the whole family very much and hope to visit them in Congo.

We had a movie tonight, all in French. Ray fell asleep but I had a swell time trying to figure out what it was all about. There was a Popeye too and we were about the only ones to understand that. How I wish I'd payed attention in my French classes!

Monday, April 25

Sat and talked with Mrs. Sprunger while the men played chess. Then we all went out on deck for awhile. Met the Swedish couple and we all pranced around. They are very lonesome as they had to leave their 6 and 8 year old children at home. The climate is very bad at Kimpese where they are going and there is no school for the white children.

Wednesday, April 27

Got up at six just as we were nearing Madeira Island. What a thrill to see mountains growing right out of the sea which has been so very level for days and days. The houses are grouped around the bay and spread up and out to the very tops of the mountains. They are all white with red roofs—there must be a law—and look very pretty.

As soon as we dropped anchor a fleet of little boats started toward us from all along the shore. They were laden with wicker chairs, table cloths, jewelry, and little boys who dove for francs (not pennies). The water was so very clear we could see them swimming under water and felt very much like joining them.

We went in to gobble our breakfast at 6:45 so we could go ashore. When we got out on deck again we found it hung with beautiful Madeira linens from end to end. Ray finally got me by them and down the gangway to the launch which took about fifty of us ashore at a time. Just after we got off I was so excited that I dropped the camera and broke my new green filter that was made specially for my camera.

We walked along some narrow cobble stone streets to the Post Office to mail our letters. We also wrote some postal cards and sent the filter mount to Rogers so that he can have a new one made.

The people who are mostly Portugese are dark skinned with curly black hair. Some are very handsome but for the most part they are dirty and ragged—their scale of living being far below ours. Some of the older people still wear long full skirts, shawls on their heads, and high boots or no shoes at all.

Thursday, April 28

Got up at seven and dressed in a hurry because we saw a very mysterious looking island through the porthole. Up on deck we found one on either side of us—very weird in the morning light with their heads in the clouds. The sun shone through every so often, lighting up a bit of land and sea. Ray ran for my camera and we made ourselves late for breakfast trying to get a good picture.

Mr. Sprunger came and helped us fill out government forms so that we can be admitted to the Congo. They are very fussy—we had to present letters of good conduct and health and a contract besides the form which gave our life history.

Friday, April 29

Another even more beautiful day. I hated to stay in even to develop my film this morning. It looks about the best so far though.

Today everyone wore their cork helmets and Ray was so glad because he has been dying to wear his ever since we got them. Even tiny boys and girls have them. We saw some whales blowing water in the air. There must have been quite a few of them as we saw six or seven fountains coming out of the sea at a time. I got so excited—I never thought I'd see anything like that.

Sunday, May 1

Had our service at 10 A.M. this morning but much to our disappointment it was all in French—even "Nearer My God to Thee."

We had movies tonight and got a big kick out of Walt Disneys penguins speaking French. The other picture was quite funny although we couldn't understand a word of it.

Monday, May 2

Awoke to a scorching hot day. Ray went over the scenario of our first picture, Bwamba, with Mr. Stenstrom who is a swedish missionary at Kimpese near Sona Bata where the picture is to be made.

Tuesday, May 3

Another nice warm day. We started taking our quinine tonight before going to bed. 5 grains a day is the rule.

Thursday, May 5

Late yesterday we crossed the Equator. The boat leaped right over just as everyone said it would while I was taking a bath. The water splashed over the edge of the tub and I almost floated out!

Ray was taking movies so I was sorry I missed out on the kissing. But Ray wasn't! He doesn't approve of my kissing anyone else, ever.

Friday, May 6

This morning Ray was too sleepy to get up for breakfast and I was too sleepy to make him—so we slept till 9:30. We had two apples and a pear that did very nicely for our petit dejeuner. I had enough to eat at dinner last night to keep me all day anyway. We had lobster and other fancy dishes that Ray couldn't eat. I hope when we get to Africa he'll learn not to be so finicky.

Saturday, May 7

Ray wouldn't get up this morning so I went to breakfast without him. I got my washing done and two letters written before the lazy bones got up. Spent the rest of the morning up on deck writing and going over methods of keeping records.

Stayed out under the moon till 1 A.M. Only one more day before we see Africa!

Sunday, May 8

Had a job getting Ray up again this morning but I decided he just had to get up for breakfast. Missing it 3 times in a row begins to be real lazy.

Mr. Sprunger led the service this morning, in English thank goodness. After it we played hide and seek with the little boys. Missionaries know how to have a good time I must say.

Did some more writing and then went on deck—it was such a beautiful night. Got to bed much too late.

Monday, May 9 [Lobito]

The night steward woke us at 5 A.M. as we wanted to see the sun rise over Africa. We hurried out on deck and found our ship drifting a mile or so off the coast, waiting for daylight to guide us into the harbor. Great black clouds of night were moving to the west as the first faint light of day stole up and put out the eastern stars. Africa was only a long dark line with a few twinkling lights as we waited with awe and impatience for the dawn. It grew into rows of hills with high mountains in the background. Our ship went on as the dawn flamed in the East and we saw the hills were like none we had ever seen. They were low and rounded, worn into a sedimentary plateau, and covered with sparse scrub-like vegetation completely browned by the dry season. We saw a long spit of land extending fully two miles into the sea, and thought how crazy some people were who had built houses there. And then the sun came out, our boat drew near the dock, and we found the spit of land only 100 yards wide was Lobito!

The first thing we heard was a rooster crowing, and the first thing we saw was a Ford sign, so we felt right at home. We had breakfast and went ashore just after 7 A.M. as we only had till 9 before sailing. First we went to buy stamps in a funny little store that had all kinds of skins hanging outside on big racks. I wanted to get a leopard to put in front of my fireplace that I haven't got yet but Mr. Sprunger says we can get one from the natives much cheaper.

We were quite impressed by the natives working. They move even slower than the W.P.A. workers. We watched five of them putting up a foundation and only saw one brick lifted in five minutes. They will have to move faster than that for us or we won't get home for two years.

Their clothes are pathetic in most cases. They have been patched until you don't know the color of the original garment and then worn to shreds. And I really mean shreds. Some of the women wear a dress, then a piece of cloth wound around their bodies, another over their shoulders, and still another over the basket on their heads hanging way down behind. Mrs. Sprunger says they do it to show that they have cloth as evidently the more they have the better they are. I'd hate to see Mother wearing the wads of it she usually has.

Best of all I liked the dear little black babies tied to their mothers backs. One pointed right at us and was so cute I would like her for my own.

I am amazed that so many natives come to live in such a place. Most of them have nothing to do and just sit around on the curbs.

Tuesday, May 10 [Mouth of Congo River]

Slept through breakfast and then worked hard to get all the last things done before we start our pictures.

After dinner we went on deck to study and write. Our ship was just entering the mouth of the Congo so we didn't get so much done. At 2:30 a small launch came out to meet us from the small town of Banana. It was full of natives who came aboard to unload tomorrow at Boma and Matadi. They seemed to have all their belongings with them, lamps, chickens, mats, and bundles of every size and description. One had only a cane!

On either side there are dense tropical growths that smell like a hothouse and we are yearning to explore them. We saw our first native hut on the shore with a great palm tree growing over it. Just like the pictures you always see.

Did some packing and went to bed early so we can wake up and see Boma.

May 10, 1938 [Letter to mother from Jinny]

Dear Mother,

We have just anchored in the Congo River for the night as there are so many twists and turns that a big ship like ours dare not move after dark. Tomorrow we spend the morning at Boma and then three hours sail up river to Matadi. It has all been so wonderful and there is so much still to come that I wonder if I can stand the excitement. I can't believe that I shall really see African villages and animals. I thought they only existed in story books. If you could see the dense tropical growth on each side of us you'd think you were dreaming I am sure.

We just went up on deck to look at the natives. They sleep on straw mats with a piece of cloth over them to protect them from the skeeters. They can sleep anywhere just like dogs. We havn't smelled any too bad ones yet and are hoping for the best.

Our waiter gets a big kick out of us. He speaks English fairly well and always laughs at Ray's table tricks. Tonight Ray accidently spilled some of his water and he said "The gentleman always likes to play" by way of excusing him. He always calls Ray 'gentleman' and me 'lady.'

May 10, 1938 [Letter to Jinny's mother from Ray]

Dear Mother,

The mouth of the Congo—what a thrill! Just 61 years ago Stanley appeared at this spot and one of the last great mysteries of the Earth was solved. How I envy him and his days.

A launch has just set out from the town of Banana. It is carrying a cargo of negroes who will unload our ship at Boma and Matadi.

We watched them come aboard. They're to stay with us overnight and so have brought all their possessions along—even their women and children. They'll sleep on deck.

Wednesday, May 11 [Boma—Matadi]

I got up at 6:30 to do some of the packing. Right after breakfast we went ashore at Boma and found a real little country town. There were rolling hills all around that are very much like our Western hills. Ray is a little disappointed that it is'nt more African. At ten o'clock we went back to the boat and met the missionary of the town, Mr. Knudson. We got back to the boat just before noon when it started up river to Matadi.

At two we finished all our packing and went on deck. The rugged hills on either side and the winding river made this our most thrilling boat trip. Just before Matadi came in sight we went between two rock walls with a whirlpool swirling madly through making the boat rock. It is called the Devil's Caldron & when the water is low it becomes a real menace. Of course we wished that it had been.

Matadi is lovely lying among the hills and overlooking the river. The Swedish Missionaries met us at the boat and helped get our baggage out. They had eight of the Mission boys to carry it and a truck to get it up to the Mission. It took about an hour so at 4 P.M. we drove up the hill and found a large and lovely home awaiting us. The view was magnificent and after tea we went out to take some stills. We found a little white church too and liked it all so much that we wanted very much to stay.

We were 16 at supper and had a great long table and a real good meal. It was nice to have the Sprungers and Stenstroms still with us. After supper we had tea and cake in the living room and then a short service. We sang to a little organ like Aunt Clara's and I felt very much at home. We got a letter from Mother at last, one from Ross, and a welcome note from Sona Bata. Our plans are still mixed up and we don't know when we will meet the Ross or when we will get up to the Cameroons.

Our bed had curtains all around it—the kind you see in museums and although it wasn't buggy we put them down just to have the fun of sleeping under them.

Thursday, May 12 [Matadi—Sona Bata]

We didn't have time for breakfast at the Mission with the others but drove back to say goodbye. I was indeed sorry to leave—Mrs. Jernberg was so very sweet and made us feel so much at home. But our train left at nine and we were delighted to find the Stenstroms seats right across from ours and the Sprungers on the other side of the aisle.

We were riding backwards until 1 P.M. when the Stenstroms left us at Kimpese and I got quite trainsick. I was sorry to see them go but very glad for their seats. As we had until 5 P.M. before reaching Sona Bata we got some typing and other work done.

Miss Anderson and Rev. Ericson met us at the station and Ray ran up to the baggage car for our 23 pieces of luggage. He took so long that I had time to say goodbye to the Sprungers properly and he didn't have time to even see them again as the train pulled right out.

We drove about a kilometer in an old Ford truck and then up a hill to the Mission. Dr. and Mrs. Freas came out of their lovely house to meet us. She is stunning—black hair and eyes and a light complexion. Then on across the large hilltop to the compound where there are school buildings, a brick church, work shops, and small houses where the natives live who work in the Mission. Our house, the Ericsons, the Lanous, and Miss Andersons are situated. They are not at all near together and have great palm trees growing all around.

We went across the road to the Ericsons for dinner but I could'nt eat very much as I had developed a case of cramps. I tried to leave them back in the States but they seem to have trailed along anyway.

Dr. and Mrs. Freas came over, and Miss Anderson who is the teacher, and we went over the scenario of Bwamba. Ray gave an excellent pep talk on co-operation and patience. I was very proud of the way he started our work with a bang. We never went to bed till 11:30 which is an occasion in the tropics.

We learned that this large station with seven workers has established many native churches as far as a hundred miles east and south of the station.

The school consists of 140 boys and 40 girls who have been chosen from the various native schools to come here. We were sorry to find that their vacation started last week, as this is about the end of the wet season. We find that the rainy season is the best time of year in Africa. The air is clearer and the rains consist of showers so we have arrived at the wrong time. In a few weeks the air will be very dusty and the green things will dry up. We have to work like mad to get our picture made while conditions are still good.

We got a letter from Rogers telling us not to let Ross influence us as the Committee has arranged for us to go to the Cameroons June 23. Things get more and more complicated but we are going to make this picture and make it good before we do anything else!

Friday, May 13 [Letter to mother from Jinny]

Dear Mother,

The Mission in on top of a large hill and all the natives who live around are very civilized. So much so that we are having difficulty in finding any who will undress enough for our early scenes in the picture. So you don't have to worry about me being eaten!

[Letter to mother continued Sunday, May 15]

Dear Mother,

Today we went out in the truck with the Ericsons to visit two of the villages about 20 miles from here. They knew we were coming by word of mouth, and gave us quite a reception. At Boko they made an arch of palm branches which we drove through and found the boys lined up on either side playing flutes and drums. I was thrilled to death and Ray jumped out to get a picture. We attended church and my husband distinguished himself by a very fine speech which was translated by a native. We had a picnic lunch with us and the chief invited us to use his dining room which had a table and a few chairs and nothing else.

We are a little disappointed to find there are no wild animals in this section other than antelope and an occasional wildcat. The country is all hills and only looks different from N.Y. state because of the palm trees. We hope to find it wilder in the jungle.

Friday, May 13

We awoke at 7:20 just in time to get to Miss Anderson's for breakfast at 7:30. We had our first native food, pai pai, which is a melon with a mild and delightfull flavor. We learned about the Mpesi, cockroach to you, who grow three inches in length and eat holes in anything silk. So I went home and packed away all my dresses that I'd hung up so nicely.

We went over to meet Mrs. Lanou who is sick and then I unpacked all our things and arranged them on shelves by the beds. We have two big beds in our room but only use one. A few of the native boys have been working at our house all day. They sweep, make the bed, work in the yard and have everything in perfect order for us. I like Africa! The other houses all have cook boys and an assistant who waits on the table. They do very well and even learn to make bread and rolls.

Ray who had been making arrangements for the picture came for me at 11 A.M. and we went to Freas to meet the monkey. He's a darling one and we are renting him for ten francs for the month. The Young man chosen to play the part of Bwamba was there and a number of ten year old boys. We decided that Mowanda's cousin looked most like him. I am going to stick his ear lobes down and paste some hair on his forhead to make the resemblence even greater. We also chose a boy to play the part of Kimbu, Bwamba's friend.

I didn't feel very good so laid on Mrs. Freas' bed and fell asleep. Ray told them about me so they let me sleep through dinner and then put me in bed with a hot water bottle. Under protest however as I had so many things I wanted to do. At five Ray came back and I got dressed and took a few pictures of our little house. Then we dressed up a little and went to Ericsons for supper. They sent one of their boys out to find about twenty boys so that we could choose some for the hunting scene. After supper we found not only as many as thirty boys but fifteen girls as well. They came in first just so we could see how silly they act. They giggle and hide their faces and are as cute as they can be. Mr. Ericson explained that we would want them a little later for the picture and then the boys came in. We chose ten very cute ones from four to ten years old. I thought it would be swell to have the little one trailing behind. We explained their part in the picture to them and told them they would wear loin cloths instead of their very varied clothing. Some have an old cloth wound around them and tied around the neck while others have little suits that are either much to small or too large. Usually they are well ventilated by long tears or the gap between shirt and pants which exposes six inches of skin. I got a real thrill out of these kids and am going to love working with them.

Ray put on a leopard skin to scare them and how they did laugh when they discovered him under it. They were quite awed by the head and teeth and their eyes grew as big as saucers.

We went over to the Freas to see some of his movies so that we can get an idea of lighting conditions. Nfienge, who is fifty years old and knows the old customs came to talk to us. He speaks quite a little English so we got along nicely and arranged to have him make the loin cloths, the fetishs for Bwamba and the witch doctor, and the spears for the little boys.

Mr. Freas let me drive home in the Ford truck much to my delight and said we could keep it at our house. It's an awful rattletrap and I surprised myself by getting in and driving it right off.

Our little house was bathed in moonlight and I find there is nothing quite like a full moon shining through the palm trees. Did some typing and went to bed at 11:30.

The boys laugh at us holding hands as in the Congo the men never touch the women in public. They met us in the road as we walked over to Freas and all trailed along with us. We shone the flashlight on them and they squealed and hid behind trees or in their shirts to get away from it. Dr. Freas came out to see what the comotion was all about. We certainly got a kick out of them and how we wish we could talk to them. We can say Kiambote (hello) and clap hands lightly which is just like shaking hands with all at once. They do the same in return.

Saturday, May 14

The little boys came after breakfast and Ray helped dress or rather undress them. They don't like their loin cloths much and sneak their ragged pants on again. We bought one of their old cloths that they tie around them for five francs to make the loin cloths of. We want them to look as if they are made of the raffia cloth they used to wear.

Mr. Ericson and Ray and I spent a good part of the morning looking for the best places to take the hunting scenes. We walked down the valley to the spring and through some real tropical country. We saw the banana and pineapple plantations that belong to the mission. After we got back we took the truck and drove around looking for a hilltop for the opening scenes. We couldn't locate one by dinner time so went back to Freas. Ray and I went alone then in the old truck which rattled and shook on those awful roads till I thought sure it would fall apart.

The little boys gathered at 2 P.M. and I put tribal markings on some of them with my pastel pencils and some water. I had quite a time cutting hair off the back of Bwamba's head to paste on the front. It was so very short. But we want him to look as much like Mowanda (the older Bwamba) as possible. Ray and Eri (Mr. Ericson) went ahead to set up the camera and we followed after fixing up the boys.

The sun went in a few times and we had a hard time trying to make Bwamba act. He is a little shy and stiff but will probably be all right after he's worked with us a little.

Ray only got two shots and we found it was 4:30—to late to go on to the next place. I got some still pictures that I expect to be real good. We find the light very deceiving. It looks bright in the sun and the meter readings are low.

The little wee boy got tired and said his feet hurt from running after the others. So he sat under a bush holding his spear and I got a few pictures without him even knowing it.

Sunday, May 15

Had breakfast with the Freas this morning. We like them so much and have decided they are the most intelligent people we have met, have our kind of ideals, and the most class. I was indeed surprized to find that out here.

Just before nine we started out for Boko in the truck. The Ericsons & I sat in the front and Ray in back with three of the natives. Ray had a wicker chair to sit in and had a grand time talking to the natives as Mfiengi was with us. He is a big help all around.

We drove 15 miles or so to Boko and found the boys lined up on either side of a palm arch playing their flutes and drums. It was a real welcome—the nicest I've ever had. Ray jumped out and got a picture and then we got out to see the village.

The houses in this section are always oblong or square and usually mud walls and grass roofs. Some are quite large with doors and windows. There are too many wooden doors to suit us. We must find an old village with mostly grass and bamboo houses for our picture. At 11 A.M. we went to the little brick church with a dilapidated tin roof that is full of holes. We sat up in front and the natives on benches that looked most uncomfortable. The men are always on one side and the women on the other. The children sit in the aisle or anywhere on the floor. We sang our first hymn in Kigonga which is very complicated. The congregation sang with all their hearts and were really ear-splitting.

Eri gave the sermon and Ray a very nice speech. I was very proud of him. Of course a native had to translate for Ray. There was a boys choir of sixteen that made more noise than any fifty I've heard at home. They sang for all they were worth and I was pretty glad to get out again. Took a few stills and then took our picnic lunch to the chief's house. He invited us to use his dining room which had a table & a few chairs—nothing else.

The chief put on his old grass cloth outfit and got out some ancient knives and drums to show us. He went on at a great rate telling about the old times. Of course Ray & I couldn't understand a word but he talked with his arms and demonstrated some things. It was quite an act and of course all the little boys in the village crowded around.

Then we left for Kifura. We had to leave the car and walk up and down hill for half a mile or more it is so isolated. The village is on top of a hill and while a long way off we could hear them singing a welcome to us. When we go up the hill a very little boy came and shook hands with us. Then almost everyone else did. We had to go in their church too and Eri told them all about

Ray and I. How we had just gotten married and come to Africa not knowing anyone. He went on and on and then Nfienge talked about us some more. Ray had to say a few words and then we had a prayer and a song. These people just have to sing loudly. Finally we got to look at the village. We still find door frames and windows. There were two Albinos—pure white skin and blonde hair. They are very queer looking with their heavy features.

Nfienge managed to borrow an old fetish that was a witch doctor's and an ancient [copper] tool like an ax. There was one adorable fat baby I wanted to keep for my own but of course no one would let me.

The sun was very dull so I couldn't get any pictures.

When we left all the children followed us back to the car. They are so cute hurrying to keep up with us. I tried a couple of pictures going up the hill but am afraid some of them were looking into the camera. Its awfully hard when we can't talk to them. Drove home at sundown—the lovliest time of day.

Monday, May 16

Eri called us at 6.30. We haven't gotten used to waking up early yet. We had breakfast with him and then walked to the nearest village. The houses are small and we think it better than either of the others we saw. We are considering having the doors taken out. The people all greeted us Kiambote so we didn't feel too strange. Another very dull morning so I couldn't take my stills.

We took the little boys out in the woods to practice the next few scenes. We found a lovely place, real jungly looking. If the sun will only shine!

At 11:30 we dismissed the boys and went with Eri to visit another nearby village. Two of the young women brought us each about five oranges as a gift. The children all ran when they saw the truck. It was comical to see them ducking behind bushes.

We had dinner with the Freas and just got through as the little boys assembled again. Went back in the forest and took pictures till 4.30. The clouds kept hiding the sun and we had an awful time getting enough light even with the reflectors. Our little savages looked darling under the enormous trees and they did very well. We are worried about the lack of light.

Got a telegram reading twentieth which means we have to leave tomorrow for the Cameroons. It's just as well as the dry season has started and it is always cloudy in the mornings here. Went to bed early so we can get everything done tomorrow morning. Our train leaves for Leopoldville about three.

Tuesday, May 17 [Sona Bata—Leopoldville]

Sent a telegram to the Cameroons so they will know we are both coming. There wouldn't be any point in my staying here. There isn't a thing I can do with school out and the sun never out. Spent most of the morning packing our things. We hope to leave some of them in Leopoldville till we get back.

Had our baggage weighed at the station and we have to pay five times as much for it as for ourselves to ride. We went third class because its so much cheaper. There is only one little section on the train for second class as this is really the natives train. They are so noisy and bring everything but the kitchen sink!

Wednesday, May 18 [Leopoldville—Brazzaville, French Congo]

Got up at 6:30 as we have an early breakfast. We walked down to the shopping center immediately after. The town is quite large and very lovely. It's like one of our Long Island towns with old rambling houses and big trees. There are so many palm trees, flowers, and natives, that it is typically African however, and we get a big kick out of that.

Luteti took our baggage down to the station so we could get it through the customs as we are crossing the river to French Equatorial Africa this afternoon. He also went shopping with us so Ray got as elegant pith helmet and a watch strap.

We slept an hour after dinner and then after telephoning Mr. Coxhill we dashed off to catch the three o'clock boat for Brazzaville. We just made it thanks to Luteti and crossed the Congo in a little launch. We put our hands in Congo water for the first time even though it is muddy.

Mr. Sodergren met us at the dock and took our luggage to the train in a truck. We went to a steamship office for our boat tickets but find it's too late to get them anywhere but Pt. Noire. Mr. Sodergren took us to his Mission for tea and it sure tasted good. We met a very nice young lady who is to be married in two weeks. She has been a missionary since 1903 and is soon going home for good.

Our train left at six and it is a very up to date one. In second class we have a large compartment with nice leather seats. I don't see how first class could be any nicer.

Thursday, May 19 [Pointe Noire]

Arrived at Point Noire at 9 A.M. both feeling quite sick. Ray left me sitting on the luggage and went to find the Swedish Mission. He took forever while I sat and tried to explain to every porter and policeman that I was just waiting for someone.

Finally Ray got back with Mr. Joonson who helped us get our steamship tickets. We managed to get the missionaries discount which is 50% on the French line! Went to the Mission and had tea and cake which was very welcome. Mr. Joonson left on the 5 o'clock train for his Mission station which is way off in central French Africa. He has to travel a week on foot. It sounds very wild and Ray wants to go there of course.

Went to the dock after his train left and took a launch out to the "Foucauld." Three missionaries were there to wave goodbye. We sure are thankful for missionaries in every port. I don't know how we'd get around at all without them.

Friday, May 20 ["SS Foucauld": Pointe Noire—Libreville]

Last night we heard a peculiar crying and up on the very top deck we found a row of cages. There was a tiny lion cub crying like a baby. I put my hand right in and patted him and Ray had a fit—he was sure I'd get a poison bite or scratch. He sure is persnickety sometimes. I'm crazy about the lion—he's so very little. Ray likes him too, now that he finds he is too little to bite. There is also a monkey, a dog, and two macaws for us to play with. But we like the lion best. He drinks out of a bottle and cries all the time for his mother. I feel so sorry for him.

Spent the day writing, working on expense accounts, and developing some of my films.

Saturday, May 21

This morning we arrived at Port Gentil but did not go ashore as it is a rainy day. The first we have had since Antwerp. Ray did five of my films yesterday and I am dissappointed to find some of them spoiled. Some moisture must have gotten in them at Sona Bata. I did a lot of typing today—recording my films, writing an article, and making out a list for customs at Douala. Ray is finally writing to Rogers.

Went to bed early so we will be well rested when we get to the Camerun.

Sunday, May 22 [Libreville]

I woke up at 6 Am and couldn't go to sleep again so got up and did my wash. We stopped off the coast at Libreville and at 8 o'clock went ashore in a little boat. It was a long way and we enjoyed the ride very much. None of the stores were open but we found a native market in full swing. We went and looked at all their funny foods. The butcher shop was th best. They cut up all kinds of animals that still have their skins on.

Monday, May 23 [Libreville—Douala]

A small boat came and took us off the Foucauld and we had a two hour trip on it to Douala. We sat on the bridge as we were the only white passengers and rode up the river.

Early this morning we saw a vague outline among the clouds that looked very much like a mountain rising right out of the sea. And then another like an illusion it so nearly matches the clouds. But as we got nearer they became a reality—two great mountains towering over the sea and land. We looked on our map and found the largest one is Cameroun Mt. 13,350 feet coming right out of the ocean. The other one, Fernando Po, is an island and nearly as high. These are the only real mountains I have seen. At Douala we were met by a French Missionary, M. Boury, who is a batchelor but well able to entertain us. Mr. Ross sent a telegram telling us where to come and saying he had seen the Governor so we can get our paraphanalia through the customs without paying duty. At the Mission we found a very nice note from Mrs. Ross which was almost as good as one from home. I am going to love being with them I am sure.

The Mission is on a hill and we can sit on the porch and look across the river and lowlands to Cameroun Mountain in the distance. It is usually wreathed in clouds or, as Ray says, wearing a hat. I could sit and look at it forever with it's ever changing shades of light and color.

We went shopping and met two ladies who had tea with us and then we went to see the town. It's much more African here to us because of the foliage. We went up on a hill and saw the sunset behind the mountain—a truly inspiring sight. Then we took the ladies home, which to my delight was an orphanage, and were invited in. The babies were darling and I got one very little one I wanted to adopt but Ray says I can't have a black one.

Tuesday, May 24 [Douala]

Spent the morning getting Matriculation for the Camerouns and permission to take pictures here in Douala.

After lunch we went to the government orphanage again and started taking pictures. One two year old baby sat in a tub and poured water over herself for half an hour to suit us. The two nurses were called in for a few minutes as a woman arrived to have a baby. It took about five minutes and then someone carried her out to the ward piggy back! Another one arrived after that so we had to take the pictures alone. What a time trying to tell the children what to do.

M. Boury came back for us at 4 P.M. and we went to a boys school. Ten or twelve of them put on a wonderful act for us. Taking their canoe out into the river and then all paddling in unison. They were marvelous and we worked with them till the sun went down. I walked in mud up to the top of my shoes and Ray rolled up his pants to take the camera in the river. It was great fun and were we tired when we got through about seven. Had to pack again and then we went to bed exhausted.

Wednesday, May 25 [Douala—Eseka—Elat]

A terrific rainstorm woke us at 6 AM and how it did rain! We got our train at 7 and started on our wobbly way. I felt miserable before long but stretched out on the seat and fell asleep. It is the best way not to be train sick—I never woke up till noon and we were nearly to Eseke. Two cars met us there and Mr. Beanland, Neal, and McNeil. We drove about five miles to Mr. Neal's station for lunch. It sure was good to get some American food again. Then we set out for Elat, 100 miles to go. The country is magnificent—more like we imagined Africa. We went up and down hill and round curves all the way. The forests all around us are truly jungle and we heard many stories of the gorillas and other animals who live there. We ferried over one river on a boat made of eight dugout canoes with boards fastened over the top to hold the car. The whole affair is attached to a cable to prevent it from being swept downstream by the strong current. The natives paddle us across and manage to go quite fast.

We stopped for tea at Lollendorf, one of the missions, and then on to Elat. We arrived at 7:30 and were so glad to meet the Rosses at last. It was almost like coming home to find them here to welcome us.

All had dinner together and then went to the Girls school building where all the missionaries assembled. We were twenty in all. Some have come to work with us and we had a grand confab. They have already appointed three people to help us, gathered some of the props, chosen the scenes of activity, and are all ready to help us in every way.

Thursday, May 26 [Elat]

Met with the committee and Rosses to arrange a schedule. We will be here till Monday. Went right out and started work. Shot the school girls going to church, 275 of them! The printing shop, exterior, and the Hope school for missionaries children, we did in the afternoon. We find much more light here than in the Congo.

We think missionaries are grand! They are real people and such fun. Everyone is always laughing and having a wonderful time. They don't just sit under a Palm tree with a Bible!

Friday, May 27

At 8 am started work in the Halsey Memorial Press. It took 2 ½ hours to get the lights just right for the first shot. I am not taking the interior shots as they are not so interesting in stills and Bob McCrackin has already taken many good ones which the Presbyterian board can use. I had the afternoon off and managed to type the article for Rogers and a letter to go with it.

Walked over to the print shop about four and found Ray climbing in the rafters to get good pictures. The natives enjoyed it all immensely and Ray got absolutely filthy.

Took showers before supper and were sorry to find our host, Mr. Harris, down from a tropical desease. He got it a long time ago from wading in the streams and there seems to be no cure for it. He has such a big job here as pastor, 4000 people come to the church here, and he has many others in various villages.

Saturday, May 28

This morning we went to the only Dentist office in Cameroun to photograph a Catholic Priest getting his teeth fixed. Dr. Weber has a swell office and two natives who have learned to do all the work. The Priest was very nice about having his picture taken by us Protestants even though he had no forwarning.

The afternoon was rainy so we went to Ebolowa to see the stores. Ray and I got khaki pith helmets, made in India, for only 32 francs. They are really swell looking—the nicest we've seen.

Sunday, May 29

Did some typing before church at 10:30. The church was jammed—over three thousand people. Dr. Ross spoke in English and Mr. Harris translated into Bulu. He was wonderful—so animated and he obviously made the people understand each point. The inspiration on their faces is a real thrill. They are very eager for the Word of God and respond with all their hearts. We wanted to shoot them all pouring out of the church but it was too cloudy.

After dinner we rested a little and then had a Vesper Service for the white people in a little chapel. Ross spoke again and we learned that Martin Johnson was in a way responsible for the work we are doing. He offered the church groups any of his film they might wish through the Africa Committee. They chose some and with shots taken by missionaries here and there made "Africa Joins the World." It has been so successful as the first picture of its kind that this expedition was organized. The whole service was lovely and we have decided that these people as a whole are nicer and more intelligent than any group we've known of other professions. They are real people!

After the service we had a meeting because of the difficulties in the amount of film we can shoot and the amount of work they all want photographed. Dr. Hope offered to pay for all the extra footage and Mr. Ives said that he was authorized to use a hundred dollars for our board. The cooperation we are getting is wonderful!

Monday, May 30 [Elat—Lolladorf]

Got up at four AM to hear the Presb. broadcast. We were disappointed to find it was the United Brethren but listened anyway. We were supposed to leave at 6 but never got off till nearly 7. It's a two hour drive but we stopped once to see a natives cross bow and again to see driver ants.

Started right in working on a translation scene with Dr. Good who does all the books. Dr and Mrs Johnson who are retiring at 70 after years of service stopped for lunch. They are on their way to the boat and aren't a bit happy about it.

I fell asleep on Dr. Good's bed while the others were working on the porch. Before long it started to rain so production stopped till tomorrow. They let me sleep and I made a very good job of it—never getting up till 5:30

Had a confab with Dr. McCrackin and Mrs. Ives about what we should shoot in the one day we have left here. Went to bed at 9:30 and I am surprized at how sleepy I still was.

The people here got all dressed up as they heard we were coming to take movies. The women and children waited around all day and nobody did any cooking. So they are all hungry and cross we hear tonight.

Tuesday, May 31 [Lolladorf—Elat—Metet]

Waited all morning for the sun. It was too dull to do anything so we pretended for the sake of the boys in the gardens. They worked diligently when they thought we were taking pictures. One way in the back leaned over howling and waved a leaf wildly with the other hand. Just so he could recognize himself if he ever saw the pictures. How we laughed.

After lunch the sun arrived just as Mr. Beanland did. We decided to go to Metet while we had the chance. We really wouldn't have been able to finish the sequences we had planned in one afternoon anyway. We hope this will assure our return in October. Everyone is so nice here that we will be glad to stay a good long time.

Arrived back in Elat about 4 and after some tea went on to Metet. We were very crowded with all our luggage.

Wednesday, June 1 [Metet]

Had breakfast at seven and then went to see the nearby villages. We chose the Leper camp about five miles away for Ngono's village when a child as the huts are all bark and grass. The cheifs village is near here and has a grand palaver house. We also chose a little girl to be Ngono who seems real bright. This morning she came up to the house and when Mrs. Wolfe asked what she wanted said she came to be in the pictures. Somebody looked at her twice so she thought she had been selected. One of the head men informed us that we sure picked the right man when we asked him about the old customs and we sure are smart! We chose a girl for the older Ngono and hear she is a widow with seven kids. The oldest being seventeen! We can't believe it, she looks so young, and are sure there is a mistake somewhere.

Right after lunch we went to the Leper camp to take the palaver for Ngono's marriage as a child. We got all set up and then were delayed a long time because the Chief insisted on wearing an overcoat in the picture. The others put on loin cloths without a fuss but the chief said his father wore that coat and it was the only thing that made him different from the other men! We finally got it off him but he wasn't at all happy about it and thinks we are nuts.

Worked till 6 and then I went home and slept till 8 when we had dinner.

Thursday, June 2

The sun shone beautifully at 1 so we gathered our parapanalia and went out to the gardens for some more of our drama. Ngono does very well even took a beating in one scene.

Worked until six and found Mr. Beanland waiting for us when we got back. He came to take some of us to Youande in the morning.

This morning we had a fire in the living room and Bob who was in another house writing said his hand was cramped from the cold. This is Africa!

Two of the women chosen for the movie arrived this morning in grass skirts with white paint and mud smeared all over them. We asked them why and they said, "Can't you see we are widows and in mourning. You aren't supposed to speak to us." We had to make them wash as they were to be the chief's wives and he isn't dead. This shows how well these people have caught the spirit of the thing we are doing. They are real anxious to help even though most of them don't understand what movies are.

Tonight another woman arrived at the house with funny white spots painted on her. Her whole get up was wild looking—all for the movies.

Friday, June 3 [Metet—Yaounde]

Got up at 5 AM to get an early start for Yaounde. It is the capital city where the governor lives. Mr & Mrs Beanland have a house on a high hill. They are head of the missionaries now that Dr and Mrs Johnson have retired. Its quite mountainous and very lovely up here on the hill.

We only drove 90 Kilometers so got here early but it was so cloudy we couldn't do a thing. Went to Mr. Underhills house. He is a mulatto and a grand fellow. I was fascinated by his collection of African things and he gave me a hunting knife and a carved nut shell. The shell was used for gambling years ago, but there are no more as the government forbids it. The natives gambled even their wives away so its no wonder. Each man had a certain design that was his for life. I'm going to make a pin out of mine.

He had a big basket of old smelly things that were saved by generations because they had some magic. They had become black as they were kept up over the fire to preserve them. The chief who owned it became a Christian and gave it to Mr. Underhill. We couldn't tell which was what but some were–

A man's tongue because it was eloquent.
A blind mans stick—it could see.
Hair & nails—they always grow.
A great many sticks and stones and animals feet.

I was so disappointed not to find any African wares this morning that Mr Underhill got a Hauser man to come up. They are the African Jews when it comes to selling. They wear long white robes & red Turks hats and travel all over peddling their wares. After a great deal of palaver to get good prices we got a leopard skin, a leather hassock cover, a camels hair blanket, and a small billfold. I am delighted with them—smell and all.

Just as we sat down for tea at 4 the sun came out. We tore down to the school yard and got ready for the scenes of Ngono at school. There are 42 girls and they have been held over a week after school was out by a great deal of pressure. Mr Beanland told us on the way this morning that once he sent a boy with a message to their compound. The girls had a fit and tore his shirt off and gave him quite a pounding so no one got the message. Considering all Ray was quite scared about going down. Miss Taylor who is the supervisor went with us so he didn't mind too much.

We had an hour & a halfs shooting before the sun went down. Mr. Underhill came over & when Bob asked Ray what he was shooting with his Leica, Ray answered, "Nothing, from every angle!" We were glad he wasn't near at the time.

Saturday, June 4 [Yaounde—Metet]

Took little Ngono to the native market this morning. She was fascinated and picked out presents for her family. A penknife for her father, beads for mother, a hat for baby, and bracelet for herself. She is a darling kid and real smart. Yesterday we asked her if she liked to be in the movies and why. She said yes she did because we take care of her. Like all African girls she has to take care of the baby and doesn't get any attention herself. Her mother almost didn't let her come to Yaounde because there would be no one to mind the baby. We finally convinced her that it was a great honor to have her child in the pictures that would go across the sea.

I bought some of the African dress material which is the wildest stuff imaginable.

By ten the sun was shining so we dashed back to the school compound. We worked till 1;30 and then insisted on lunch. Ray kept right on for another hour though. He works us all to death when the sun shines. We went on during the afternoon till the sun went in about four. The school here is in an ideal place on the side of a hill. The background is all mountains and clouds which will make these pictures some of our best. Started back at five so we could get to Metet in time for supper.

Many of the native towns are along the road now according to government rule. It is easier for the tax collectors. The houses must be built of mud and painted white. Ray says they look like Canarsie shacks.

So the nice bark houses are few and far between much to our regret. The towns are fairly close together in some parts so the road is usually full of goats, sheep, and chickens. I never knew there were any sheep at all they look just like goats. But I hear the difference is all in the tail. The sheep wear theirs down and the goats stick theirs right straight up. It's simple to tell them apart now.

Messages are still sent by the drums. Mrs Wolfe was talking to a native today when a drum in another village started beating. The native said, "Now isn't that too bad. A man caught a big pig in his trap, enough for us all to have some, and it got away." Each man has a certain drum call that summons him back to his village. We went to get one of our actors and found he was off in the forests so the drummer began beating his call over and over on the drum. They say it can be heard 4 or 5 miles. Here in the mission the drum wakes us up, tells the time of day, announces church and Sunday school, and a lot of other things we don't know about.

Sunday, June 5 [Metet]

The church here is made entirely of Palm leaves and is an enormous affair. It must have taken ages to build. We sat in chairs we took with us up in front. We no sooner got settled than a terrible smell assailed us. So we picked up and moved to the other side of the church much to the amusement of the congregation. It was just as bad and then someone discovered a dead chicken under the pulpit. They removed it but the lovely odor stayed with us most of the hour. A little boy near us kept us amused. He sang till it looked as if he would burst. (Right now a group of little boys are looking in at the door and watching me type.)

Monday, June 6

Another day of waiting for the sun. All morning we worked on records and hoped Elsie, Bob and Mrs. Beanland would come from Yaounde bringing the sun. They arrived for dinner without it but it did come out before too long. We rushed down to the compound and sent for the characters and props. We had quite a wait as one of the young women who is a wife of the chief ran away. The other women laughed at her for wearing leaves for the picture and she wouldn't do it again. They sent a drum call for her and we finally got her undressed. We had only an hours shooting and the sun went in again. It was 4:30 by that time so we had to give up for the day. And I only got one still.

Read an article in National Geographic by a woman who lived a year and a half in Boma, our first stop in the Congo river. It wasn't very good and we don't think entirely true.

We still think Africa is swell even though the sun plays tricks on us all the time.

Tuesday, June 7

Waited till after dinner till the sun showed its head. Then we all went down to the compound again where the chief's hut is located (for the picture) Mr. Beanland arrived from Yaounde just in time for his act. We had another palaver, this time in a real palaver house, and the missionary gets Ngono away from the chief. We just started the next scene when the sun began playing hide and seek with us again. The natives are very patient under such circumstances, more so than I am. At 4:30 we had to quit again in the middle of a scene.

Notwithstanding the terrible weather we have been able to do some shooting every day. It's been mighty little at times and we are hoping and praying that we will get the picture done before we have to leave for the Congo.

Wednesday, June 8

The sun came out at 10 oclock much to our joy and we rode off through the woods to a little stream with a crude log bridge over it. Here Mrs. Beanland finds Ngono bathing and takes her back to the mission as she has been cruelly beaten and needs medical attention. Mrs. Beanland arrives on the scene in a Tepoy carried by four men. Ray and I had a ride in it, of course, and it feels just like riding on a horse. The same rocking chair motion. It took us till 1:30

to finish the scene the sun was so contrary. It was in and out a hundred times and usually in much longer than out. We sit three quarters of the time. Had dinner at the other house with Dr. Evelyn Adams and Esther Bartlett. Just as we got through it rained! We went to bed in disgust and slept till five.

One of the actors asked dr. Adams why they can understand Ray and no other Americans. That's an example of how he talks with hands, feet, and all the rest. He gets lots of response too.

Thursday, June 9

This morning dawned grayer than ever. I worked on my white skirt and got it nearly finished by 10:30 when the sun came out. We worked on the scene at the mission house when Mrs. Beanland brings Ngono in from the forest. Esther gave Ngono a doll to play with and she loved that. Ray couldn't get over it because she has a real baby to take care of all the time. When we finished the scene which is the last for little Ngono we let her keep the doll. She went home just beaming all over.

Gathered the Chief and his wives again and continued the scene in the village. The sun was as inconstant as usual. One of the medical students came and took the Garners picture! He just got his camera from France and we sure got a laugh out of him coming for our photo. We had to stop at 4:30 again as the sun was down behind the treetops.

When we want Ngono to talk we tell her to say John III 16. All the natives know it we find and it sure comes in handy for the closeups of them talking. We hope it will look as if they are saying something like the title that will be on the screen

Ray tried to buy one of the old chiefs spears and got it for a present. First the chief said it would cost an awful lot as he would have to buy tinned meat for his family if he sold his spear and his living would be a great deal higher. Then he gave Ray the spear as we are guests and he couldn't sell us anything.

Friday, June 10

Took our first pictures of the older Ngono. She is sweell and looks so young I just can't imagine her having seven children. Took our most dramatic scene of the chief's son having a spasm and passing out. Ray showed him how to do it and was so good I'm beginning to think he missed his calling. The natives howled at his antics and the scene went off very well.

The Nealy's stopped for the night as they are on the road and wanted a good bed for the night. We had a great bonfire out in front of the house and a buffet supper out there. It was great fun. We took a flash picture but couldn't show the moon which was nearly full. Ray and I were so tired we went to bed at nine with all the children.

Saturday, June 11 [Metet—Elat]

Started at ten this morning and worked like demons so we could finish today. We had lunch at 5:00 and then packed our stuff in the truck including the stars, Ngono and Eman, and set out for Elat. There was a lovely sunset and then a full moon.

We discussed operations and found that Bob has some new ones that have been very successful out here. One of them is to hold kid's ears in. His little girl was born with ears that stuck straight out. When she was about nine months old he tried the operation and it worked. She has swell looking ears now and no one would know anything had been done to them

Monday, June 13 [Elat]

Started out at 8 A.M. with good intentions for a days work. We had to get our lights from Harris' and as long as we were there took all the rest of our paraphanalia that we left with them. Then we had to go to the Industrial School for chains for the tripod. I ordered some ebony salt dishes and decided to pay my bill so I wouldn't have to change my money again when we go down to the Congo.

We rested until two and then went back still intending to do some work. We got Ngono in a nurses uniform and a group of nurses for a classroom scene. Ray had me take down all the curtains in the room and then he decided to wait till the sun came out as it would light the room up better than our few lights. After Dr. Weber fussed so long to give us power for the lights. He even ran a wire from another building. We went to choose places for our other scenes and then found it was so late we might as well not start. I said we tried so hard all day not to work that we might as well declare a holiday and enjoy it.

Tuesday, June 14

Got to the hospital early this morning to make up for yesterday. Ray decided he needed the lights for black faces so we set them up again. We found the cutest fat baby and had Linda show Ngono how to wash it. Of course Ngono has had seven to Lindas two but we won't tell anyone that. Then we did the classroom scene with Linda teaching the whole group. Ray wanted her in it to dispell the fact that missionaries are old foggies as everyone thinks. She is so young and cute looking.

After lunch and a sleep we went back and took an operating scene. We had Ngono administering the chloroform. Bob did a great deal of clowning and had us all in stitches but it did look like a real operation.

Ray wanted to shoot one of the love scenes at sundown [& needed me to help direct]. So we got that done too. The sun went down too soon for me to get any stills though.

Wednesday, June 15

Started early this morning at the White Ward. We set up an office scene which Bob was in so there was plenty of clowning. Before lunch we set up the living room for the Mission meeting. We had to interrupt the executive meeting to get Mr. Beanland to be in it. We had an awful time making the fire burn and I finally had to hide behind a chair and fan it. It took till 2:30 to finish the scene. Once as Ray was taking it a native walked right into the scene and straight at the camera before we could stop him.

Then we moved all our lights over to the Chapel for the wedding. Ngono wore a white dress that we dipped in tea so it wouldn't glare. The buttons got black so we pinned roses down her front to cover them.

Mr. Harris performed the ceremony and had to explain to the audience that it wasn't a real marriage for fear they'd think Eman a bigamist. We didn't have any trouble getting the audience—they just appeared from every direction. We had a lot of trouble with the lights as usual but finished in time to get some outdoor scenes before the sun went down.

Thursday, June 16

After rest hour, during which Ray had me giggling as usual, we went up to the hospital to shoot the last scene. We saw a big elephantitus that had been cut off a man this morning. It looked quite gooey so we took a good look at it in order to harden our stomachs for photographing our first real operation.

The clouds got thicker than ever so we went back and got Linda and went to the Industrial School to buy Ginny some dress material. Then the sun came out and we dashed back to the hospital where we worked until the sun went down at 5:30. We finished the picture! Phew, what a relief to have one completed picture behind us!

Friday, June 17

We all went to Weber's to see some of his movies. I took Ray off in a corner to see if I could get his good behavior on. On the way everyone lectured him on how not to criticize Dr. Weber's movies. I was scared to death at what he might say but he did very nicely.

Said goodbye to the group and went home to bed early as we have to get up at four in the morning to continue our travels.

Saturday, June 18 [Elat—Eseka—Douala]

Dr. Davies came for us at five AM and we started for Eseka, about 100 miles. It poured rain all the way and was such a curving and hilly road that we felt quite sick. Finally arrived just before nine o'clock and had our baggage weighed and checked in at the station. The train was not due for over an hour, there was no rest room in the station and I just couldn't wait. I thought I'd DIE before we got to Nealy's, about five miles away, where we went for lunch the day we arrived.

We wrote letters all the way to Douala, a five hour ride.

We spent the rest of the afternoon, having a blood test for sleeping sickness, having the government authorities check our passport, getting through the customs, and making reservations on the boat.

Sunday, June 19 [Douala]

It has been raining ever since we finished the last scene on Thursday. The sky was just holding back till we got through and now all the water in the heavens is let loose. We havn't had a glimpse of Mt. Cameroun it is so deep in clouds.

Monday, June 20 ["SS Asie": Douala—Ponte Noire]

Got up at five thirty to have time for breakfast. We got down to the dock too early and had to wait for the launch to leave. It finally did about seven. The sky cleared at last and by the time we got out to the Asie the sun was shining.

Tuesday, June 21

Typed some letters while Ray fixed the shutter on the movie camera so that it works perfectly again. He had me scared for awhile as he found an extra spring and he didn't know where it belonged.

It was swell on deck tonight, there were so many stars. The air is so cool and clear out at sea that if feels as if we are going north instead of south. There are only about 25 passengers in all so we go anywhere we like on the ship. No one has said any thing to us so we guess it's all right. This boat isn't nearly as elegant as the others we've been on—even in first class.

Wednesday, June 22

We remembered some old film that has been in the extra magazine a long time and decided to use it up. The first part of it is our first view of foreign soil after crossing the Atlantic and our baptism when we crossed the Equator. So we decided to make some sort of picture for Mother. We talked about it all during lunchtime and got real enthused over it. I wrote a letter for the titles and then we portrayed each part of it. We were sorry we only had 50 feet of film to work with. Ray figured out two contraptions so we could turn the camera on and off and be in the picture at the same time. He really is marvelous even if he does say it himself.

Thursday, June 23 [Pointe Noire]

The boat docked in Pointe Noire just as we finished packing. We had quite a palaver in our terrible French about luggage and passports before we could get off the boat. Finally we took the luggage we could carry and went ashore in a launch. There we got a taxi and went to the Swedish Mission. About six natives came out to meet us and we finally understood that everyone is in Brazzaville at the conference but we could stay there anyway. We had a grand time explaining that we wanted a swim in the ocean and lunch at noon. One boy could speak a little pigeon English but we can understand French as well as that.

Just as we were about to leave for the swim two missionaries arrived who are on their way home. They saved our life when it came to buying train tickets.

Took a rest, got our train tickets, and then the missionaries left on the boat we just got off of. We got our train shortly after five o'clock. We were horrified to find a French couple, fat and sloppy, and two dogs in our compartment. Not that we are snobs but we had to sleep in close quarters.

Friday, June 24 [Pointe Noire—Brazzaville—Leopoldville]

Last night we had the two upper bunks made up for us while our companions were in the Bar. We figured there would be more privacy up there than if they were climbing over us. They never appeared at all although their baggage was in our compartment. We can't figure out if they drank all night, found another place to sleep, or they had to sit up on account of the dogs. At any rate we didn't have a bad night and arrived at Brazzaville about nine. We took a taxi to the mission for help as all the baggage we left on the boat had been shipped through and we had to get it through the customs. Mr. Sodergren had to be at the conference so he sent a young man with us who knows about as much English as we do French. We managed nicely between the three of us. He put us on the ferry for Leo, which is a launch, and we arrived safely after a shaky half hour.

Being experienced travelers we took a taxi and customs officer to the customs house where we got through ourselves and then went to the U.M.H. [*Union Mission Hospice*] where we found the Rosses. Many of the Missionaries are here so we have lots of company.

Saturday, June 25 [Leopoldville]

Mr. Ross woke us up this morning to tell us about the arrangements he has made for us while he is away. He and Mrs. Ross are driving to a conference in Angola and will be gone a week or so.

Had breakfast with the Freas who were glad to see us and are full of plans for when we get back to Sona Bata. Mr. Watkins came and took us out to the air port which we will photograph as soon as we get a good day. Mr. Van Beethoven, the chief engineer, showed us around and we were surprized to find the natives doing important mechanical jobs. Two of them working with a white man, were reassembling a big transport plane. It was slightly out of line so they took it all apart.

Got wind of a cable to Ross that Mr. Coxill had so we phoned him. Imagine our delight to hear that it read:

Your film worthless due to excessive panning and lack of tripod.
Subject matter uninteresting.
Garner's stuff excellent.

Sunday, June 26

Walked over to the little Baptist church and found to our delight that there is a service in English for the white folks in town. About thirty attended in their Sunday-go-to-meetin' clothes and I made the collasal mistake of not wearing a hat! The service was very good and except for the hymns which dragged terribly we enjoyed it immensely. We sure needed Mother and her good old hymn singing.

Monday, June 27

We have been married just four months today and it already seems like years. Folks have been kidding us all day for celebrating but we have had a lovely time.

We tramped around town and discovered a park and a small zoo. It was quite wild looking and most of the animals were not in cages but fenced in huge jungly looking places. We saw a chimpanzee, leopard, young lion, and many birds.

Tuesday, June 28

A big transport plane was being all gone over by the natives. What a thrill to see these boys, one generation from cannibalism in some cases, working on a modern plane. They wheeled it out of the hangar for us and Ray was delighted at that. He says he likes to have things moved around for him, especially [big things like] airplanes! After a few shots the sun went in and we spent till 5 PM learning about planes. Ray learned to put a roof on today too.

Wednesday, June 29

Dr. Kellersberger, A.P.C missionary, took us to the government research laboratory this morning. The head DR. Dr. Bruetsart showed us all over the new building which is a beautiful white concrete structure. They are just moving into it, having been in the Congo since 1898 doing wonderful work for the natives. I was thrilled to death over the whole thing and we decided to photograph it when we come back to Leo and they are really settled in their new home. They breed Tsei flies, with and without sleeping sickness, and feed them with live chickens, monkeys, guinea pigs, & other animals, according to the experiment. The box of flies with a screen side is held against the animal until the flies tummies get full of blood and swell up. I felt real sorry for the many chickens who had their feathers off and merely exist as a meal for a fly. They die after about a month.

We saw natives working with microscopes and performing experiments and marvel again at what these people can do with a little training. We saw the germ of sleeping sickness, trypanosomes wiggling in the blood. My first look in a microscope and I was completely fascinated and had to be dragged away. Then Dr. Bruetsart asked if we would like to see an operation he was about to perform on a rabbit. Of course we did in order to be ready for the ones we must photograph later on. The rabbit was tied to a little operating table and chloroformed just like a person would be. This operation was to determine if the lady was pregnant and her stomach was opened. As she had an operation yesterday, this was merely cutting out the stitches in the skin and then the abdominal wall. The Dr. then groped for the ovaries and much to my horror the rabbit wiggled and all the intestines oozed out! I tried hard to stay but everything got blacker and blacker and I had to go sit on a chair in order not to fall over. Ray was so white that I was afraid he might but he stuck it out. I went back as soon as the intestines got pushed in and saw the sewing. Ray said I was a sissy but his face was like paper for an hour and my color came right back. He looked really funny because he is always so very pink.

Next we visited a big native hospital that is maintained by the government for the natives. It has all modern equipment and is fixed up nicely by the nuns. The baby beds in the maternity building have the mosquito nets draped from a crook over the bed and are tied with colored bows. And the walls have a border of cute little black babies all around. They have 75 babies a month here. There are three wards, first, second, and third class as the natives who have any money at all always want something better than the others. First class is really for chiefs wives. We saw darling new babies, most of them are quite white when they are born, and two sets of twins. The mothers have the babies by their beds and they all sit up with their feet hanging on the floor no matter how young the baby may be.

There is a separate building for each branch of the work, surgery for men, surgery for women, venereal diseases, etc. We were overcome by the surgical instruments and the doctor explained all their uses. It looked like a carpentry shop, hammers, saws, screws, chisels, and all kinds of horrible tools. I sure hope I don't ever have to have an operation by one of these butchers.

Thursday, June 30

Went to Leo east, about 7 kilometers from here, and met Mr. Coxill who took us to Chanic. Mr. Marcuad is in charge of the big ship building yards. He took us all over to see the work they are doing. They are building barges and tugs, riverboats and a Mississippi river boat is being repaired. We went up and down ladders and all over the boats in every stage of building. We are going to take some shots of the natives who work almost entirely without supervision. There are almost 1000 of them and only 35 white men. We hear that Chanic also assemble Ford Cars for all of Congo and maintain a plant to manufacture acetylene and oxygen. The Fords are assembled entirely by natives and never one screw is left over!

Friday, July 1

Dr. Kellersberger left for his station this morning. He is going by air as he has been away so long for the conferences and is the only Dr. at Bibanga.

I started developing films and Ray going over all the different films we are to make. He is listing all the places we are to go to and just what is to be taken in each place. We hope there will be no more mistakes after todays.

Ross had us come all the way from the Cameroun for the Fete today so that we could get a parade and the Governor General for one of our scenarios. Now we find that there will not be one! It is an athletic meet for the soldiers and not what we want at all.

Worked until 3:30 when we went to the stadium. It is a grand big field and we had the privilege, from the Gov. Gen., of going anywhere we liked. Ray took his camera even though he did not want any pictures and we had a wonderful time watching all the events close by. I took stills for an hour but then the light was too bad to continue. What a thrill to see these natives, many of them right from the bush, taking part in athletic events. High jump, pole vault, hurdle races, relays, and javelin throwing were the events and they were all interesting. The big moment was a mule race that everyone bets on. Horses can't live in Africa so even the cavalry are mounted on mules. They really go too, with lots of prompting.

Saturday, July 2

Ray developed a film for me the first thing this morning and we found it an absolute blank. It apparently had never been exposed! Mrs. Salmon, the English Baptist ministers wife invited us to go to the rapids today. The two ladies who are staying here went too, so Ray had a grand time with four women. We took the launch to Brazzaville but not before some trouble with the customs as we were going into French territory. Then a taxi 7 kilometers to the rapids. We walked over a swinging bridge, made of bush rope, and then half a mile to the mighty Congo. Here this river, 3000 miles long, pours through a narrow gorge. There are so many rocks and so much water that it rushes and roars and throws spray high in the air. It looks like great waves and breakers of the ocean. They say there is enough water power here to supply electricity to all of Africa. The many little tributaries that go into the Congo here are dry during this season except for one rather large one. So we could walk among thousands of rocks right out to the brink of the rapids. We had lunch and then I put on my jodphurs and Ray and I went exploring and picture taking.

Sunday, July 3

Tried to get up for a baptism in the river at 6:30 but we just could'nt make it. We dragged out at 7 feeling a little depressed by the continual cloudy weather. It is so bad that we can't take any pictures, hardly any of the time, at any rate.

After dinner we developed some film and were horrified to find one of the best spoiled by weather. It is the only one we hope.

Monday, July 4

Did my wash this morning while Mr. Garner loafed. Mr Coxill came for us and we went over to Leo West to Texaf, the big cotton mills. The director took us all through and we saw the complete process from the raw cotton coming in on a railroad to the finished cloth being packed and shipped to all parts of the Congo. I was completely fascinated by this lesson. This mill produces 40,000 meters of cloth a day which is not sufficient for the 10 million people in Congo. They would consume 85,000 meters a day as they save cloth rather than money and use wads of it when burying the dead.

Ther are 2000 natives working in the mills on eight hour shifts, night and day. Still it is hard to believe they produce so much, it is such a long process.

The machines are very modern and efficient. One is unique in its complete process of dyeing Indigo blue. This is the preferred color, one of the hardest as it has to go through chemical processes of dyeing and oxidizing that take quite a while. This is the only machine which does the whole thing in the world.

Tuesday, July 5

Mrs. Salmon stopped for us at 8 this morning so we could go and see the B.M.S. school. The girls come in the morning and the boys in the afternoon. They range in size all the way from one year to old grandmas. We attended their service in the Church and heard them sing. Then they all went to their classrooms which are open on one side and really make the nicest school compound we have seen. The chauffer took us all around the native city for an hour and we were quite fascinated. There were homes of all kinds—from grass huts to cement cottages with electricity. In some sections little open huts with a table and chairs were built in large numbers. We found later that they are drinking booths! Ten thousand natives live in this section of Leopoldville as near to one another as we lived on Glenwood Rd. Every house has a fence all the way around which gives them a little privacy. Everyone cooks in the yard and it seems so funny to see the women sitting on the ground in back of the modern houses, dressed in brilliant cloths, and cooking over an open fire.

We got back to the school in time for the dismissal, with singing, and then had tea and cookies. I was horrified to find one class of married women who are just children. Mrs. Salmon says when she calls the roll in this class the answer frequently is, "She's dead" They are so young that they die in childbirth.

Wednesday, July 6

We went to the native city again and shot the Garden City which is an improved industrial area, maintained for the workers of Otraco, a transportation company. We had an awful time with the women who giggle like kids and once two of them ran away just as Ray turned away from them to the camera. There was no chance of getting them back either.

This afternoon we went to the shipyards and spent an hour fixing the tripod hole on the movie camera. Then we frantically shot pictures in order to finish by 5 PM when the place closes. We didn't though and will have to go back some other time.

Thursday, July 7

Went to the Post Office the first thing to photograph the government clerks for one of the scenarios. We got telephone and telegraph operators after some difficulty with the lights. At 11 we rushed out to the air port to get the transport plane coming in from Europe. It was so dark we decided to leave it till the rainy season so we can get clouds and all.

The Halls invited us to a special movie being shown by the museum and then to dinner. We went at 5 so that we would have time to see the museum. But they put us out shortly after and said that they were closing. And we had dismissed the chaffeur and were at least 3 miles from anywhere. We sat on the steps and sat and finally Coxills went by and just happen to notice us sitting there like orphans. They took us to the theater where the picture was and we couldn't find Halls. They thought it was at the museum and then they looked for us and finally found the theater when the show was half over. It was on the island of Ceylon and very well done.

Friday, July 8

The Rosses arrived at noon much to our relief as we are leaving tomorrow and they expected us to be here till Tuesday. We did some of our packing till three when we had a date with the Gov. General who is the whole cheese in Congo. It was dark but the Gov. will be away for the next six months so we had to get his picture today. We got him coming out of his house and shaking hands with his secretary and an officer. Then close ups of him talking. Ray was trying to take both 16 and 35 mm and it was terrific as we had just a few minutes and he had never used the Eymo before. It jammed before we were through for some unknown reason.

Ross sent our film, got it through the customs, and I sent the negatives I'd developed. Gave Ross 24 of my Finopan. Spent till 10:30 going over all the scenarios and deciding which should be taken where and which should be 35 mm. This is the last time we will see Mrs. Ross but we are doing nicely without her to take care of us. We do wish she was though.

Saturday, July 9 ["S.S. Berwinne": Congo River Trip]

We got our nineteen cases ready and said our goodbyes by seven o'clock and Lutete took us down to the "Berwynne". We stood on the deck waiting for someone to assign us a cabin and talking to Lutete. A Belgium, apparently the captain or of some authority, came along and told Lutete to get off. We were quite taken aback and when Lutete turned to us the Belgium went into a rage and screamed and yelled at him, in English this time. I was so mad that I couldn't do anything but shake hands with Lutete. Ray did the same and then walked up the stairs and to the gangway with him. He told Lutete that in America we wouldn't do that and that we consider Africa belongs to the native. The Belgians and every other white man are guests in this country and should behave as such. We hope this eased the hurt somewhat and also the fact that we always have talked to Lutete as if he were one of us. Ray tells him all the oddities of America like snow and red men etc. We would like to have gotten right off the boat as we felt as if it had happened to us as much as to Lutete. The Belgian politely showed us to a cabin and we looked very icy I am sure. Ray almost socked him but I think our actions toward Lutete spoke louder than any words or violence might have. At least we hope so. Too bad this is the only Kasai boat for two weeks.

At nine we started up the Congo and have been marveling ever since at the scenerie. There are grassy plains with hills in the background, lush vegetation with masses of vines, high mountains, and tiny villages. It is an ever changing panorama of beauty. The colors are amazing, all shades of browns and lovely greens. We can even find blue and purple shadows and feel as if we were looking through rose colored glasses.

After supper we stopped to load on wood. The boat only carries enough for about twelve hours and has natives cut and pile it at various town. The wood fire causes lovely red sparks to fly out of the smoke stack that look like a million tiny Roman candles at night. We hang over the rail as soon as it is dark to watch them as it's so much like Fourth of July.

The boat only draws a little over a meter of water so we go in near the shore. Then two natives jump over board with a cable, swim to shore and attach it to a tree. The first time a twist held up the cable and we drifted down stream, then had to get up steam again and try over. When the first one is firmly attached four more are taken ashore. Then the gangway is let down but as it won't reach the shore they rest it on a wooden horse and then use two planks from there to shore. The first to walk on one of the planks skidded, sat on his tail, and went into the river. How we laughed—[Ray hardest because, he said] it was so much like me. Then about every fourth man did the same till we were nearly hysterical. They most all took the slippery plank even after the others fell. Finally they got ashore and piled great loads of wood on their shoulders and head. We waited breathlessly and before long down one went and spilled the logs all over. All the natives who travel on the lower deck in the open, hooted and yelled, so finally one came with a broom and scrubbed the slippery place.

As we came up the river to this place [Kwamouth] we had a huge searchlight to find the markers which are placed at intervals all along the shore. The water is so low during this season that they have to be very careful. The natives had huge fires on the shore so that we would know where to stop and they looked so pretty blazing in the darkness. They lit torches of Palm branches which give a good light when they are dry. It was a real thrill to come up to this little village this way and we are liking Africa better all the time.

Sunday, July 10 [Kwamouth—Mushie]

Woke up early as the boys made so much noise scrubbing the deck. The scenery is still wonderful and we think this river far more beautiful than the Hudson which is reputed to be tops.

At eleven we stopped at a little town and stayed a few minutes to let some natives off. Then we turned into the Kawai river. The place where the current sometimes makes boats turn around six times and where Mr. Martin's boat overturned when he first came out.

Took two of the pills Bob gave me and felt well enough to eat dinner. Started some crocheting while Ray read to me. We have a Bible and a Geology book so are studying both of them. Ray thinks that the Bible is so full of begats that in the old dayes people did little but begat! It also says that men are the rulers of women. Heaven help me now!

About four we stopped for wood again. The light was good so we took some stills. There was a very picturesque village in the background.

Played games till dinner time when we stopped for the night at a real large town. We saw a few white people so imagine some company has a plantation here.

Monday, July 11 [Mushie—Banningville]

Got up early to see where we are. The country is a lot flatter now but still wild and beautiful. The river is so low that we see a lot of sandbanks—some extending for half a mile or more. There are two natives with bamboo poles on the front of the boat who find the depth and yell it out every once in a while. Two natives in a canoe paddled like mad to catch hold of the side of the boat and then sold fish to the natives. There was a terrific din as everyone wanted a fish and there weren't enough to go around.

We stopped at Banningville for the night and after supper took a walk in the moonlight. There were huge palm trees that looked just like feather dusters.

Tuesday, July 12 [Banningville—Dima]

Got up early to take a picture of the "Feather dusters" before we set out again. At eight we started pushing our way upstream against the amazingly strong current. The river now looks like all the movies of Africa. A rather narrow stream with dense growths on either shore.

Stopped at Dima and a crowd of native women came to sell manioc to the natives. There was a great deal of haggling and it reminded us of the seventh avenue Jews.

The towns are all set among Palms or on a hillside and are by far the prettiest that we have seen. Ray is always bemoaning the fact we didn't have one like this for our Cameroun picture.

Wednesday, July 13

Another beautiful day on a winding and rushing river. The sun has been lovely every day and in Leo we never seemed to have any. We have had very bad luck and wasted a lot of time because of the sun.

Thursday, July 14 [Mabenga]

At sundown when we stopped for the night we went for a walk as we are getting so little exercise. We went up a hill to a native village that was real wild and very picturesque. I saw a lot of good stills but it was too dark to get anything at all. The women were all cooking supper in front of their huts and the babies running around in their skins. We think bare Africans are not a bit nude looking because of their color. When they are in swimming they have a beautiful shiny skin that looks swell.

Friday, July 15 [Mabenga—Mangai—Mangbay]

Got up early to see the elephants but we looked and looked and never saw even one. We had our cameras out and everything. Until nine o'clock we waited and watched and then gave up in despair.

Stopped at Mangai this afternoon, where the Sprungers get off the boat. We climbed a hill to the village and got two pinapples for 50 centimes, just 1½ cents. Walked around and got a still of a tiny baby sitting in the dirt and howling because he didn't like us. One women had hair that stuck out fully two feet all around her head. Ray says she must be from the Sudan and is a "Fuzzy Wuzzy".

We stopped just before supper at Mangbay. Had frankfurters and sourkraut for supper! I thought it was only an American habit.

Sunday, July 17 [Mangbay—Port Franqui]

Got into Port Franqui at 10 and had to wait for all the natives to get their paraphanalia off the lower deck so that we could get through with ours. We had quite a palaver to find where to go and what to do but met a white man who did not speak English but seemed to know what we wanted as he piled all our luggage in the back of a station wagon and drove off with us. Up on the top of a hill we were put off at an elegant looking hotel. We were a little afraid of the price, especially when we got put in a lovely room with bath and a balcony overlooking the river, but had to stay as we didn't know what else to do. The train only goes on Mondays so we decided to enjoy our night of luxury. We walked around in the afternoon and saw nothing but a few houses and wild uncivilized country all around the hill Port Franqui is built on. How they could have such a swell hotel here is beyond me. We set up the still camera and with a string attached took some portraits of ourselves.

Monday, July 18 [Port Franqui—Mweka—Loebo]

With some difficulty we got all our luggage in a compartment and set off on the dirtiest journey that ever was. At 4:30 we were eating and had our stuff all out when somebody yelled "Mweka" and we had to get off. Mr. Jackson and Ross were going to the train but were late getting in. We had an hours drive to Loebo, the Southern Presbyterian Mission or MECM. The country is different again with giant palm tees, hills that are almost plains, and densely wooded valleys. The Mission is one of the largest we have been to, about like Elat, and there are nice brick houses. There are seventeen missionaries here and of course being Southerners they fell all over us. After we scraped the dirt off we had dinner at another house and then met with most of the mission. The seven men present, with me to guide them, had a special meeting. We hashed over all the problems and decided to come back here on our way back to Leo for the most important work to be done in this section.

The Bakuba tribe, about 100 miles from here, are the most interesting in Congo. The people live in an area of over 30,000 square miles and the history of the kingdom dates back to the thirteenth century. They are the only tribe who still have all their ancient crafts, government, and customs. The king is paralysed and has the use of only one hand. He has nearly 600 wives!! The power behind the throne is the kings old aunt who can even dethrown him if she wishes! It was done not so long ago and Mr. Washburn was given the royal anklet for six weeks during an epidemic. The children keep the mothers name and belong to her side of the family. So the successor to the throne is never the kings son, but his oldest nephew. At last a place where women are recognized as the power behind the throne! And everything else!

Tuesday, July 19 [Loebo]

Spent the whole day going over scenarios, expenses, and travel with Ross. This is the last time we will see him and we had a million details to clear up. As the schedule now stands we well get back to the Cameroun in December and after a month start home.

I am most excited by our decision to use the 35 mm film on the Bakubas. We have had no instructions from home and as this is so interesting feel sure it is the best thing we could do. I have big plans for a scenario and a picture all our own that will knock 'em dead. We must make it good enough for March of Time as the 35 mm is all that can be used commercially. I am all excited over this and wish we could start right in.

Wednesday, July 20 [Loebo—Tshikapa]

Had breakfast at Miss Black's with Ross. We talked over the last few details and then set out for Tchakapa in the truck with Mr. Jackson. Ross went to Mutoto with Mr. Craig. We crossed the first ferry with them and then took different roads. If they can be called roads. They are just one car wide and rather overgrown in places. The natives find a certain type of ant hills here that are very hard. They look like big chunks of iron ore and not at all like ant hills. These are pounded down till they crush and form a hard road bed. They are just used in the wheel tracks, the rest of the road doesn't matter.

I sat on the outside and had to wave at all the kids in the villages. When I did they would howl with delight. Very few cars come through so they race out to see every one.

We suddenly went up a hill and from then on over plains. We crossed the Kasaii and drove into Tshikapa at five. Up on a hill we found Mr. Kirk's house and sat down for tea. He is an American and does all the entertaining, distribution of food for the fifty whites, and care of the natives. There are fifty thousand in this zone which is reserved for diamond mining. No one else can come into this large area. Most of these work for Tshikapa in their many different industries for the white community here, and in the mines.

A party of five indepentdent missionaries arrived shortly after we did. They had just spent two weeks at Mukedi, with the Sprungers. Mrs. Aimee who is heading up this new venture in the Kiva used to be with their mission. They are carrying most of their equipment in a big truck and a carry all. In order to reach their destination they have to go way south and then back up to the Equator on the east coast. There are no roads beyond Leo as the river goes all the way to Stanleyville and roads are not needed. This is quite an adventure as they are going into the beautiful Ruwenzori mountain country that has not been touched by civilization.

We are sleeping in the bed that King Leopold and Astrid slept in when they were here. Everything we've had is good enough for a king.

Thursday, July 21 [Tshikapa]

Woke up when the drums beat at 6 AM but Leopold's bed was so comfortable that we went to sleep again till 8:30. We didn't have breakfast till 9 though as Mr. Kirk has charge of all the natives getting to work in the morning. Mr. Blosser, the other American here, took us around the station to see the part of the work that is done here. There are three magazines, an Industrial school where furniture, mattresses and anything the whites might want, is made, and a repair shop where all machines are assembled, repaired, and made for the 48 different mines. Mr. Blosser has 20,000 natives working for him in these mines!

We went through a big barbed wire fence to get into the picking station and then through locked doors. One man has the keys and no one can get in or out unless he lets them. The fifty natives who work here are made to change their clothes on the way in at 6:30 and at 3:00 when they leave for the night they have to take a shower and be completely examined. They have their heads shaved so that their hair won't have to be gone through every day.

The alluvial gravel, of 16mm size and under, is brought to this station by truck in locked cans, similar to our big milk cans. Careful records of each days collection and the resulting diamonds are kept. Each can is tagged with a metal tag having numbers and pictures on it to show at a glance where it came from, what day it was mined, and the tag follows the gravel in the can through all the concentration processes. The diamonds are put in a small can and sent to Antwerp with all the information.

When the gravel arrives it is sent through a pipe to the picking station. There is goes into an enormous machine which washes and sizes the gravel and it comes out in three different bins, being graded into three sizes. Each, in turn is put through a magnetic machine which attracts many of the stones but never diamonds. The magnetic action of the center plate is so great that it holds a big hammer so tightly that we had difficulty pulling it off.

The gravel next goes through a machine which shimmys and is made of great greased pans. The grease attracts the diamonds which stick to it along with a small amount of crud. The diamonds are then washed by hand and gone over in flat pans till everything else is removed. They are put in small cans with all the information attached, weighed, and sent to Belgium parcel post. I got to hold a whopper that was formed so nicely that it looked almost as if it had been cut. It is amazing that they find them in gravel and entirely separate from any other stone or mineral. There were so many that I think they were awful piggy not to give us at least one.

After a grand lunch we drove five miles to the nearest mine. We got a few movies and a lot of stills. I feel sure Life would run a sequence on this!

Friday, July 22

After an enormous breakfast Mr. Blosser took us out to the mine again in his car. We went by all their gardens this time and it was the best we've seen in Africa. They grow everything they need for the whites who work for Tshikapa. The mine was in full swing this morning and all the natives sing a chant to help them get their work done. They have a certain allotment to do each day and can leave when it is finished. We took quite a few pictures and they all enjoyed that. The ones with the wheelbarrows wiggled their hips as they went and did a regular dance so that they would show in the movies.

Then to the picking station where we shot thousands of carats and didn't manage to get even one. They produce 70,000 carats a month and won't give any away, the pigs! Ray managed to break two more bulbs, blow another of our lamp fixtures, and cut off all the juice so that all the machines stopped. I took some stills with my flash bulbs and scared the natives nearly to death. They were so surprized at the flash that they would howl and shrink back in terror.

Drove across the hill and got some long shots of this beautiful community and the very neat native village here. We stopped in the village and I got some portraits of some real cute kids.

Saturday, July 23 [Tshikapa—Loebo]

Got up at eight and got all ready to leave. About three we stopped at Charlesville to pick up some shipment for the Mission. We met Mr. Graybar of the C.I.M. (same mission as the Sprungers) who invited us to lunch. It was so late though we decided to go on without any.

When we reached Loebo [the town] we ran out of gas on a steep hill. We got some natives to push so we could turn around and roll back to a gas station. We had to cross one more ferry to reach the mission and were so glad to finally be back.

Sunday, July 24 [Loebo]

Had dinner at the Pooles and decided that he is just the slowest man alive. About four Mr. Jackson took us down to a nearby village to the Backsliders Meeting. One of the natives runs this for the Christians who have slipped. It is his idea and we think a good one for New Yorkers. He has such a swell program that he gets mobs of people backslidders or not. We took pictures till the sun went down and then enjoyed the program. [Tshisungu] has a pawpaw ochestra of little boys, an old organ that he made work, and two piano like insrtuments that he tuned to a piano. These are played by his two sons the way a xellophone is played.

Some of the young men put on a drama that had a swell idea behind it. They showed a sick Christian going back to the witch doctor for medicine. They went through a lot of crazy antics that amused us all enormously and then declared the sick person well. An Evangelist then arrived and told them all how foolish this was. This is all after the story of Simon in the bible. The diviner becomes blind because he fought against the will of God. The natives really got the point better than I did. Went to bed right after supper with Miss Black.

Monday, July 25 [Loebo—Mweka]

Dinner with the Jacksons with ice cream and cake. We sure hate to leave this place. Some of the folks came over to say goodbye to us and we went round and saw the rest. They all seem sorry to see us go—they say we made them feel ten years younger! They refused to let us pay board even after Ross had arranged it. Mrs. Jackson says they like to entertain on their own sometimes and this is one of those times. We were surprised at this as this Mission is so very poor right now.

Mr. Shive drove us to the train at Mweka and we promised to meet them in N.Y. in 1941.

Tuesday, July 26 [Mweka—Lulua Gare—Mutoto]

The porter woke us at 3:30 and we nearly died by the time the train got to Lulua Gare at 4:30. Mr. P.smith and his daughter, Ruth, met us there in a Ford truck. We got all our stuff in the back and Ray, and set out for Mutoto. Had breakfast there and then went out with Mr. Edmiston to see his agricultural work. Took a few shots of the many commentaries that are written in Buluba for the students here.

After lunch I fell asleep and Ray had an awful time getting me up again. Mr. E who is a negro missionary, took us out to a big field to take the natives burning off the brush. It was an enormous field covering the side of a hill. The natives spread out all around it and at a given call all light the edge of the field. We were all set up with our cameras to get good closeup views expecting an ordinary grass fire. In a few seconds the flames were leaping at our cameras, singeing the hair on our arms. It turned out to be a regular forest fire! Ray had the big camera on the heavy tripod so close to the blaze that the case became too hot to touch. He jumped in front of it to protect the camera and almost got a hole burned in his back. It looked as if the fire would jump across the path and cut off our retreat so we took a few close ups of the ever growing flames, picked up our equipment, and ran madly down the hillside with the scorching fire on our left and impenatrable underbrush on our right. The natives thought we were crazy and long before this had all run away. We ran across the stream and up another hill to get telephoto shots. It was a raging fire by this time, sweeping in toward the center from every side. Ever bush and tree writhed in agony and then went down under the terific heat. It was a magnificent sight and the most thrilling thing that has happened to us. Later we went back and got some shots of the smoking ruins. A pitiful burnt and blackened place after the luxurious growth that once was here.

Mr. E. then took us to the gardens by the stream. We said we never rode in a hammock so he got two of them and the natives carried us up and down hill. Boy, I like that.

We said we like to hear the natives sing so much and tonight just as we were about to go to bed they came to serenade us. A [trained] choir of about 15 stood outside our house and sang for half an hour or more. It was thrilling and they were exceptionally good. I could have listened all night. As they went off in the distance we could hear them singing until it died away into the sounds of the night.

Mr. E. is swell. His wife died out here last year after 35 years out here with him. He looks about 45 but must be much older. We think it is tops to have a

Negro missionary. The Southern folks here treat him very well and have him to meals all the time. He is pretty humble though.

Wednesday, July 27 [Mutoto]

Got up at seven when we should have been to Smith's for breakfast at 6:30. They had two English missionaries visiting so they all had to wait for us. This is Dr. Smith not the one who is working with us and who met us at the train. We all went to see the hospital and I was once more overcome with the desire to work in one of them. The native medical boys held a short service for the fifty or more people who are waiting for medical attention. Its all so wonderful to be able to help these poor ignorant people. They just know nothing about taking care of themselves or their babies. There is one tiny orphan here that has been fed the terrible manioc and bits of meat for six weeks. They just push this stuff down the baby's throat.

Took pictures all morning of Mr. Edmiston and his class. Even the tiny boys like this class and we got a row of them peeking through the fence.

Thursday, July 28 [Mutoto—Lake Mukamba]

After lunch we went right out to the rose garden and manioc field to finish our pictures. I usually sit on my camera case but here Mr. Edmiston always produces a chair. It appears like magic no matter where we are and I am getting terribly spoiled! I found a little boy with no seat in his pants, carrying a Wheatena box around with him. I got some stills and hope it will net us a little profit. Imagine finding this way out here in this section which is surrounded with cannibals!

At 3:00 we decided to go to the lake where this mission has a vacation house. Lake Mukamba is set in the plains, down in a valley, and is shaped like an enormous four leaf clover. The natives believe it is full of spirits and will have nothing to do with it so it is all for us. The rolling plains are beautiful and we would like to stay a while. Had a wonderful swim before supper and after eating with the two families staying here we went to bed in a little mud house like all the natives live in.

Friday, July 29 [Mukamba—Lusambo—Minga]

Ate an army's breakfast and then set out on our journey to Minga, Southern Methodist Mission. After five Kilometers of "what a good driver I am" Mr. Smith turned the car over to me and I kept it till midnight when we arrived. I did let him put it on one of the dinky ferries just so I wouldn't backslide in the water, like he did. Ray crossed in a native canoe and got some pictures of the ferry.

About three thirty we got to Lusambo and went to the English Mission for some food.

We have seen and done so much here that I feel the need of some time to let it all sink in before any new countries. Of course we will grab at the opportunity if it comes.

We drove on in the gathering darkness through tunnels in a pitch black forest. A new moon came up and a star to guide us.

I was revived after eating and went on driving. It was fun in the dark going through the jungle. We saw four big black monkies, a wild cat, and a coyote. Many great birds sleep in the road and were continually darting up before us. The jungle was alive with sounds and real scary. The headlight way in front of us made tree trunks look like ghosts standing tall and straight, sometimes with an arm outflung, or old and bent. Palm branches caught at us with their snake like fingers and banana leaves tried to wave us off the road and into the jungle.

The road got better and by midnight we found ourselves in Minga. We drove in to Mr. Davis back yard and he found us beds in the guest house which is brand new.

Saturday, July 30 [Minga]

Woke up at nine and found ourselves in a glorified native hut. The walls are mud, painted white, and the roof thick grass that should keep out the rain. The floor is good old earth covered with cotton seeds which are lovely and soft, and woven grass mats. The ceiling is made of mats too. They are held up by long strips of bamboo, reaching all across the room. If the wall gets a hole in it you can just go out for some mud and plaster it up. The trouble with these houses is that the white ants get in them and slowly eat them to pieces.

Sunday, July 31

Johnny called us for breakfast just before eight. Then we had to read funny sheets to the kids. Mrs. Hughlett took me to the girl's Sunday School and Mr. Hughlett took Ray to the boy's. We spent most of the afternoon reading as everyone seemed to be in bed and then at church for the natives.

We saw the hospital, home for Leper children, and small light plant, with Miss Allen and Miss Reynolds who are visiting. One is from Bibonga and the other from Bulape so we will see them both again. Ray has arranged a cake eating contest with Virginia Allen when we get to Bibonga next week. I have arranged an ice cream contest and only hope it really comes off. There are cows there so we have a chance.

Had supper with Miss Forman and then all the folks came over for prayer meeting. Dr. Ross spoke and we sang some good old Methodist hymns.

Ross certainly is up on everything. No matter what the discussion he seems to know all about it. We think he is a little dumb about movies though. Ray keeps hollering all the time because he expects us to get them done so fast and every where we go we feel so rushed for time. This project can't go on forever though and there just isn't enough money for us to stay any longer than we planned.

Monday, August 1

Right after breakfast Mr. Davis and Dr. Hughlett took us out to a native village about five miles from here. There we called all the people together, by drum, and set up an examination scene for sleeping sickness, yaws, and leprosy, that is given every year to all the people, by government requirement. Dr. Hughletts work is subsidized by the gov. for his part in this and his traveling expenses are paid. We are using this scene to show gov. cooperation with the Missions.

After lunch we took the children of the Lepers who are cared for in a little house here on the mission. The parents are allowed to visit them and they are free from the danger of Leprosy. The best shot was feeding them cod liver oil! We also took Mrs. Davis' nursery which she has to care for the babies while the mothers are working in their gardens in the hot sun. About thirty babies and very small children were brought, by request as this was not the time of day they usually come, and they all screamed and yelled when they got left. It made a good shot but then we couldn't shut them up and get them playing. Finally Mrs. Davis fed them some bananas and we were able to finish the sequence.

Tuesday, August 2 [Minga—Wembo Nyama]

We went through the most beautiful plains country we have yet seen. We stopped once to see a great rocky hole that is thought to be one of King Soloman's gold mines. There is no authority for this but it sure looks as if it might have been.

At ten o'clock we decided we would like to try to get a Roan Antelope. They are as big as cows and would give us plenty of meat for our stay in W.N. So we stopped at the next village and changed our clothes. I wore my brown jodphurs, which are really too tight, Ray wore his scout pants, and Mr. D wore Ray's brown slacks which were much too short. We had one native with us and got two more from the village and set out. Mr. D. had his rifle with him, the natives had spears and machetes, and we had cameras.

We crossed a stream on the natives backs so we wouldn't get our feet wet. I thought it was very sissy-like. After the first mile I began to work up a few blisters but there really was nothing I could do about it. We went up and down long hills (I puffed like a steam engine) at quite a good pace. The natives scouted out on either side of us so that we covered a good bit of territory. They can spot an antelope two miles off. After three miles with my feet screaming, we came on top of a vast plain. We cut over to our right and went on over the plain and down into the next valley. When no one was looking I took my shoes off and slung them over my back with the camera. It was too cloudy to get any pictures and when the sun came out later one of the natives was off with the camera. It was like heaven in my socks and I tramped on very happily for a time. We were dripping wet and pretty tired and realize now how soft we have been getting. We sighted two small antelope and circled around after them. They were quite near but ran lickety split when they saw us. We went through a field of high grass and then my troubles really began. It was push, push, push, against the thick tough grass and I felt as if my toe nails were being torn off. It was bristly underfoot, the sun poured down on us, and I began to get a Charlie horse in my right leg. I struggled to keep up, feeling as if I would die at any moment. Later we came across one of the natives. By this time we were forcing ourselves on with the utmost will power. We didn't get the antelope but we saw some wild Africa.

I ate six bananas in the village and an hour later when we arrived at Wembo Nyama, drank five glasses of water. We got a royal welcome here when we arrived and are sure we will like it even better than Minga.

Wednesday, August 3 [Wembo Nyama]

Mr. Lovell, Miss Armstrong, and we set out for a village, seven miles away, in the worst old rattle trap I have ever seen. I drove and with no brakes had quite a time stopping when we got to the village. In the village we got an old man teaching two tiny boys to drum. I got some girls pounding and sifting millet too. Then we got a whole group of women doing pottery with the little girls helping. It was swell and I got a pot too.

After lunch and a sleep we went to a nearby town for weaving and toy making. The boys here make cars out of bamboo that are swell. Ray got a tiny girl learning to cook and I went over to the hospital compound and got a whole sequence on making peanut milk. Miss Armstrong and a doctor at John Hopkins worked out a formula and it produces very nutritious milk. We felt that we accomplished a good deal today.

Thursday, August 4

Got up feeling like a lot more sleep and had breakfast with the Lovells. We read for a couple of hours and then I did some writing and packing for our trip to Lodja tomorrow. We will have to take our sequence on the Bibles in the morning.

We have decided to go right to Lodja in the morning and take the Bible shots when we get back.

Friday, August 5 [Wembo Nyama—Lodja]

Got up early and packed in a hurry. We left right after breakfast in the old Chevy. We chugged along [with Bill Chapel] making very little speed on the hills. Bill made it allright though and we got safely to Lodja in the next hour.

There are two couples here, the Reeds and the Wheelers who have two little girls.

Saturday, August 6 [Bena Dibele—Lukfungu—Lodja]

Right after breakfast we started out in a good car for Bena Dibele. Mr. Reed, Wheller, Bill, Ray and I. The people wear less and less as we go on and are now down to a long fringe in back and front. It looks just like a horses tail swishing along in back and probably has the same purpose—fly chasing.

We stopped on the road for lunch and an hour later arrived at B.D. We had some shopping to do there in the one horse town. I got a pair of sneakers (45 cents) to cure my sore feet and to play tennis in.

Bankutshu, a tribe of little forest people, were the reason for this trip. We found one of their villages and were greeted by the most ferocious looking natives we have ever even seen pictures of. Their hair is quite long and tied to form many tiny strands about ¼ inch thick. It is heavily oiled and as these people never wash, smells to high heaven. Their faces are cut with deep tribal marks that have rubber in them so that they stand out in ridges. Their teeth are filed and they have wild horrible looking faces. The men wear a grass loin cloth, woven, and the women a short fringe skirt which looks and smells like their hair. I got one of them for 2 francs and wonder if they will let me back in the U.S. with it. The men all carry beautiful knives that are handed down from one generation to another. We had a hard time buying them for this reason but did get a few. I got a lot of stills, two inside the tiny houses with a flash bulb. We scared the people half to death in doing it. The houses are made of leaves and bamboo and have everything under the sun in them, even a fire and extra food. There is just enough room left to climb over the two foot high door jamb, stoop over the fire to cook, and lie along one wall to sleep. I don't know where the whole family gets but they seem to squeeze in somewhere. Mr. Wheeler amused the folks by taking out his teeth and shooting his pistol, Ray with the zipper on his jacket, and Mr. Reed with the horn on the car. I was too busy taking pictures to join in the fun.

Later we stopped at Lukfungu where the people wear horsetails. It was too late to get many pictures and we had no success in trying to buy some of the copper anklets from the women. The men put them on as a sign of ownership. These people have such wild looking faces. What a difference in those who have been influenced by Christianity. It's almost unbelievable.

It soon got dark and when it came to getting on the ferry I almost spilled us all in the river. As I hit the two planks to go on, they jumped forward and the wheels sunk in the mud. I managed to back up the hill and the next time the natives put the planks too close together. I stopped half way up them with one wheel 3 inches off and two inches of tire keeping us from falling in the river. The men got out and pushed the car back on and I finally got safely on, much to my surprise.

Sunday, August 7 [Lodja—Kondola—Lodja]

Slept till eight we were so tired and as soon as we had breakfast set out for Kondola, 25 K from here. This is the largest village we have seen, having 3,000 people. The streets spread out in every direction and are lined with Palms, making it a very pretty village. The little girls met us, waving flowers, and the little boys, singing as hard as ever they could. We had a service in the church and then got everyone lined up outside for pictures. We need a mass meeting and so spread out about 500 people so they would look like a lot more. It was an awful job as they all wanted to be in the front line. We got through finally and went home for lunch. Twelve wild looking men in full regalia met us on the doorstep and after we ate we got some stills of them.

Another meeting in a nearby village. We took a few more pictures and came home just as it got dark. Mr. Wheeler is always taking out his false teeth and the natives are a scream. They look horrified and then try to yank theirs out. I got a still of one of them

Tonight Ray talked at Prayer meeting, on the project and all its ins and outs.

At Kondola this morning we were admitted to an enclosed compound where the chief and his wives live. One hut contains the grave of the old chief who died a few years ago. His hat and shoes are there and a table set with food and wine. Also some soap so he can wash. There is a great long stick, which was the height of the Chief. It is trimmed with fetishes and was carried by the head wife. Mr. Reed picked it out of the little pan it was in and before it could touch the ground a women ran in the doorway and grabbed it out of his hand.

Monday, August 8 [Lodja—Wembo Nyama]

At nine we started home by another route in order to go through Katako Kombe and get some shots of the natives bringing in elephant tusks. We bought a few pieces of worked ivory, got some gas and went on.

About eight P.M. and twelve miles from home we ran out of gas. Luckily we had bought a new bicycle at Lodja for a native. We sent the native we had with us, home for help, and sat down for a long wait. We had food, water, a flashlight, and Lexicon so we didn't mind much. Mr. Lovell found us playing at nine when he arrived on his motorcycle.

Tuesday, August 9 [Wembo Nyama]

After lunch we got set up for the Bible pictures. It took a lot of fussing and it was after four when we finished. Ray went to play tennis and I did some writing. I haven't had time lately to get anything done.

Wednesday, August 10 [Wembo Nyama—Tunda]

Went bicycle riding after breakfast to get some exercise. Then we packed to go to Tunda this afternoon and rode until lunch time.

We stopped at a village where they have shields and waited over an hour for the men to come in from the forests. And then they had such punk looking shields that we didn't want them. I took some stills while we were waiting, of some cute little boys.

Tried to buy some bracelets at another village but no one would sell us any. They ask if we would sell our cameras!

Thursday, August 11 [Tunda—Enyamba]

Got up at dawn and after breakfast set out for Enyamba, fifty miles from here. We need pictures of the rural dispensary out there that is run by a native. The government built the hospital and is cooperating with the mission on the project.

The sky was so gray that we couldn't do a thing. We saw the nearby village and some native dancing that wasn't particularly good. It looked just like "trucking" to us. Doris could have shown them how to pep it up a little.

A Belgian working for a cotton company invited us to dinner at his house. We couldn't say much but enjoyed the dinner anyway. The sun came out just as we were ready to start home. We had just enough time to get the sequence before the sun went in again. Ray had to pretend to take the Chief's picture as he got all dressed up in a white suit.

Friday, August 12 [Tunda—Bibanga]

Stopped at the Methodist lake for lunch. No one was there and it reminded me very much of some of my trips back to camp in the fall. I wanted to swim but we just didn't have time as Bibanga is a long way. One of the young missionaries was drowned in this lake a couple of years ago and his poor wife had a baby a few months later that was born dead. I'd just die too if any thing like that happened to me.

Bought some native mats that are very artistically woven. I have never seen them before but the Baluba people all make them

Got to Bibanga just before supper and had time to take a bath. We have an elegant house as one family is now on furlough. The houses are built out on a point and we can see for miles in three directions! The houses are facing out so we drove up to the back doors. This is by far the loveliest station we have seen.

Had dinner with Virginia Allen and then went over the scenario Mrs. Kellersberger worked out. Mrs. Kelly, as everyone calls her, wrote "Congo Crosses," one of the best books we read on Africa.

Saturday, August 13 [Bibanga]

Decided not to take any pictures until Monday so we can plan our work well. After breakfast we worked on our records. They have been getting far behind and so we got Mrs. Kelly and young John Miller to help us. We had three typewriters clacking away all morning and got quite a bit done.

Sunday, August 14

A native came with a note before we were out of bed. I got up but could not get my house coat from the closet without going by the open door. I told Ray he would have to get the note and I retreated into the dining room and bumped smack into the native [who had gone around the other way]. So I grabbed the note and a clock he had brought and ran. I guess he doesn't think pajamas are immodest anyway.

Went to the Leper camp at nine with the Kelleys and were thrilled to find it a beautiful village out on a high point of land like this one. The valley on one side has little lakes and streams where the lepers bathe, and all their gardens. The Chamoulgra oil trees, 1000 of them are planted in the valley too. These provide the life giving medicine and are the only ones in Africa. We came back to church here and were glad to find about 1500 earnest people. Our churches at home will seem boring I'm afraid, after this. Worked on records till dinner time. I went over all the Leper material and drew up a tentative scenario. Ray thinks it is swell and Mrs. Kelley was very enthusiastic when I showed it to her tonight.

Visited the tiny children in Sunday school at four. Mrs. Kelley teaches them songs with motions and they are darling. Dr. Kelley took us through his hospital and showed us his museum. He has babies from three weeks old to eight months. Premature babies and they all look like an almost complete baby, even the one only as big as my pinky. He has one petrified baby that was in the mother eight years! It was outside the womb and nature built a protctive sack around it. Most mothers die if the baby is not removed at two or three months. We saw goiters, hernias, tumors, appendis and other stuff, all prserved in formaldehyde. These prove invaluable in teaching the medical boys.

I am completely taken by all this and would like to stay right here and work in the hospital. Dr. Kelley hasn't even a nurse to help him and does a terrific amount of work with this good sized hospital and 800 lepers. He has planted trees all around the station and since 1918 has been building this station into the beautiful and successful place it now is. His lepers support themselves for the most part. He receives only $250 from his church board for hospital work each *year*. But somehow through government help, individual gifts, and a few native fees, he carries on as big a work as any we have seen regardless of the number of doctors. He is a real Christian personality as well. He gives jobs to the outcasts, like an old woman witch doctor who became christian and was put out of her tribe. And a man who had to have his leg cut off and is helpless in African society. His head medical boy was crazy from sleeping sickness when he came here 15 years ago.

Monday, August 15

After breakfast with the Andersons we attended a five minute prayer meeting. As the weather didn't look at all promising we went home and wrote some letters to get off this afternoon by air. Worked until lunch time. We are now having our meals in one house each day. We got our mail ready by two and then the sun came out. Unfortunately we had sent the Lepers all back to the camp and they are not well enough to walk all the way back here to the station. Some of the ones we are using in the first scene have almost no feet and have to hobble along on stumps.

Young John Miller, 17, took us out to the cotton company as we need a shot of fields of cotton. We drove twelve Kilometers out over the hills and saw some of the most beautiful country we have ever seen. I have never seen such velvety hills with a few trees scattered along the ridge, sihouetted against the sky. We stretched our necks all the way so that we would see everything.

There was no cotton in bloom and we came back and went out in another direction to see if we could locate some. I got a few stills along the way in a little village on a hill. We discussed religion quite thoroughly and found that we agreed on some points. Ray has worked out a good philosophy which he firmly upholds. Mainly that Christianity condones no force, of any kind.

Tuesday, August 16

Johnny drove us to the Leper camp at nine AM and we found them all lined up along the road waving flowers at us quite frantically. Ray took a shot for Mrs. Ross as she always enjoys this so much.

We took the Leper evangelist leading a service and his tiny boy walked into the scene and right up to his father. It was the cutest thing and will make the picture a hit without doubt. Next we took the outdoor school but had a lot of sitting around to do as the sun kept going in. We had to give up at one o'clock and all washed in water full of some strong antiseptic that would kill anything [we hope].

The afternoon was rainy and we couldn't do a thing so far as movies are concerned. Read and slept awhile and then did a little writing.

Mrs. Kelly is simply grand and full of interesting stories. In one of the brush fires here a mother and baby elephant were trapped. The mother got on top of the baby to protect it from the fire and was burned to death. When they found the singed baby it was trying to bury it's mother, according to elephant custom.

The monkies out here eat the unripe coffee bean and get so drunk they stagger around. What a movie shot that would make.

Wednesday, August 17

The sun wouldn't shine so we sat out in front of the house and talked. Then Ray and Julia Lake (everyone calls her that instead of Mrs Kelly) did all his movie records while I developed some film.

Julia Lake seems to be blessed with everything or the ability to think everything is a blessing. I never knew anyone with as much happiness as she has. Her native name means giver of happiness and it certainly fits.

We are wild about Bibanga and all its beauties. This is a place where I could spend a long time and find lots of happiness.

Thursday, August 18

This morning one of my life's ambitions was granted. We went to the operating room right after breakfast and saw Dr. Kelly do an elephantisis. The bite of a fly caused a gigantic growth, usually in the sexual organs. In this case the testicles had grown until the man could not walk. This huge lump of meat, the size of a basketball, had to be opened, the organs located, and then all the excess flesh cut away. It was wonderful and we didn't get sick at all! The man had a local anesthetic, injected in the spine, so that the lower half of his body was without feeling. A tourniquet was put around the elephantisis until it was opened and the organs located. When the tourniquet was removed the blood spurted all over. Every blood vessel of any size was caught with pincers and then tied with cat cut. The trick in this operation is to leave enough skin to construct a new scrotum sack and to cover the penis. It is really very neat after all the blood vessels are tied. Dr. Kelly was such a bloody mess that we took his picture. I never saw such a sight in my life and I loved it!

We went out to take some pictures but it was so cloudy that we decided to wait till this afternoon. I tore back to the operating room and Ray didn't want to miss anything so he came too.

The next was a rupture and to complicated to describe. There is an awful lot to a stomach operation. Then a woman had phalaria worms removed from three places on her body. Deep incisions were made in her shoulder, side, and thigh, and the worms cut out. The digging and tearing of flesh in this were awful. These worms, also from the bite of a fly, cause blindness. In one section near here a great many people are blind from them. This woman has had about 75 of the worms removed from different parts of her body.

Enjoyed lunch even after all the goo and blood. I am going to see a birth next. Some fun! Went to the Leper camp with Dr. Kelly this afternoon. We went down in the valley and got a sequence on the Chaulmoogra oil trees. The leaves were all full of holes from a heavy hail storm! When it rained here the other day it hailed for about an hour out there. And this is Africa! We had to cut off some of the good branches and hold them in the proper light and scene.

Friday, August 19

Were so sleepy that we sent a note to Mrs. Anderson saying we didn't want any breakfast. She sent us some at eight and directly after we went out to the Leper camp with Johnny and Julia Lake K. and Dr K. He spent the morning interviewing his lepers as he does every week. We took pictures of the children in school and playing all sorts of games.

We had a picnic lunch [in the Leper camp] and then shot Dr. K doing his work with the Lepers. It was a swell day and we felt that we accomplished a lot.

I play with the kids when there is nothing else to do, show them pictures in a magazine, sing Hi Ho which they sing after me, draw in the sand, or something to amuse and delight them. It doesn't take much and whenever I sit down Now they all crowd around to see if I will do something. Ray got them all saying "Well, smack me down."

Some of the Lepers are real bad—without fingers, toes, and sometimes feet. Many of them have "lion faces" all cracked and lined, with deep furrows. They begin to lose their voices when they get bad and are pitiful when they try so hard to speak. Leprosy is not as contagious as people think and it usually does not cause death. People die because they are outcasts and haven't the proper food.

Saturday, August 20

My darling hit the quarter century mark today and is beggining to feel (but not act) real old. When we woke up a tray arrived from the Kellys. It had a little black doll holding a big piece of cake, which Ray ate first thing. A box of little ivory elephants, and an autographed copy of Julia Lake's book. I gave him a little monkey that you work with your hand and he amused the kids with it all day.

We worked at the Leper camp till one and then had dinner with Julia L. More cake. Rested and read and looked at sterioptican pictures. Dr. K lent us a whole set, by Burton Holmes, that take you around the world.

Sunday, August 21

Julia L. sent us our breakfast this morning, including a large piece of cake. She thinks we might like to eat alone at our own little table, once in awhile! We ate in bed though and then Ray looked at his Steroscope pictures while I read. I slept again till ten of twelve! We got up and had dinner at the Miller's and then went back to spending a lazy day. I did develop one film and typed up one record as an excuse for not doing any other work. Ray has been nearly around the world with his pictures. They are pretty good and he likes them a lot. I thought those things were out of date after our mothers courtship days.

Mr. Miller gave a sermon tonight by special request. I said I hadn't heard one since March except in Bulu, Otetelo, and Bakuba. That was my way of getting out of talking as he wanted me too, and it worked very well.

We just drag ourselves around no matter how much sleep we have had, and we get fatter all the time too. It is an effort to lift a shoe and put it on. When we go out to take pictures I feel like laying down in the dirt and going to sleep. We wake up feeling swell and by ten are all fagged out. I suppose Africa has to have some effect though.

Monday, August 22

After breakfast with Big Jinny I dashed off three letters to the next places we stop at, as we are behind schedule. Went out to the Leper camp and worked like mad till 1:30. We got a lot done and went for lunch so thirsty that we drank and drank and then had to stuff the food in. Took a nap and slept for exactly eight minutes when someone called and said Dr. Kelly was waiting for us at the hospital. We took the sequence of extracting Chalmougra oil from the nuts. Dr. Kelly has been growing the trees for six and a half years.

They don't bear fruit till after the first five. No one else groes the trees here in Africa and the oil they buy for the Lepers from the Orient is very expensive.

Julia L. washed my frill for the black net dress and it looks just like new. Everybody sure looks after us in every way.

Tuesday, August 23

We had 65 Lepers come in from the camp this morning to reenact the scene that took place seven years ago when the camp was first opened.

At 10 we started our work up near the hospital. Dr. and Mrs K. started the group of homeless lepers off to their new camp, that had just been completed. We showed the whole procession in sihouette on their way. The ones without feet rode in carts, the women carried baskets on their heads, and the crippled hobbled along with sticks to help them walk. It really was quite a scene and should be very effective.

Wednesday, August 24

After breakfast with the Millers we went out to the Leper Camp for the last time. We worked hard and were through by one, luckily, as Ray was feeling tired and not in a photographic mood.

We had lunch alone as the Millers couldn't wait for us and then we rested till 3 PM. The last few scenes we were to take here where the Lepers once gathered before they had their camp. We got only one shot and a great bank of clouds covered the sun. We waited hoping to get a little more sun to finish. It came out for about 15 minutes and we shot all but the very last scene. We should get enough light to finish that tomorrow.

The Andersons had everything packed and were ready to take us out in the bush to spend the night in a native village. Someone shoved some letters at us just as we were going. Ray and I sat in the back of the pickup with the luggage and read to one another. Rogers finally wrote to us and is delighted with the pictures we have done so far. There were a few minor critisicms but on the envelope he had written, "Just saw the first six reels of Ngono. It is marvelous." We sure were thrilled over that. I was a little disappointed about the stills as Rogers seems to have given me credit (or discredit) for some of Rosses pictures. He talks about not having people look into the camera and I never, never do. I hope by now he has my records and has it all straight. I may have some faults but will never commit that sin if I can help it.

We got a letter from Mother and Doris written a month before the last one we got but time really added to our joy in reading it. We like so much to get poems and such in our letters especially when someone as dear to us as Mother has chosen them.

A river stopped our reading and we put all our baggage in one native canoe and ourselves in another to get across. The country is more lovely than ever and we are sure going to miss it after tomorrow. Mrs. Andy and I rode bikes for the few miles to the next village and the men walked.

We were greeted, in the dark by all the population, and then set ourselves up in a little house. The Evangelist and his family vacated it for the night and had it all swept out and as neat as a pin. They have no furniture so we had plenty of room for the beds. Ray and I had one room and the Andys [Andersons] the others.

They brought their cook and in short order we had a meal on a little table out in front of our hut. The natives formed a circle all around and watched every move we made. Then they sang and I entertained them with the monkey. My fingers have gotten used to working him now and I can make him do all kinds of things. The natives all love it and laugh and shout whenever I get it out. It takes them a while to figure out that it isn't alive.

Thursday, August 25

We just got to bed last night when Ray who had been feeling badly all day, got a terrific fever. He was burning up even though he had taken a lot of extra quinine to offset any malaria. And he has dysentary as well. He had to get up very often and had such pains that he couldn't sleep at all! This is the first time we have really felt Africa and it sure hits with a bang when it comes. How I escaped I don't know but luckily I feel fine and can take care of him.

At four we decided to get up and start back to Bibanga where we could get some medicine. Mrs. Andy stayed to get all the stuff packed up when it got light and we rode down to the river on bikes. We borrowed the extra one from a native and didn't take long. If Ray hadn't been so sick it would have been glorious riding along in the early morning light. We did plenty of hollering at the river to wake the boatman and have him come over for us. We tore along when we got in the car and before long I had my darling in bed. Dr. Kelly made me official nurse and I am taking temperature, giving doses of paregoric and quinine, and feeding the patient beef broth. Having never been sick Ray is sure he is about to die and he sings HI-HO to keep his spirits up.

I fell asleep on the couch this aft. and when I woke Mrs. Kelly told me to run to the hospital as someone was having a baby. I tore down but was too late. Heck! Dr. Kelly had to take the baby with forceps as it was much too big for the mother. It was the cutest, fattest baby I ever saw and I was so sorry not to see it get born. Better luck next time.

Friday, August 26

My patient only got up twice in the night and is feeling better today. He has no fever and is passing almost no blood. I'll have him up in no time. He has some pain at times and during fifteen minutes I wrote down all the things he said in reference to it. "Lots of people die from Malaria. Gee, I got such a belly ache, Jin, in my belly. Jinny really, I am deathly sick right now. I'm only eating so I won't die. No, no, no, get it away from here. Terrible stuff!! Gin, I'm sick. Awww! It's appendicitus as sure as I'm alive. Why do you laugh at me when I holler, you know I'm sick. I feel awful bad. Mmmm I do feel sick. Why am I so sick Jin, can't I get up." The last remark was all in one breath, too.

Saturday, August 27 [Bibanga—Kasha]

Ray seems almost well this morning. He didn't get up all night. We had the Lepers come in again, fifth time, to get our last shot. Ray got up at ten and we worked until one to get it! I did most of the work so he could sit in the car. We held a branch from the roof of the car and arranged the Lepers under it with their [mutilated] hands outstretched in appealing fashion. Just when I got it right the cloud we were using for a background would move or dissolve. Then I had to move the car and start all over. It took at least half an hour to set it up each time. I was exhausted and then dashed home to finish packing!! Mr. Miller decided to take us to Kasha, one of their stations, and Ray can rest over Sunday. Then we can go on to Songa Monday, instead of waiting till Tuesday for the next train.

Sunday, August 28 [Kasha]

I stayed with Ray all day reading, and then Mr. Miller dragged me out for a walk. Ray seems much better and he enjoyed his broth and a coddled egg tonight. We'll have him eating everything he doesn't like before long. To-night we had a little service, that I enjoyed very much. We each read part of a chapter in the Bible and Mr. Miller interpreted it for us. It is so different when you hear someone talk on the subject and can have some understanding of it.

Monday, August 29

Woke up early and sneaked out for breakfast while Ray was still asleep. He is feeling much better today and is beginning to holler for food. Mrs. McKee does not weaken however and is still feeding him porridge and thin soup. He wrote a letter to Rogers this morning which I typed up and then worked on the Leper scenario with me.

Johnny and I went monkey huntin' with a native this afternoon. I squeezed into my brown jodhpurs and looked quite African tramping along with a gun. A native led the way and we went across the plain and down into some deep forest. At last I could crawl along in the darkness of a real tropical forest! My meter only registered 2 in there so there wasn't any chance of getting a picture. We saw one wee monkey but didn't think he was worth shooting at.

The sounds in the forest are wonderful. It is full of silence that sounds like a sea shell held up to your ear. In the distance an animal grumbles and all around the birds and crickets take turns singing. It was a heaven for monkeys, with long vines to play on and thick tree tops to hide in. They are very good at hiding so we came home empty handed.

Tuesday, August 30

Mr. Miller called me in the wee hours to take me monkey hunting again. I tried to dress quietly but dropped a shoe, kicked a glass, and knocked over a chair before I got out.

We went deeper into the forests this time and Mr. Miller very gallantly carried me over three streams. Ray has been raising more than his eyebrows at this.

We worked our way through some real heavy undergrowth to reach a place where our guide swore there were monkies. I got all tangled up in the vines and almost didn't get through. And still we could find no monkies. On the way home we saw three little ones but they went like lightning and then hid way in the tops of the trees. I got a stiff neck looking for them all to no avail. We went home for breakfast with nothing more than an appetite.

Ray feels a little better today but we got a report from the laboratory in town saying he has amoebic dysentery. After much discussion we decided to go to Lubondai tomorrow where the nearest doctor is. I dashed off some more letters to the people who have been expecting us at Kanene, Kamina, and Elizabethville. They must think we are crazy we have changed our plans so many times. Ray got up for dinner and supper and pestered us all to death for something more than soup. Mrs. McKee "stuck to her guns" though and just gave him more soup.

Wednesday, August 31 [Kasha—Lubondai]

We put a cot in the back of Mr. McKee's "hearse" so that Ray could take it easy on this trip. We don't want to get him down again. Mr. Miller, McKee, and Johnny went with us. I sat in the front between the two men and Johnny just folded up among the luggage in the back.

I drove awhile over a terrific road and then Mr. Miller took us into Lubondai. It is a grand place—just like a college campus. The palm trees are gorgeous and it sure is an ideal place for a school. There are about 35 children from different missions all over the Congo. One girl comes by air from Leo!

They range in age from nine to seventeen and are a grand bunch. There are 3 teachers, one of whom has just come out. She looks fresh out of college and is just about my age.

Thursday, September 1 [Lubondai]

Mr. McKee, Miller and Johnny left right after breakfast. They sure have been swell to us and so has everone in this mission. We have stayed with them so long and havn't paid for a thing. Thank goodness as my money will last so much longer.

Worked on our leper scenario before and after dinner so that we have it nearly finished.

Friday, September 2

Spent the morning finishing the Leper scenario out on our porch. It is a nice place to work, under some swell palms, and we accomplish a lot.

After dinner I slept a couple of hours while Ray lay on his bed and read Time. It is swell for the news and very compact. In fact we think we would rather read it than the newspapers.

We are undecided whether to go to Bulape or Elizabethville from here. It is all kind of mixed up as we are due in Bulape by Sept. 15 when Mr. Washburn will be ready to work with us. I wrote to Mr. Booth in Eliz. but have had no answer yet. ?????

Saturday, September 3

The kids don't have school on Saturday and have been having a grand time all day. The girls have a house up in a tree like Totty and I used to have. I think every kid has a bicycle and they have been bumping into us all day. The school now has kids from five missions and next year will have them from two more. They hope to make it much larger and that the other boards will contribute in the upkeep. It certainly should be a cooperative project, instead of all the burden being on the Southern Presbyterians. They have less money now than any other mission board according to Mr. Ross.

Sunday, September 4

Decided to take a sequence on the school because it is the only one in Congo and it is far superior to the school we took in the Camerouns. They only have Grammer school and only 14 students.

Rays bed fell in last night and we had more fun fixing it in the dark. It reminded me of the house we had in Brookhaven where all the beds fell in. We like Africa better all the time even with all our longing for movies and ice cream and Mother. The time is flying and we never grow weary of one another. Husbands don't wear out I guess like most of the things I've had.

Monday, September 5

After breakfast we went to take pictures of the Grammer school kids. It took us till almost eleven o'clock to get everything ready. We put a flare just outside one window and then couldn't get it shut to keep out the smoke. After much pounding we called a carpenter to take the frame off so the window would close. The other flare we put on the other side of the room outside the door. When they were finally lit the smoke poured in the room through little spaces between the window sashes. So we couldn't take a thing. The kids were scared but went on acting the way we had told them too. We gave up for the morning and I went home to bed with a tummy ache.

Ray took the pictures at half speed this afternoon and the kids had to do everything in slow motion. They loved it.

Tuesday, September 6

Ray went for breakfast alone as I was just too sleepy to get up. When I finally did I started in on my sewing and got all the mending done. It was too dark to take pictures so I got out the blue cotton dress I started long ago in the Camerouns.

Ray has been working on his records today and has them almost up to date. I've been squeezing mine in at odd moments and hope to get them done by Friday when we leave. We got mail today from Mother, Sherm, Bert, and Stan. We read them all twice.

Wednesday, September 7

Took pictures of the High School kids until after one o'clock. They had a grand time and so did we. Some of them had to stand outside with mirrors and thow sunlight into the room.

After lunch it was too cloudy to do any more so I finished my dress and Ray got his records all finished.

Had prayer meeting and everybody had to pray!! After a little too much of this we always say some hells and things when we get out. I can't say I like praying in public even with only six people present. It feels like an exhibition of my inner soul.

We are anxious to get to Bulape now and start our work there. It is some of the most important as we will do the 35 mm film and its got to be good. I guess we will stay a month or more and hope for good weather.

Thursday, September 8

Last night we had a real rain and how it did pour. I got a chance, at last, to wear my raincoat. By the time we had eaten our breakfast it had stopped and the world took on a beautiful new coat of green. All the dry season dust was washed away and everything looks so bright and clear, as if God had spilled new green paint all over his earth.

Tomorrow we have to get up real early to get the pictures done before we leave, so we are going to bed with the children tonight.

I have my expense accounts all straightened out now, and hope to keep them up to date. I have an awful time with three of them and it's such a relief to get them typed up and off my mind.

Friday, September 9 [Lubondai—Tshimbula RR]

Got all my packing done after breakfast and then went down to the school to help Ray finish the pictures. We got the kids out playing basketball and tennis and riding their bikes so we were very popular. Then we did the science class after waiting ages for the steam to come up. At last we got it all done and after dinner and many goodbyes set out for the RR station with the Cousar family.

About five we left Tshimbula, going north again to Mweke. For an hour we just sat and looked at the sky. At last we find that there are wonderful sunsets in Africa. Before this there has been so much haze in the air that the sun just disappears behind it and there isn't even a glow in the sky. The twilight here is very short anyway as the sun drops down so quickly when you are near the equator.

Saturday, September 10 [Mweka—Bulape]

Arrived at Mweka at 8:30 while we were still having breakfast. We couldn't see Mr. Washburn and as the train stayed half an hour we went on with our meal. In the meantime poor Mr. Washburn was looking for us and thought we hadn't come. But he found us and we got our 18 pieces of baggage safely off and in his truck.

Drove twenty miles to Bulape and got settled with Miss Reynolds, the girl we met at Minga. Met the Andersons, parents of four of the kids at Lubondai, the Chapmans, who are young and have a two year old girl, and Mrs. Washburn.

Sunday, September 11 [Bulape]

Bulape is located in the forest country and is on a hill like all the other stations of this mission. There are people of three different tribes here, the

Baketi, Baluba, and Bakuba. The Bakuba, to the north, control the whole section and make slaves out of many of the other people. The whole Baketi tribe
are subject to Lukenga's [*Lukengo's*] rule, king of the Bakuba, and many
smaller tribes as well. The missionaries here have to learn three languages.
Our little Baluba is still good here thank goodness, as we know more of that
than any other language in Africa.

Monday, September 12

Spent the afternoon on our own porch overlooking the valley. I did some
mending and Ray read "The Leopard Hunts Alone" (by Conway T. Wharton)
to me. It is about the Bakuba people and recounts some of Mr. Washburns
adventures here since 1914, referring to him as the "Kentucky Gentlemen".

About four we begged the Washburn's bikes and rode down into the valley
looking for the lake. After two miles of flying down hill we found ourselves
at the brick kiln where Mr. Anderson is working. He wasn't there however
so we went another way, through some dense jungle, and suddenly before us
saw the lake. It is truly like a jewel shining in the black forest, and a wonderful place to swim.

Tuesday, September 13

As we had our meals here with Lena today we hardly even saw anyone else. We worked out on the porch, getting some letters written, and Mr. Washburn came over to talk business with us. Tomorrow night the two natives who are to work with us will get here and the next day we will spend in conference with them.

Thank goodness the natives here have some individuality. They are the first we've seen who have any pride and who uphold their dress, customs, and government, regardless of the white man. Mr. Washburn is really the only one who has access to the kingdom and to the capitol city. A number of years ago the people were dying off like flies in a dysentery epidemic. The king wouldn't obey his mother so she dethroned him and gave the royal anklet to Mr. Washburn, knowing that he could help. He burned villages and did all he could to clear up the disease and the people made him keep the royal anklet for several weeks. Then the old mother restored the king to power. She really is the power behind the throne and I guess this is the one place in the world where women are recognized as such. Some fun!

Many years ago a Baluba woman and her infant son were captured in the forest and put into slavery by the Bakubas. Every five years the king demands a slave from each family so that the royal family is well supplied. So the little boy was taken from his mother and sent to Mushenge. Here the king, his family, and his 1000 wives, live in a capitol city. So Katshunga grew up there and became valuable to the king. These people rely on memory and this keen minded boy became the king's memory.

When he grew into manhood the king promoted him and made him a tax collector. This is a prize job as when the king asks two goats from every family the collector demands five and keeps three for himself! So Katshunga bought six wives and became a powerful and terrible man. As he traveled over the 25,000 square miles of the kingdom the people became more and more afraid of him. In one little village the people heard of his coming and all ran away in the forest. But one old man couldn't run fast enough and when Katshunga caught him he cut off his head and stuck it on top of a pole. A symbol of what he would do to the rest of the people when he caught them. As he went on his way he met a woman with a baby in her arms, from the village, but she had been away and knew nothing of Katshunga's anger. He was so enraged that he snatched her baby and threw it into a crocodile infested stream. And the poor women jumped in to save her baby and was lost.

That's the kind of man Katshunga was. When he returned home he found that one of his wives had been attending Mr. Washburn's meetings, in the village, for six months. He beat her into unconsciousness that night and the next day some of her friends sent a note saying, "Don't give up your religion.

We are praying for you." Then Katshunga saw that his wife had learned to read and he thought, of course, that she was getting love letters. But when a number of people interpreted that note for him he turned back to his wife with forgiveness. He suddenly realized that he was just an animal but she could read and write and was a human being. So she taught him to read and after many months of study from the Bible, the only book they had, Katshunga went to Mr. Washburn and said he wanted to be a Christian. He gave up all his wives but the one who had taught him how to live and with her he started life anew.

Today he is an elder in the church and is studying to be an Evangelist!! And tomorrow he is coming here, to spend the next month helping us and teaching us everything he knows about the Bakuba.

Boy, am I having fun!

Thursday, September 15

Mr. Washburn took us out to look at villages this afternoon. We will need three for our first picture alone. I got some presents along the way, a pan of peanuts which are very good raw, and half a dozen eggs.

The houses are made of palm fronds and look as if a good wind would carry them away. We saw seven villages and found three photographable ones without any trouble.

I have been so sleepy all afternoon. I got up at 5.30 to see the sun rise and get some stills. It was beautiful enough to get up for but Ray was so sleepy I let him stay in bed. I roamed all around and even went down into the native village near here. We are so glad that the haze has been washed out of the air and we can enjoy the sun rising and setting again.

Friday, September 16

After breakfast we got all our exposed film ready to send to Eliz. I dashed off a letter to Mr. Booth asking him to check it through the customs for us & mail it home.

We then set out to find the king and ask if we may take pictures in his kingdom. Going through Mweke we left the films and our mail. Followed a back road looking for the village where Lugenga [*Lukengo*] is staying to set up a new court. We had to stop and fix a flat and finally about one o'clock we found the king. His people were building a great fence around the chief's house and the area where the palavers will be cut.

After some red tape we were led into this enclosure, up and down alleys, and into the kings presence. He was lying on a mat and we had to go and take his hand. He is completely paralyzed except for a little motion in one hand and

has been for years. Even before he became king. His slaves and henchmen were sitting with him under an open air house, having just a roof. No movies have ever been taken in this kingdom and we were getting a little scared about getting the old king's consent. Mr. Washburn explained the whole thing to the king's son. Everyone listened including the king. And then the son had to tell the story all over again. Finally Lugenga spoke, then the son spoke, and at last Mr. Washburn told us what his answer was. We will be permitted to take any pictures we wish and as soon as Lugenga gets back to the capitol city he will cooperate to the fullest! Ray ran out for the monkey after the formal proceedings were over and I worked it for the king. He grinned from ear to ear.

Saturday, September 17

Mr. Washburn is getting the cast for the pictures lined up and making arrangements for us to stay out in one of the villages while we are taking it. We think that will be fun and we will surely get our work done faster.

After dinner, with Lena, I was reading in the front room and heard a funny noise outside. I looked out and there was a little native boy dressed in a mask and raffia costume that he had made himself. I let out a whoop and Ray came running. There were 15 other little boys to entertain us too. They sang and clapped while the masked boy danced and he sure could dance! Not one of them could have been more than eight and there was one tiny naked one. We took some stills of them, they all had sticks like spears, to scare us with. Then we gave them each a piece of chocolate. They smelled it warily before they would eat it and then some of them spit it out. They would have liked salt much better.

Sunday, September 18

After breakfast with the Washburns we worked on our 100 envelopes to send the mimeograph letter in. Ray rigged up a thing on the bike to draw on the ground as you are riding. He says he can write with it and has been fooling with his crazy invention most of the day.

This afternoon we borrowed Lena's bike so we could go riding together. We went through the village which is fully half a mile long and all the kids came running behind us. The pied piper had nothing on us! They all stare at my anklets and talk about them right in front of me.

Monday, September 19 [Bulape—Koshi]

Got one pair of Ray's slacks that a native made for us. He couldn't do button holes though so I had to undertake the job. The material frayed so that I had to make bound ones—too elegant for pants. Going to Lena's to stitch them I fell off the bike and put a hole in them with the scissors.

Mimeographed our letter and then packed for our stay at Koshi, a native village where we will do "How an African Tribe is Ruled."

Arrived at Koshi late this afternoon and settled ourselves in a little hut at the end of the village. We have our personal boy with us to wait on table etc. and Mr. Washburn brought his cook. They cook in a little hut in back of ours.

Ray and I had a grand time amusing the natives until dark. He jumped over my shoulders and over groups of natives and I jumped rope. They are amazed at Ray and say he is awful strong. He is so glad he is at last appreciated. The natives are so funny explaining to newcomers what he did and their actions make us almost understand their language.

After supper on our porch we interviewed possible stars for the picture. Went to bed hoping it wouldn't rain the roof is so full of holes.

Tuesday, September 20 [Koshi]

Got up just as the sun was coming up and after breakfast went down into the village. The people stood around watching us so long that we had to come back to our hut so that they would dress up and get ready for the pictures. We worked on our scenario for an hour and then got started. The Bakuba costumes are really elegant. The men wear a red-orange skirt, always at least ten yds. long, gathered across the front so that it is very full and looks almost like Scotch kilts. Every man wears a big knife inlaid with copper and iron designs and a tiny conical hat, held on with a long metal hatpin. For dress up most of them have feathers and beads added to the everyday hat. Some wear anklets, bracelets, and necklaces of cowery shells and beads. The women have a long cloth wound around them too but it is covered with embroidery, beautiful outline designs, and draped around their hips. These are the most colorful costumes we have seen anywhere.

The confounded sun went in so often that by 1:30 we had only the scene with the witch doctor. Then we went home for lunch and it rained until 5. The whole village came over then with a tall man to see if Ray could jump over him. He could. I cut paper designs for them and then Ray did some more jumping. Since they got their dress clothes on this morning they have been dancing. They came up and danced for us in the pouring rain and are still at it tonight. Once they get started they don't stop for a week or more. We heard so much noise that we went down tonight and found only five little boys!

Wednesday, September 21

It rained all night and part of our mud house washed away. Mr. Washburn was so afraid the roof would blow off in the terrific gale, that he lit a lamp so we could get out fast. There is enough house left to live in, however, and keep us fairly dry.

I finished Ray's pants this morning while Ray & Mr. Washburn changed a tire that went flat over night. Then we worked on the scenario for the Mission picture till dinner time. The people were all dressed up again and dancing like mad so we went down, as the sky looked a little brighter. We got enough sun to shoot some dance pictures for the Mission Picture. The men do a wild jumping around dance yelling and hooting, while the women, who are very ladylike, do a wiggle like Doris does, and keep up a chant. The women are really much nicer than the men. This is the first time any movies have been taken of a Bakuba dance and we are sure they are good. They are still dancing tonight and their drums and chanting are booming in the quite night.

Got a very discouraging letter from Rogers about the stills. He objects because they are too pretty and there aren't enough close-ups. He seems to forget that they should be enlarged and even recomposed before they really look like anything.

The little boys are still hanging over our porch and will be untill we put out our light and go to bed. They sure are cute and not afraid of us any more. African mothers always make the white man the bogey man to scare their kids.

Thursday, September 22 [Mushenge]

Another day dawned bright and clear but before noon, clouded over. We spent the morning working hard but finished only one sequence and rehearsed another.

I wrote a letter to Sue Weddell after lunch and then we decided to go and see Mushenge, the capitol city.

It is an enormous city and a maze of fences. There are about 3000 people living there. The king and his harem form one part, from 600–1000 wives. No one knows just how many. Each family of Bakubas must always keep a girl in the harem. If she dies she is immediately replaced by another girl. In this way the king keeps control of every individual in his kingdom. In former years if anyone rebelled his daughter in the harem would be put to death.

After going through numerous gates and even some houses, which are entrances, we reached the harem which is a good sized village in itself. Mr. Washburn succeeded in getting a chapel in here, a number of years ago, and there are a number of Christians. My monkey made his biggest hit here. We told the women that his name was Brooklynite and it is so funny to hear them say it. About 200 wives crowded around Ray and I and screeched and yelled at the monkey's antics. We didn't know how we could ever get away and more kept coming all the time. We laughed ourselves sick and once the monkey grabbed a bar of soap right off a woman's head and she about died of fright. We finally got away and as the women have to stay in their fence they couldn't follow us.

We met the king's old aunt who really has all the power. She is about 90 and all wrinkled and withered. Then we met his mother, who is the second lady of the land, and fairly old too.

These women have a seperate "fence" which means houses etc. enclosed in a private compound. All the kings sisters and their families live in another fence and are the royal family. The nephews on the women's side of the family are the heirs to the throne. In Bakubaland the children take the mothers name and belong to her family!

The king has a brother however who is next in line for the throne. He lives in still another fence and has 150 wives and a million children floating around. We sat in his house which is much larger than any we've seen in Africa, and has beautiful carved posts and hand made mats in it. These people are very artistic and work out intricate designs on everything. The brother looks like a fat sloppy guy living on the fat of the land. He looks like a hard cruel man and I hope he never gets to be king.

There are a great many dilapidated houses at Mushenge but the mucky-mucks have a number of large and beautiful ones. They are made of palm thatch like all the others but are woven in lovely designs instead of just fastened together. There are sliding doors on all houses covered with a fancy mat which can be rolled up and fastened at the top of the door. You have to step up two feet and bend down two in order to get into the house.

The natives here have started dancing again tonight. I hope this one is a sun dance!

Friday, September 23 [Koshi]

A beautiful clear day at last. We worked like demons in a blazing hot sun all morning. After lunch we laid down to take a very short rest and when we got back on the scene our villain was gone. He decided it was a good day to go burn his field off. After a long wait we got the rest of the people out but couldn't find the man who was to dress up and be chief. We had some wala bakodi (big palaver) but couldn't take any pictures. Maybe these people shouldn't be so independent after all. And the Bakuba sure are even if all the others we've seen lean the other way.

After much palavering in the village Ray and Mr. Washburn went off to the next village. We hope to work there tomorrow and take the rest of the scenes we need there.

Ray came back quite elated because he was appreciated again. When he jumped over the car a native came and told him that the white man excells them in everything, brains, food, machines, and now in brawn. Mr. Washburn told them it was because Ray ate lots of lettuce and green things. HA HA!

Saturday, September 24 [Koshi—Bulape]

The villain arrived first thing this morning with a chicken for peace offering. He didn't say it was but that he'd been looking and looking for a chicken ever since we came.

Went up to the next village and worked all day, finishing up the last few scenes. The sun was broiling hot and we drank gallons of water. The natives can't seem to stand the sun as well as we can. The are always trying to get in the shade but when they light their pipes they pick up a hot coal. Their skin is so tough that it doesn't burn them. Dr. Poole says they need salt and calcium, which they have very little of, in order to stand in the sun.

Packed up all our stuff to go home and just got it all in the car when it started teaming.

Sunday, September 25 [Bulape]

After breakfast Dr. Poole, who is here to give Dr. Chapman another injection, came over. A few minutes later some cake arrived for Ray and after the first few bites he got a mouthful of quinine. Boy what a fuss he made. We began to see why Dr. Poole honored us with a visit.

After dinner I wrote letters to Doris and Jean while Ray mixed my chemicals so I could develop a film. It turned out fairly well except for one picture that is out of focus. Will I be glad when I get Rosses camera. We sent to Eliz. for it and should have it in a few days.

Didn't go swimming as it was rather cloudy and we were so very busy. We sure have plenty of work to catch up on when we have a day off from pictures.

Monday, September 26

Set out to the north this morning in search of two villages to use in the mission picture and some beautiful forest and plain scenes. We stopped at five or six villages and my monkey made a great hit as usual. I make him dance now like the natives do while Ray drums on the side of the car. The step the women do is wildly received.

After miles of jungle country we came out on a huge plain, high up over the surrounding country. It is so flat that we drove out over it. Suddenly an antelope jumped up right in front of us! He ran like the wind and we drove right behind him for fifteen minutes or more taking stills. We twisted and turned with the antelope and had more fun trying to keep up with him.

We started back toward the road when a jackal jumped up out of the grass in front of us. He led us on another merry chase and we got real close to him so should have some good stills.

Went back to Bulape lake for a shot of the beautiful jungle around it. Took the boat and stopped on every shore trying to get the proper camera angle. It got too late to take the picture but we did locate the place. Took a quick swim and then home to supper. Ray and I worked late on the cover for his white helmet so Mr. Washburn can wear it in the movies. It's an awful job.

Tuesday, September 27

Got our caravan of 28 men together and all the camping equipment Mr. Washburn carries when he travels by hammock. We went out on the plain near here and rehearsed scenes till lunch time. It was too cloudy to take pictures at all today.

Went home late in the afternoon and developed a couple of films. Ray fell asleep and when he woke up and it was time to dress for dinner there was no water for our showers. I had used it all up in developing.

Got a letter from Rogers that says how delighted they were with the rolls of "Ngono" they have received. And if "Bwamba" is as good that the pictures alone will be worth the cost of the expedition. This was the nicest present we could have gotten for our seventh monthiversary.

We know the pictures we are making now are much better than those we rushed so in the Cameroun.

Wednesday, September 28

Went out to take the pictures we rehearsed yesterday. We had to choose a new spot for the first one as the sun was in another position. Ate lunch in the car in a great hurry so we would get a lot done today. Spent lots of time waiting for the sun to come out anyway.

When we wanted clouds in the last scene about 4:30 they all went away. Ray says when he is flying around in heaven he's going to spend most of the time kicking the clouds around.

I am getting terrifically worried about the 35 mm picture. At the rate we are going here we won't get to it till November. Then there is a Mission Meeting for two weeks and we couldn't stay all that time doing nothing. We will have to somehow rush this through and try to work on it the last two weeks in October. The natives and Mr. Washburn are so terrifically slow at getting things set up and rehearsed. It just about drives me nuts to be always sitting around waiting for them.

Managed to finish quite a little by sundown even with all the difficulties. The mobs of children in the village here are so cute that even Ray wants one of the little ones now. They have very fancy haircuts in this section, intricate designs are shaved on their heads. It reminds me very much of the way Dad used to decorate our cats.

Thursday, September 29

A nice bright morning at last. We drove out to a village to work but had to wait a long time for the caravan to arrive. They started walking about 6 AM. Got set up and rehearsed the villagers about ten times so they would do everything right. Then the sun went in. We spent the hour eating lunch and then gathered the people together again. What a relief when we finished that shot!

Worked hard and got three more before the sun went down. We will have to come back tomorrow though to finish. Got home to our shower just as it got dark and then wrote a letter to Ross before supper. We are sending him the leper scenario we did at Bibaṇga and hope he likes it as well as we do.

Ray and I have to figure out a way to rewind all the film in the magazines that Ross gave us. The magazine camera doesn't work very well and we want to put the film on spools so we can use it in the Special. It's going to be an awful job but we can't waste 1,000 feet of film. We wish we had a lot more anyway as we are shooting so much more than we expected to. We ordered some more and hope Rogers has sent it before now.

Friday, September 30

Went out to Bukoyi bright and early so we could finish up there. But the confounded sun was completely hidden and we couldn't do a thing all morning. Mr. Washburn took a nap in the tent we set up for the scene, Ray read, and I typed up a scenario for the 35 mm. It doesn't look as though we will have time to do it at the rate we are going now.

Ate lunch and then walked down the road to a great clump of bamboo where our next scene will take place. We had the natives clear a space for the car so Ray can get on top to take some of the pictures. This is supposed to be the begginning of Bulape station. Mr. and Mrs. Washburn lived in a tent under the bamboo for a month or more while waiting to have their first little house finished.

The sun finally broke through and we took the caravan to the bamboo and shot the scene of the first arrival and the men begginning to clear away the brush. Ray wants morning light on the village scene so we have to wait till tomorrow for that.

Got home at five o'clock quite worn out as usual. I wouldn't say this job is any cinch. We work harder than we ever have in our lives and it gets discouraging sometimes when so many things go wrong.

Saturday, October 1

Went back to Bukoyi early this morning hoping to get the scene there. We waited and waited for the sun to come out and it just wouldn't. I took a nap on the cot in the tent that is part of the scene. About noon Mrs. Washburn and Lena came out with our lunch. We had quite a party—even a table cloth today.

Finally it cleared about 2:30 and we shot the scene in the village. We had hoped to do the scenes under the bamboo with Mr. and Mrs. Washburn as well today. Better luck next week I hope.

Ray took a few stills of me playing with the kids. I drew pictures for them—all kinds of crazy ones to keep their attention. One tiny boy came and put his nose right on the book I was drawing in.

When we got home I went down to the village with Lena, on bikes, to see a new baby. It was an awful little one and the funniest looking one I've ever seen. I hope I wasn't as bad as that!

After supper with the Washburns we printed a few negatives. I hoped to have something I could use for a Xmas card but none seem good enough. We borrowed a gasoline lamp to have a bright light for exposing the pictures. Some of Ray and I that we took with a string attachment turned out very well.

Sunday, October 2

We got a big book on the Bakuba by an English scientist who was out here in 1906. So far as anyone knows he is the only one who has studied these people. Unfortunately the book is written in French.

We are sorry we are 20 years too late and cannot be among the very first to get into this country. But we are making the first movies of them and that is something.

Monday, October 3

Went out to our bamboo taking Mrs. Washburn and lunch as usual. We had to move the tent from Bukoyi and set it up before we could shoot. A beautiful clear day and the sun actually kept shining all the time. Were we happy? And we got all our scenes out there finished by five o'clock. We had to retake one scene because Mrs. Washburn forgot to wear the right hat.

Mr. Washburn took a few stills of Ray and I in front of the tent. It was such a nice setting and Ray wants a picture to put in our African trip book.

Got a letter from Carpenter who is to help us in lower Congo saying we should arrive not later than November 1st! He has to start on a trip the middle of November. But we will be here till November and can't possibly get to Sona Bata before December! We certainly are working under terrific pressure everywhere and have made a mess of our schedule. The committee seems to have forgotten that missionaries have a lot of work to do and can't be helping us every minute. Mr. Washburn runs this whole station, is the only evangelical man here, and has to stop and give some time to his own work, quite frequently. Sometimes we don't get off in the morning till ten o'clock. Well we are doing our best and the next time will insist on unlimited stays in every place we visit.

Tuesday, October 4

Went down the lake road to the jungle this morning and took four scenes of the caravan. Ray shinnied up a very tall tree and the natives said, "He's no American. He's an African. Look at the way he goes up that tree!"

We hoisted the camera up to him on a vine and he took a shot of Mr. Washburn coming along the trail with his caravan and then one of me. Riding in the hammock is like a cradle and how I love it. Ray's feet fell asleep he had to wait so long for the sun to come out and I thought he'd have to fall in order to get down. He had to sit on a skinny little branch that looked as if it would break any minute. I sure was worried about the camera!

Ate lunch by the lake and wished for bathing suits and time for a swim. Took a scene of surveying a new road through the jungle and then went to the village to see the new chief installed. We sat under a shed of palm branches with a million other natives. The chief came in with his lengthy family behind and gave a speech on his ancestors and why he should be chief. Then a guy shook a rattle all around, the speaker said something and everyone yelled approval. The chief was then allowed to sit on a mat, a native strolled in with an eagle feather. He went to stick it in the chief's hat but everyone yelled no, until he held it at just the right angle, at the side of the hat. There was a great yell, and the feather went in. He was crowned chief! Thunder roared and it began to pour so everyone got up and ran so their Sunday clothes wouldn't get wet. Rained all afternoon so we went home & read.

Wednesday, October 5

Clouds and more clouds. We read and do records, develope films and write letters. And go out to look at the sky. Soon I shall die of acute impatience!

At 2:30 we went down to the lake road and after lots of waiting around managed to take four short shots. If we keep on at this rate we won't go home till next summer.

Katschunga picks leaves, waves them at the sun, and goes through some crazy incantations, to amuse us. If the sun happens to come out when he gets thru he is delighted. So are we. Today when it didn't work he said it was because we haven't paid him and you always must pay a witchdoctor. He demanded a chicken, no less!

We have lots of fun with him and are teaching him lots of English words. He remembers them too, even scram, and I can see why he served as the King's memory when he was a slave. He really still is a slave but has as much freedom as anyone else.

Rewound some of our fifty foot reels that are for the magazine camera, so that we can use them in the Special. It's quite a job in the pitch dark and Ray is afraid they will be spoiled from so much winding and rewinding.

I developed a roll of film I took with the Rolleiflex and what a difference. The negatives are so much sharper than those I have been taking with the old camera.

Thursday, October 6

Another day of waiting for the sun. We went to the plantation about 2:30 and managed to take 25 feet of film in two hours. As soon as we are set up and ready to shoot again, another cloud sneaks over the sun.

This awful waiting around for the sun to come out is more tiring than anything else. Instead of using this time we find ourselves tired and discouraged and manage to do only a few letters or records. This is supposed to be the rainy season but it hasn't really gotten under way as it should. If it would only rain some more maybe the sky would clear up. Today we told Katschunga we would pay him a tie if he could make the sun shine—but he couldn't do it.

Two missionaries from the north country are visiting. They are from a Canadian mission and have a station among a real wild and untouched tribe. The government hasn't even been able to collect taxes from them. They are cannibals and although the missionaries are permitted to live in their country they make absolutely no headway. Last year the roof of their house blew off and it was four months before they could get some natives to make them a new one. Fortunately it was during the dry season.

Friday, October 7

After a rather late breakfast—I couldn't get Ray up—we developed a film and gave up hoping for the sun to come out. It surprized us by appearing at

11 AM. So Ray climbed the very slanting and high church roof while I waited below ready to catch the camera when he fell. He was up and down about six times before everything was ready to shoot. He even took the big tripod up there and the school boys eyes nearly popped!

After two shots the sun went in so we all went to eat. By the time the kids all got back it was nearly three o'clock. We had to wait some more for the sun but managed to finish just before it went down. Except for the stills—there wasn't much time to give them and I got very few. My stills really suffer on account of Ray's movies—I have to give him so much time and attention.

Saturday, October 8

Went to the plantation this morning and although there was lots of waiting we got through. Then back up to the girl's home. It took till 2:30 without benefit of lunch for us to get through there. Later Ray thinks the shutter was closed and he didn't get any pictures there! Grrrr!

After lunch we went to the boy's home and had to wait ages for their food carts to come so we could get an eating scene. They serve the food on plates, set in rows along the ground and then four boys dive at one plate and whoever eats the fastest gets the most. Some fun!

While we were waiting a boy showed Ray a trick. He ran, jumped on a mound of earth, and turned a somersault in the air, landing on his feet. Ray went one better and did it with out the mound. Then he showed his other tricks and the natives decided there was no beating him.

The two missionaries who are visiting go all around with us to see us take pictures. One speaks German so we can't talk to him.

Sunday, October 9

We planned to go swimming this afternoon but darn if it didn't rain. We were supposed to take pictures of the church congregation this morning but of course it was cloudy. Had dinner with the Andersons and got caught in a terrific downpour. When it rains in Africa it rains elephants and hippos, not cats and dogs.

Our German friends had supper with us and were probably horrified by Ray and Mr. Anderson who referred to the cheese as rat food and made other unbeautiful allusions, most unfit for table talk. These two young men are supported by Canadian churches. Both were born in Germany, however, and one doesn't speak English at all. Fortunately!

Monday, October 10 [Mweke]

Went to Mweke with Mr. Washburn this afternoon and felt almost as if I'd been let loose in Macy's with a hundred dollars to spend. I only spent a hundred francs however, in two tiny hick stores. I frequently dream of all the places in N.Y. where we can get anything we need. Especially the five and ten! How can Africa ever progress without that soul satisfying institution?

Saw the King at Mweke and tried to persuade him to go on home where he belongs—so we can get the pictures we need. Then to the state administrator to register. We have never showed our matriculation cards before and they say you can't go anywhere in Congo without them. A young Belgian invited us to his house for tea. He and his wife both spoke English so we got along nicely with our tea drinking. They have two little girls, one only a month old, who look just like pale faced china dolls.

Got back to the station after dark. Stayed up till 11 rewinding film.

Tuesday, October 11 [Bulape—Mbela]

Spent the morning sewing and packing for our trip into the northwestern territory. We had hoped to take a few pictures on the station but there wasn't a Ray of light.

After dinner we loaded the car and set out. When we got to the plains we felt well repaid for all the waiting we have done on the sun's account. Beautiful mass formations of silver tipped clouds made a border all around the horizon. We took pictures of plains and clouds, Ray and clouds, and me and clouds, for an hour or more.

Then on through more jungle and finally about five thirty we reached Mbela, a native village, where we were to spend the night in a rest house. It was a one room affair so Ray and I offered to sleep on the porch, which was really just an extra piece of roof stuck out over the front of the hut. Katschunga and our cook tried and tried to dissuade us. They were sure a storm was coming up and we would get wet and we would go back to our foreign country and tell our Mothers that the black man didn't take care of us.

Looking at a lovely sunset today made me wonder just how much of all of this I'll be able to remember?

After some deep thinking, as deep as possible in Africa, I found that I no longer remember things in terms of beauty and effect. Ever since we left New York I have been remembering things in terms of our relationship. There is more beauty and magic in that than any of my other memories but I find I forget just how the ocean and other things looked. From now on I'll just have to take an extra long look at everything so that I can have more than just an impression to keep for always.

Wednesday, October 12 [Mbela—Mesumba]

It never did rain last night and Katschunga says we must have strong medicine. But someone presented me with a rooster last night (I was so honored) and it began to crow at 4 AM. It got all the others in the village going and it was just impossible to sleep with the chorus.

Got up as the sun was rising but when it saw us it sneaked behind some clouds and stayed half the day. I got a whole book read before we packed up again. We crossed the Lubudi river on a ferry and drove up the road a way to get away from the tsetse flies. Ate lunch and changed a tire that had a leak in it. Then back to the river where we got some sun at last and took quite a few pictures. We got a sequence on the caravan crossing in canoes as they did in the old days and one of the car crossing on the ferry. It was so hot and all the kids were swimming in the river. But I married a photographer and I have to work when the sun shines.

Drove on to Mesumba a beautiful place high on a plain. We can see for miles in every direction when we stand on top of the car. We saw the sun set from there and felt truly on top of the world. All the little black children crowded round and laughed at us. There are a million here and all so cute. Our tricks have them all jumping up and down in great glee. And they don't stop but even now are dancing up and down around our house. This is a little palm house, two rooms and a porch effect.

This is the Bangonga tribe, another sub tribe of the Bakuba. They have control of about fourteen other tribes, most of them having been conquered in days gone by. Every family in this great kingdom must supply the King with a wife. (A family includes relatives to the last cousin.) When the wife dies another must be sent to the King and so on forever and ever. In this way he is able to control each family in all his kingdom. No one is anxious to rebel or disobey when their sister, cousin, daughter, or aunt will be killed as a result. And then another girl will have to go to live in the harem. Not a bad idea really. Travel out here is so difficult and natives so irresponsible that a police force certainly wouldn't work and this plan that has been in use for generations works beautifully. I hope Hitler doesn't get on to it!!

Thursday, October 13 [Mesumba—Mbela]

Had breakfast as the sun rose and took a still with all the kids crowding around. And quite a few grown people too. Now I know just how the freaks in the side shows at Coney Island feel. I always felt so sorry for them but it isn't so bad after all.

The sun went in and stayed till ten and then we took a series of shots of a woman doing some hair dressing. It just happened that she was a bride, not for the first time though, and she was fixing the groom's hair. He has collected the necessary dowry, a basket of cowerie shells, and will present them to the former husband. Someone will bring a pot of food and everybody will eat. That concludes the wedding ceremony! The divorce that went before is even simpler. The woman decided to take a new husband and merely gave the old one a bit of charcoal and said "Our marraige is finished." I tried to get stills of all this but the old husband was so mad at the new one, we were afraid we'd start a war.

The sun went in to stay about noon and we discovered that the footage indicator on the 35mm camera doesn't work. So we couldn't take the sequence anyway. We hope we can fix it but are rather worried about the camera. It is pretty old and has jammed twice during the 50 feet of film we have shot.

A big dance was organized near our hut and we looked all the fancy costumes over and tried to buy some knives and things. We had an awful time as these people just don't want to sell a thing. We finally got two carved cups and a fetish about eighteen inches high that is quite artistic. Katschunga is going to try to get me a necklace that I liked very much but couldn't buy. This is his village and he may be able to pull some strings.

I almost broke up the dance by having the monkey dance too. Everybody crowded round and screamed and yelled at a great rate.

Packed up and left about five. We expected to go way back to the plains tonight but had to cross the ferry and were tired so decided to stop at Mbela again. The kids are so glad to see us again that they are laughing and jumping all over.

Friday, October 14 [Mbela—Bulape]

Got up not long after our rooster began his morning alarm clocking. After breakfast Ray and I took a hike to a stream to take some stills of a fetish. The natives have set a carved figure under a little shed and as they come up from the stream with water they spill a little before the fetish. The evil spirits are supposed to let them alone for that day. Sometimes they pull a claw out of a chicken, sprinkle some of his blood around, and scatter some of his feathers. Then the spirits come and see it and think a chicken has been sacrificed but a dog carried it off and ate it! Having received this offering the spirits go off and don't bother the village. The natives think the spirits are as dumb as they are.

Mr. Washburn had a palaver on his hands this morning and had to meet with the whole village. We finally got off about ten and on our way back to the plains. We had lunch at a rest house and got our caravan together. They were waiting there for us even though we were a day late. Then out on the plain where the sun at last appeared, for the first time today. We got some very good shots with beautiful cloud effects. Worked until sundown and then I got a ride over the plain in the hammock. It was swell and I would like to have gone home that way. About twenty natives ran along with me hooting and singing and all wanting a turn at carrying me. It was some fun and I was sorry to have the car catch up to us.

Packed the car again, back at the rest house and then started home. I spotted two monkeys on the way and we got out to see them. There were a lot of them and we saw one great big brown one almost like a chimpanzee.

A little further on a tire went down and we had to stop and pump. When it got good and full of air it burst and all the air shot out like a fire hose. Our spare was flat so we had to patch a tube. Some fun in the middle of the road in the dark. During all this I felt ants crawling on me and by the time we got the tire back on we were all jumping with them. Was I glad to reach Bulape and get out of those pants!

Saturday, October 15 [Bulape—Loebo]

A bright and shining day—because we can't take any pictures. Dr. Taylor, Educational Secretary on his way to India, is coming this morning. He is fresh from America having left Sept. 17 and we are moaning because we didn't know. He could have brought us mail, some clothes, and maybe even a cake.

Ray took his 35 mm camera apart this morning and tried to fix it. I finished my dress and wrote a couple of letters. I am worried about the camera and all the expensive film. It seems a risk to use the old camera when so much money is involved and our reputation as well.

Mrs. Washburn invited us to tea this afternoon and we had a chance to talk to Dr. Taylor. He saw our first roll of film at Columbus, Ohio, in July! Rogers had just received it and took it out to the International Education Conference of all the churches. Then sometime recently he heard someone give a talk about us. He can't remember where but thinks it might have been Sue Weddell. Of course, he never expected to see us so didn't pay too much attention at the time. How we wish we could hear about some more of our pictures. The suspense is really awful.

Went swimming late this afternoon and tonight set out for Loebo. Sixty five miles on an African road in the dark takes quite a while.

Sunday, October 16 [Loebo]

Took a short walk and felt badly about this beautiful day going to waste. We never seem to be taking pictures when we should be.

Had supper with Miss Black who is old and jolly and has the most genuine love for the natives that I have ever seen. She takes care of any little orphans and has two little boys that are almost like her own. There are about 20,000 natives living in and right around Loebo so she has plenty to love.

Monday, October 17

Spent the morning in Mr. Longeneckers dark room, rewinding our films. It was beastly hot with everything closed up and we thought we'd never get thru. Had the half tone process for printing photographs explained to us. This is the only place in Africa that we know of where this complicated process is done.

When we were coming home we found a snake almost three feet long blocking our trail. Ray pulled up a fence post and killed it. My Hero!

Tuesday, October 18

Had breakfast here with the Longeneckers and then Ray took his 35mm camera apart again.

Had dinner with the Pooles and then went to bed with some magazines. Ray got his camera together and working (genius) by four o'clock. Then we went and took pictures of Phil. Ray even took a few movies he thinks he is so cute. We had him all worn out by the time we got through and I forgot my date with the doctor.

We wish we didn't have to go back to work tomorrow but there is no getting out of it. The weather has been gorgeous here and I suppose when we are ready to shoot it will be all cloudy again.

Wednesday, October 19 [Loebo—Bulape—Mushenge]

Packed before breakfast, with Miss Black, and then hiked around the station saying goodbye to everyone. We took till nearly nine to do it and then set out for Bulape with Kirk Morrison. We met Dr. Chapman on the way, taking Dr. Taylor to Loebo, and stopped to tell him what to say to Sue Weddell when he sees her in India. Then to Bulape where we found letters from the three places we go to next.

We had to answer the letters, setting another day for our arrival, pack the exposed films to send to Elizabethville, and get ready to go to Mushenge. So we were good and busy until we set out to the bush again.

Half way we heard a crash and stopped and found that my precious typewriter had fallen out. It still works though so I guess I'll have to finish paying for it. While we were putting it back in the car the back tire blew! So we gave up and Ray and I had to walk to Mushenge! When we reached the outskirts of Mushenge a mob trailed along behind us so we held hands and skipped. They just loved it and tried so hard to skip too.

Thursday, October 20 [Mushenge]

After breakfast we went to the chapel in the harem for some pictures. The women took ages to get there best clothes on—they are as bad as Ray in that respect. I am always up and dressed fifteen minutes before he has his socks on. Took a few pictures of the women looking at the monkey and then went home to wait Lugenga's call. It was one o'clock by the time he was dressed in his finery and ready for us. Then of course the sun had to go in. We managed to finish one sequence in short spaces of sunlight.

Then to the royal family fence where we took the old queen who is the power behind the throne. We tried to get some fetishes for another sequence but had a great palaver. We had to send the keeper of them to the king and he is doubtful about moving them out for fear they will stir up the spirits. It got so late we had to give it up for today.

Friday, October 21

Found some beautiful sun shine awaiting us this morning. So we ate breakfast—I was so impatient till Ray got his "shikadela" (last pancake, which is always four times the size of all the others). But he finally downed it on top of at least a dozen others and we went to the kings court house to start our pictures.

We waited and waited and no king. All the judges of his court arrived and the natives from Koshi involved in the palaver for "How an African Tribe is Ruled." And still we waited. It seems the king wished to wear a certain costume for this picture and no other would do. His attendents brought him twenty before they found the one he wished to wear! With all his fancy clothes to choose from he had to keep us cooling our heels for so long that the sun went in. And it stayed for the rest of the day!! We didn't expose one foot of film.

After dinner it began to rain. Ray and I spent the afternoon in our tent reading and loafing. We crawled out for supper and then worked on our scenario for two hours or so. I had to yawn broadly and continually before the boys took the hint and let me go to bed.

Saturday, October 22 [Mushenge—Bulape]

After much palaver this morning we finally got the keeper of the idols of the kingdom to bring them out. We had them set up in an enclosure so the great crowd we always attract would have to stay out for once. No one would or could touch the idols but their keeper and she would grab up the head man and take him away at the end of each shot. He was a very elegant idol and as we were making a whole sequence on him we had to chase after her and get him back each time she carried him off. The last scene involved a very complicated fade and each time we were ready to shoot it the sun went in. We had to shoot the first part with a woman before the idols reading a bible. Then she had to remain absolutely motionless while we took away the idols, backed up the film, and shot her alone. This will make the fetishes fade out of the scene while she stays.

Got the king out this afternoon and managed to get two sequences. Sorry to say we had to shoot the palaver scene in very poor light. We can't keep our actors from Koshi as the hero's sister went and died and they have to go home for the funeral—which is a week of dancing.

Drove back to Bulape, leaving most of our equipment behind, as we will return on Monday and try to finish up.

Sunday, October 23 [Bulape]

Woke up at five AM from the terrific din at our front door. Washburn wanted us to get up for a sunrise picture. We staggered out in our dressing gowns and managed to turn the camera on long enough to get something. Then we went to sleep again until eight, when Mrs. Anderson sent our breakfast.

The church bell rang before we had the last muffin in and we had to dash to get ready for our pictures. Ray climbed the shakiest tower, put up just for him, and he was so full I was afraid he wouldn't make it. Later he climbed the bell tower which has a ladder up its side. A rung came out in his hand and I died three times before he caught himself from falling thirty feet or more.

After the church service we set up our three 16 mm cameras and got ready to take pictures of the service with flares. We had three set off, simultaneously, and one of them shot fire in the air like a roman candle. Everybody in the church jumped two feet, except the blind elder, the kids dove under the benches, Mr. Washburn started a hymn with the words of one and the tune of another, and I was too excited to set my camera and just kept snapping pictures. The flares only burn ½ minute so we hope we got some pictures. Mr. Washburn weakened this afternoon, it was so sunshiny, and let us finish the evangelical work. Hurray!

We got a grand sunset picture today—it was the lovliest we have seen in Africa and how I wished for some color film for my still camera.

Monday, October 24 [Bulape—Mushenge]

Finished the school work this morning as we had wonderful sunshine and clouds. We got a witch doctor dressed up for a shot too, and this afternoon started work at the hospital.

About three o'clock we had to stop and get ready to go back to Mushenge. We had a shower and had to delay our start as we have to go in the open Chevy. I was sure glad we didn't have any flats this trip as I am doggone tired.

Tonight there is a new moon and until recent years this is the night a slave is sacrificed to the moon. The slaves arms and legs are broken and he is thrown into a deep pit where last month and the month before, for years back, a slave has been left to die. There is not a sound in all the village and the slave lies among the flesh and bones of his unfortunate companions, waiting to die.

Tomorrow night the historical sing is held and we are going to be there to photograph that. Here's hoping it doesn't rain.

Tuesday, October 25 [Mushenge]

Got a number of characters together to stage a poison cup scene for us. It took considerable time to get permission to do this and the king says "never again". We set up the first scene and then waited all morning for the sun. Finally we ate dinner and went back to it about one, when the sun came out.

We were able to finish the whole thing even to the funereal pyre, after the victim had died from the poison and been stuck with spears. A pleasant ending just because another man accuses you of bringing trouble to his family or quarrels with you and challenges you to drink the poison cup. Its a matter of honor, like a duel, and you must do it if challenged.

After supper we set up in the King's court to take the sing- song. His many wives came out and sat in a semi-circle around him. An old woman leads the song and all the others join in the chorus. The first row of women beat an accompiament on the ground with gourds. The story goes back 300 years to the first great Bakuba king. The history of every king until the present time follows and there must be no break or mistakes, on pain of death.

We set off one flare to get the women over being scared. Some of them jumped and ran and we were afraid there would be a panic. But the old woman leader went right on singing and everyone followed. We then got them all back in place and set off three flares. They smoked pretty badly but we were running three cameras and should have some good pictures.

After we packed up and left the women went back to the harem as the king was tired of all the fuss. But we could hear them carrying on their song far into the night.

This is the only tribe who has kept any history in a formal way and even this has never been written down. The old leader is the only one who knows it all. She has three understudies now so that when she dies the story will be carried on.

Wednesday, October 26 [Mushenge—Bulape]

A beautiful day (at last) enabled us to finish our work with the king of the Bakuba. He has grown rather weary of us, our cameras in every direction and our infernal flares. We are now about to leave our life in a tent and go back to civilization—of a sort.

We finished our last two sequences and are so glad to get out of this slow poke place. The [king] wouldn't come out for us this morning and Washburn had to spend a half hour persuading him. We rushed so he wouldn't get mad and leave us flat.

Had to say goodbye to our good friend Katschunga at Mushenge. We will certainly miss his nonsense, help, and wonderful sign language.

Thursday, October 27 [Bulape]

We've been married eight months today and what a wonderful eight months it has been. Every day we are thrilled all over again by our good fortune and the fact that we are really in Africa and together for the rest of our lives!

A cloudy morning prevented our doing any work at the hospital but right after dinner we went down with Lena and were able to accomplish quite a little before sun down. Mr. Washburn has taken the four main characters in "How an African Tribe is Ruled" to Mweke. We are going to shoot the scene with the state man tomorrow and we still can't see why we couldn't all pile in the car and go then. But Washburn is afraid of over loading the car and so has to make three round trips to Mweke before he is through and think of the expense. Ordinarily we have the natives walk but we have worked these people so hard that he thinks we should let them ride.

Washburn has rather taken over all arrangements even to sometimes setting up the camera! Of course Ray moves it and shoots what he wants to but it is rather annoying to both of us when he tries to be the director. He does not seem to know his place—which is merely translator. Any way we are about through with the picture and we do feel that it will be good. There are a few slow moving scenes that Washburn insisted on and as he is buying the film for this one, they had to be.

Friday, October 28 [Bulape—Mweke—Bulape]

Went to Mweke right after breakfast to get our scene with the state man. We found the head administrator back from furlough and he refused to let us do it. He didn't think anyone should make a picture on "How an African Tribe is Ruled" without the Governor Generals approval. Ross got that for us but not in writing so we were at a stand still. Finally we were sent to the 2nd administrator who is really still in charge till Nov. He had OKed our proposition before so decided to stick by it. He gave us a young man to play the part though—probably to push the blame off on, if there is any.

We got the scene in short order before anyone could change their minds. Then back to Bulape—stopping for lunch on the way. We set up the operating scene but by the time the doctors got there a rain had come up. We were so disgusted that we took the scene anyway at half speed. If it isn't any good they can use one of our other operating scenes.

Wrote to Beanland about our return trip to the Cameroun and to Bob Mc-Crackin. We hope he will be able to work with us as he is the only one we have met who is patient under any and all circumstances.

Saturday, October 29 [Bulape]

After breakfast we went right to the hospital to finish up there. It took till noon time as we had to wait for Dr. Chapman for one scene. On our way to Washburns for dinner we took the shot of their house. Our last shot here and are we glad! Ray has begun to call this place a morgue it is so dead and we are both anxious to get away and start some new work. This has dragged out so that we have all gotten rather stale. We are glad we decided not to do the 35mm here. It would probably take us six months at the rate Washburn goes.

Went home and read this afternoon until four o'clock or so. Then we worked on the final scenario with Washburn till after supper. He and Mrs. Washburn went down to the lake for over Sunday. We wish we could get away like that for just a bit.

Sunday, October 30

After supper I got some of our packing done. We have an extra box now as we collected so much stuff here in the Bakuba country. Ray has a mania for knives and as they have very beautiful ones here he is always trying to buy them. Fortunately the people are not anxious to sell their pet knives, which are really just part of their costume, or we would be loaded down with them.

We are happy to have reached the end of this very tiring time and to start out on a new adventure. We have gotten some good pictures here—things we can never get anywhere else—and a wealth of experience.

Monday, October 31 [Bulape—en route RR]

We had to spend the whole morning with Mr. Washburn finishing up the scenario. It is pretty bad in places, especially some of the titles, but the Africa Com. will probably understand that it wasn't us.

After dinner we had a great rush to get everything packed and ready to go. At the last minute Ray had to get one more shot and as soon as he was through we said our good byes and set out for Mweka. The train certainly looked good to us—because it is going places. And we have overcome our train sickness that was so bad when we first got out here.

The sun was sinking just as we started out and we enjoyed an hour of unsurpassable loveliness. Darkness crept slowly up in the jungle and the last rays of light touched all the tree-tops with gold. They're like tall black sentinels with golden halos round their heads.

Tuesday, November 1 [Wobbly African RR]

We like our little compartment very much because it is so private. If the train was crowded though we would have four other people in with us. But as it is we have room [to] spread ourselves and our stuff all over.

Whenever we go by a village all the children and many of the grown people run out to see the train. We always stop whatever we are doing and wave at them. They are so delighted that they jump up and down and some start dancing while they wave back at us. When we stop our monkey attracts large crowds and we keep them amused till the train pulls out again.

Wednesday, November 2 [Kamina—Songa Mission]

I woke up about two and couldn't go to sleep again for fear the porter would forget to wake us up when we got to Kamina.

Dr. Rouhe met us (for the third time at four AM) and we had to wait about an hour to get our stuff out of the baggage car. Dr. Rouhe is quite young and has only been out here two years. He said if we stood him up again this time he was going to let us walk to Songa when we finally did come. We woke up the store keeper so we could buy a few things and while we were there a messenger arrived with a note for us. We had not heard from Mr. Hartzler and were wondering if he could meet us here when we are through at Songa. We sent a note back to him, planning to meet him Friday at noon.

Drove seventy miles to Songa over a plain that is covered with stunted trees. Mrs. Rouhe met us with a hat on as she shaved her head about a month ago. She wanted to see if it would come in nicer the way people always say it does! She has a cute little boy about two.

Thursday, November 3 [Songa]

Started our pictures of the mothers and babies clinic this morning. It is rather difficult to show the items listed on our scenario. They just wrote, pre-natal care, delivery of babies, and care of babies. We did the best we could under such circumstances and got nearly through this morning.

I stayed in bed this afternoon as I felt pretty rotten and Ray did a scene with the anxious father walking up and down outside the hospital. The funny part of it is that African fathers think nothing of childbirth and usually stay home and let their wives walk miles to the hospital by themselves!

We like this mission so much because it is fixed up so much nicer than the others. The houses are not nearly as nice but have such cute curtains and such gay colors here and there that they are more attractive than any others we've seen. Most folks haven't time or energy to fuss over the little things that make such a difference. Mrs. Rouhe puts bright appliqued designs on her curtains and bedspreads that make her rooms look so cheerful. She is really quite artistic.

Friday, November 4 [Songa—Kamina—Kanene]

Got up rather late and got packed and ready to go. Mr. Hiten and Miss Mote drove us to Kamina so they could have a visit in the big city. We have had fun here and so were not anxious to leave in the hurry we thought we would when we arranged to go to Kanene today.

Shopped around Kamina (in the three stores) and wondered if our note reached Kanene safely. Finally after a heavy rain L. Sarah arrived in an elegant new Plymouth coupe. He is young, has only been out a year, and is not at all the pious Methodist type. He says his car isn't really proper for a missionary—it has a spit in your eye effect!

We all enjoyed the eighty mile drive to Kanene after that remark and arrived about eight to find a chicken pie awaiting us. Mrs. Hartzler, Miss Everett, and Mrs. Sarah were excited over our coming and we all had supper together. Mr. Hartzler was out in the bush but was expected as after ten days his food usually gives out. Luckily for us, he arrived just after we sat down at the table. We were a little concerned as he didn't know when we were coming, after our many changes in plans, and he had to be here to help us.

Even in the dark we were a little disappointed to find our own stamping ground such a poor looking place. We hear the church was built with someones gift of 150 dollars! We are staying at Hartzlers and were too tired tonight to do anything but fall into bed. It seems to be the bed of their youngest son cause it certainly is too short for us.

Saturday, November 5 [Kanene]

Slept until about nine this morning as it was pouring rain and no one does a thing in Africa when it rains. The natives won't even come out of their huts to go to school. When it stopped we went to look over the camp, as it is called here. There are 400 natives living here on the station. Many of the men attend the Congo Institute which is a well known, though poorly equiped, Bible training school. We chose one street in the village that might do for "A Day in an African Village".

Had a late dinner with the Hartzlers and then read and slept all afternoon. We are still tired out, not because we are getting old or sissy, but because this is Africa. The malaria in our blood does not cause a fever but it does make our bones ache when we are tired.

We find our Methodists quite liberal and are glad to find that they would like to unite with other missions so that there are no doctrinal differences in the confused minds of the African. Most protestant churches are working to establish the Church of Christ in Congo but they do maintain their own doctrines.

Sunday, November 6

After breakfast we thought, being good Methodists, that we would have to go to church. But Mr. Hartzler said we wouldn't be able to understand the native preacher so why not go looking for a village. So we [all] set out in the car to find a picturesque place for our picture. We left the main road after about ten miles and set out over a native foot path that proved to be the wildest ride we have ever had. If Mr. Washburn was persuaded to drive over this road he would get out and feel the ground every six feet or so. But we bounced and pushed our way through the heavy under brush at quite a rate.

The country is real wild and barren and we passed only one small village. We came to a lake where we hoped to find a village but didn't and then went on another five miles. Here in the thick of nothing we found a beautiful little village. It is near a lake and has a background of forest behind it. Kyungu is truly like a painting rather than a lonesome little village off in the wilderness. The people Bene-Nsamba are quite different than any others we've seen and we are thrilled over the prospects of the picture we can make here.

Monday, November 7 [Kanene—Kyungu]

After dinner with the Sarahs we set out for Kyungu on bicycles (by choice) with a native guide on foot. We rode very fast and he ran all the way so he could catch up to us at each fork in the path. We followed native paths all the way and had a grand time going over some real wild country. Ray spilled all our water out of the bottle that was on the back of his bike [going over bumps] and we nearly dried up before we got to Kyungu. We crossed three swamps where Gaston carried our bikes. We tiptoed across two of them and managed to keep fairly dry. But one was so long and deep that Ray took his shoes and socks off, rolled his pants up over his knees, and sat me on his shoulders. We started out all right but I got laughing and very nearly fell off a couple of times. Ray's legs sunk in almost to the hip in some places and my extra weight made each step an awful pull out of the mud. I had visions of falling on my face in all the muck.

Later we crossed a beautiful plain, the most scenic we have seen. In one village where we had to wait for Gaston we got our monkey out. These people are so far from any civilization that they went wilder than ever. Then Ray jumped over me and they shouted until we left.

Mr. Hartzler, who came by car, had the camp in good order. We set the tent up inside the hut because there are so many holes in the roof, and such large ones. We would have prefred to have it outside but we hear the rain and wind in this section are terrific and the tent wouldn't stay up more than five minutes. We went down to the lake for a bath, being stopped three times on the way and told (mostly sign language) that it was just full of crocs. Having never seen one real close up we went and took our baths anyhow. They say the crocs are treacherous and sneak up on you under the water so they will be sure of a good meal. But we used nearly a whole cake of soap and didn't see a one.

Had a swell supper and read a little while before going to bed. I am reading 'The Exile' and am glad we didn't go to China, at least not this first time. Ray is reading a new life of Stanley that sounds marvelous, so I get it next.

Tuesday, November 8 [Kyungu]

The chief here is so old and decrepit that he isn't any help in getting the people to work with us. We managed to get some groups together though and shoot quite a few scenes. The sun shone all day but there were no clouds at all for our long shots. We have to leave all of them until we have a real beautiful day.

This is a fishing village and all the men go off so that we have difficulty getting actors. The women have to plant cotton now, according to a state rule, and are afraid to give us any of that time. The cotton companies buy the whole crop and then the natives use the money to pay their taxes to the government. Sort of a vicious circle, I'd say.

We got the whole process of palm oil making this afternoon and a village street scene. Quite an accomplishment in a couple of hours. This morning we took a number of short shots and will finish the sequences when we get some good cloud formations.

Wednesday, November 9

This morning the women went to work in their gardens [about two miles from the village] before we had a chance to grab a few of them. Ray took his tripod all apart, cleaned the bearings, and made some adjustments, so that it works better than it ever has. Then he fixed two things on my typewriter that were out of order. It is so complicated that I was a little afraid to have him fuss with it but he fixed it perfectly.

About ten we got a woman and child and started the manioc story. We will take it all the way from digging roots to cooking and eating the "bedia" Stopped for lunch and a short rest.

Thursday, November 10

The men left this morning leaving us alone in the wilds in a village of not too friendly people. We wrote to Ross while waiting for Gaston to come from Kanene and translate for us. When Gaston came it was too late to take pictures before lunch as the sun was too high. So we waited until about two (we have no watch) and then managed to get some pictures. It was pretty hard as Gaston doesn't know very much English but we got the manioc sequence finished and a native cutting palm nuts out of a tree. I am crazy about them when they are cooked even though they are rather oily. They have a wonderful flavor and Ray won't even try them.

Two more helpers arrived from Kanene. They came to us with the old chief, the Kapita, and a crowd because no one would sell them food. Ray had a palaver on his hands for the first time. He told the Kapita that his wife *must* prepare food for our helpers or the Bula Matadi would get after them all. This proved effective because Gaston tells us that they all got food. We give them a franc a day and that is ample for a good sized African meal. They only eat once a day, in the evening.

Friday, November 11

I finished the typewriter cover I've been making out of heavy cloth, similar to canvas. The case has gotten banged up quite a bit and I'm sorry I did not have sense enough to make a cover long ago. It will keep out some of the dust too, which seeps in so much when we are traveling.

The sun didn't show itself at all today and we are beginning to doubt if we can make Wednesday's train as we had hoped. Probably we'll go on Saturday—if we are lucky as to sunshine [only two trains a week].

Saturday, November 12 [Kyungu—Kanene]

Another cloudy day kept us playing Pick up Sticks. The hunters brought in a deer this morning and we looked for a spot of sun so we could take the hunting scenes we need. Just before dinner time it looked promising so we went out toward the plain. Ray thought he knew the way and while the natives were tieing the deer on a pole he led the way into a tangle of under brush. We beat around the bush for half an hour or more and then decided we'd better go back and find the natives. By the time we got back on the path a storm was coming up so we went back to eat. We hope we will be able to get another animal by Monday because this one will be finished off tonight [divided among villagers].

After dinner we got ready to go back to the station [Kanene] but hung around awhile hoping it would clear up. By two thirty we decided it wouldn't so went back to the station. We left our cots and most of the camping equipment behind as we will have to come back and stay a few more days.

When I squeezed into the little bath tub and soaked some hot water into my self I felt like a new woman. There is really not anything in the world like a bath—especially when you are living in Africa.

Sunday, November 13 [Kanene]

This morning we decided it was too much trouble to get up for breakfast so we stayed in bed till time for church. We didn't want to go but felt duty bound to suffer for an hour as we are good Methodists.

Walked around and visited the Girl's home which is brand new. There are only eight or nine girls as it is so difficult to get them away from their families. Girls bring a good bride price and don't have to know anything anyway so why do these crazy white people insist on teaching them? Every native in Africa would like to know the answer to that one.

After supper, Mr. Hartzler [was better], got up, we talked religion for a couple of hours. Ray just loves to third degree people on the evolution subject and all it involves. I am getting to the place where I don't give a hang whether I came from a fish or not.

Talked till midnight after we finally got in bed without settling the affairs of the world.

Monday, November 14

Woke up and found it raining. We got Ray's records up to date as a result so weren't too sorry. At noontime the sun came out and we planned to take a few shots in the nearby village this afternoon. By the time we got through eating it was raining again so we gave up and went back to our Pick up Sticks tournament.

Tomorrow we will have to go back to Kyungu and stay a few more days. We are growing very anxious to get to Elizabethville and hope we will not be delayed anymore than this week. I hear they have some big stores there and I am writing up a shopping list.

Tuesday, November 15 [Kanene—Kyungu]

When we got to Kyungu about two the sun broke through and we started right to work. The sky was beautiful too so we got some important shots off our minds. Leslie left about five and we set up another scene of a family eating the evening meal. We were not able to get it however as the sun went behind some clouds and then dropped down behind the horizon very quickly.

After supper Ray got the Kapita here and told him about the fishing and hunting scenes we want to get. We offered to pay for the gun powder as it is so expensive for them. They make mussle loading guns and get right on top of the animal before shooting in order not to miss and waste their gun powder. After much discussion while we waited and expected to pay about fifty francs, they said "two francs" all together.

I got out my monkey for the first time here and in two minutes the whole village was at our door. I never saw Africans get to us so fast before in my life. They must have a special call in case of emergencies. They went wild and wouldn't go home.

Wednesday, November 16 [Kyungu]

Today was the most beautiful we have had here and we accomplished quite a lot with our native director. We went down to the lake for the fishing scenes right after breakfast. A shower drove us all under some bushes for a little while but it blew away and we got some good pictures on the lake. We even saw a few crocs who came looking around to see if we usurping their place of lord of the lake.

Took time out for lunch and a game as we don't like to shoot with the sun directly overhead. Then we went to the village and took some weaving and cooking scenes. We hoped to do the evening meal scene but the clouds on the western horizon scared us away.

We bought a pan full of peanuts for a franc and a young chicken for dinner tomorrow for two francs. That is six cents for a real good chicken! The boys presented us with some fish too so we are eating very well. And I sure like having a cook along so I can spend all my time working or playing with Ray.

We are having a grand time by ourselves and like the idea of making a picture with only native help. The little boys follow us around all the time and carry our chairs or something. There are very few children in this village as it is fairly small and so many of them die.

Thursday, November 17

The weather was too good to last. It rained in the night and this morning was very gray. Fortunately our beds are not under too many holes in the roof.

We wrote a long letter to Ross this morning about the complications involved with Washburn's claiming of the picture we made with his film. If the Committee does not have the commercial rights, as Washburn thinks, then the whole thing is a loss to the Project. It took us all morning to present the facts and finish the letter.

Maybe we can finish up tomorrow and still get the train. We have to go 85 miles but the train doesn't come in till 4AM. I am trying to persuade Ray to go in any event and he says I am a sireeen. Somehow I feel we should go and take the last scenes in the lower Congo. Must be woman's intuition or African witchcraft working in me. I feel sure something dreadful will happen here. Tonight we ate just about the last of our food.

Friday, November 18

Awoke to another dull day. It showed promise of clearing up a few times but never did. About noon Leslie arrived and said we would have to leave immediately in order to get the train tonight. The trains come any time between ten and six in the morning—you never can tell. We were still undecided about going or staying. There are only two more scenes to be taken and we could stage them somewhere else. Finally we flipped a coin which said stay so here we are. Leslie went home again and until he sends a boy with some food we are living on remnants and eggs which we bought from the natives.

Ray is swell to the boys, always giving them left overs or crackers, and they like working for us very much. Gaston is getting a liberal education as Ray talks a blue streak to him about America, the land of the free.

Saturday, November 19

Still no sun! This morning we sent the boy back to the station with an order for shirts, film, and food. Then we worked a little on the scenario until the little boys came around and we had to play with them. We made them pinwheels and they have been playing with them incessantly all day. They think them the grandest toy they've ever had—they have so pitifully few and even they are not real toys.

We took turns playing a game and doing a record so we wouldn't think we were working too hard. After lunch we heard a terrible yelling and thought sure a war had started. It appears someone arrived with news of the death of a son who is off working. Everyone crowds into the little hut of the mother and begins wailing. The death chant is awful and goes on and on endlessly. The only lull is when a newcomer enters the hut and everyone stops to tell him the news. Then they all go at it again harder than ever.

The Kapita came and told us he had to go on a long journey to the funereal. We wonder if we can get someone else to hunt an animal for us. We must have a hunting scene!

A boy arrived [from Kanene] with some gas for our lamp tonight so we are doing some writing. It is real cold and rainy again tonight.

Sunday, November 20

This morning our cook went off to hunt an animal for us so I took his place in the little kitchen shed. When the native women went by on the way to their gardens they laughed at me as though it were a great joke for a white woman to know how to cook. I took a guess at the recipe for pancakes and made some fairly good ones. And for dinner we had chicken, noodles, carrots and peas. It was lots of fun and I wish Ndi had not come back in time to get supper.

It began to clear up today and by 3 PM we were able to shoot another sequence in the village. We had a hard time of it as the people all duck when they see us coming with the cameras. We did manage to get the scene though just as the last ray of sunlight went up over our heads. It meant a lot of rushing and I couldn't get any stills as I had to help Ray.

The little boy who has been in a lot of the pictures got very mad today because the others were teasing him. He is only about four and yet is a typical African. He grabbed up a firebrand and chased the other kids, then ran in the house and got a knife which he threw at them. We couldn't stop laughing he was so much like Donald Duck when he is mad.

Monday, November 21 [Kyungu—Kanene]

Got up at the first crack of dawn so we could finish the sequence we were doing last night when the sun went down. We worked in a different part of the village and as the sun was very low it looked like evening—we hope.

Ndi went hunting again so when we were through I cooked the last of our eggs and made toast of the last of our bread. The other two boys then began packing up the beds and things so we can go home. Mr. Hartzler surprized us by coming about ten. His back is much better now. Ndi soon returned empty handed so we went back to Kanene without our hunting scenes. The game here is very scarce now.

Got most of our packing done so we can leave early tomorrow. This afternoon we both fell asleep and were brought out of our dreams by Dr. Rouhe and Mr. Hitten. They had brought back the man who had to have his leg cut off a few weeks ago. [infection] They decided to stay all night and take us to Kamina tomorrow as it is on the way to Songa.

Tuesday, November 22 [Kanene—Kamina]

Spent the morning [re-]writing the scenario for "A Day in an African Village". We changed the original scenario so much that we had to start all over again. We didn't leave till after dinner as Dr. Rouhe is sure we can get our baggage that we left in the RR at any time.

Said "wafwaco" for the last time and set out on our eighty mile drive to Kamina. When we were within five minutes of our destination and were boasting about having made it in three hours, we blew a tire. It had an enormous hole in it, both the tube and the shoe. Luckily Dr. Rouhe had a new one with him so we all set to work putting it on. We had a chicken in the back of the car who got loose in all the excitement. As he was a very good one we had to find him and so all beat around the bush for a half hour or more. I finally captured him and we went on to Kamina.

Of all the dead towns this is about the worst. Even the stores are ugly and uninteresting. How all the Belgians can live here we don't know. Although they are all taken with the new bar that is being built.

Wednesday, November 23 [Wobbly African RR]

Intuition woke me just before 4 AM and we got up and went to the station. Dr. Rouhe and Mr. Hitten went with us to help get the baggage out of storage. Fortunately we didn't have any trouble and when the train arrived at 4:30 we were ready to get on. Saw a glorious sunrise from the train and then set to work. Ray wrote a letter and I finished my records and worked on the expense accounts. I had a hard time of it—first I lost 700 francs and then I found it plus 300 more. I stopped then because I am sure we'll find a way to spend the extra.

Thursday, November 24 [Elizabethville]

Here we are at last! Bishop and Mrs. Springer beat us here though so we have to live in a hotel. Not that we mind except for the expense. Mr. Booth took us to his house for tea this morning so we could meet the Springers. They are really swell and not a bit Bishopy. Mrs. Booth and the little girl are still in Capetown, where she went to recover her health.

Mr. Booth had 14 letters for us so we went back to the hotel to read them. I haven't had so much excitement in a long time. We heard that "Ngono" was about to be previewed and that there was a write up about it in NewsWeek. Then we went shopping for Ray's new shoes. We ran out of money and had to go to the Mission for some more. The church here is the largest and most beautiful we have seen. There are three houses but two are rented as there are no more missionaries to be had. Its a shame the Methodist stations are so understaffed.

Friday, November 25

Got up when we woke up and had breakfast at our hotel in the open air dining room. Its quite elegant and we felt even more so when a letter, on a tray, arrived for us. It was from Cooks giving information on the trip to Matadi via Lobito. We have decided definitely to go that way.

Walked over to see Mr. Booth and go over the pictures we want to get here and in Jadotville, which is seventy miles away. Then we went to meet Dr. Moutoule, director of Union Miniere de Haut-Katanga. We had a rather lengthy conference with him and the General Manager. They will not let us take any movies without authorization from Belgium! They will cable and ask about it but we have our doubts because Dr. Ross wrote us from here that

Dr. Moutoule "will give you all facilities here and at Jadotville for filming the Union Miniere works". They will allow us to take any stills we wish and will even take us to Jadotville—which doesn't help our scenario any. Either Dr. Ross misunderstood about the movies or they have changed their minds on account of Hitler's recent threats regarding Africa. They are really right because movies can be very detrimental if they have the wrong titles.

Went back to the Hotel Albert for lunch and this afternoon Dr. Moutoule had a man show us all over the foundry where the copper is separated from the ore. We took some stills, got very dirty, suffered with sulpher in our noses and throats, climbed all over the giant sheds, cranes, and furnaces. When we were sufficiently dirty and exhausted Dr. Moutoule took us back to the mission. There Mr. Booth persuaded us to climb the church tower and see the town. So we struggled up stairs, and two lengthy ladders. After that we went back to our hotel quite worn out and ready for bed.

After dinner we revived enough to go window shopping. All the stores are lit up in the evening and have lovely window displays. We had a grand time picking out Christmas presents for all the folks at home [without buying any]. Then we visited the movie theatre to see what pictures were playing. A French one is on tonight but tomorrow afternoon there is an American picture. Hurray!

Saturday, November 26

Dr. Moutoule, the handsome man with the beard, called for us at eight AM and took us out to the workers camp. Ray grew a goatee and moustache while we were at Kanene but shaved it off on the train. The purpose of it was to make the natives realize he isn't "just a child". After seeing Dr. Moutoules beard though I am glad Ray shaved off his imitation.

Saw the hospital, laboratory, mess hall, and schools for the workers and their families, The children are examined every week and have blood tests once a month, and they are all fed three times a day! We have never seen such a healthy lot as here in the mining camp. Dr. gave us most of the morning and then invited us to go snipe hunting this afternoon! We had to work though as there was the American movie at three o'clock but we will go with him next week.

Before coming back to the Hotel for dinner we stopped to see the General Manager to see if an answer had come from Belgium. We suspected that they hadn't really sent a cable and would just say "NO". But they said Belgium wired to not only let us photograph anything we want but to arrange to buy a copy of the film! Apparently Dr. Ross had visited the autorities there.

After dinner we worked on our Xmas cards awhile and then went on our movie jaunt. We had ice cream in a little shop and then bought lollypops, long licorices, and chewing gum. Imagine finding such things in Africa! We bought loge seats as they were only 5 francs more and we wanted to see what they were like. 50 f in all. We sat in the very front of the balcony in wicker chairs with cushions and we were the only ones in the whole balcony. So we could hold hands and snap our chewing gum all we liked.

We saw "Stars over Broadway" which was really swell and not at all like the title sounds. It even had a good bit of "Aida" in it so we had a swell time. The Belgium kids filled the orchestra seats and talked most of the time as they couldn't understand the English so we were glad we sat up in the elite seats. Titles in French were projected beneath the screen. But they were written in long hand and were few and far between.

Got a few of our prints on the way home. They ruined some of the negatives by overdeveloping and did all the prints on hard paper so that they are much too contrasty. I was so disappointed but Ray says he could make a good picture from almost every negative I have. I do hope we have a chance to do some of them when we get home because no professional seems to be able to do them really well.

Sunday, November 27

Got up late this morning and had a nice breakfast. We would like to have spent the day together and just doing things we felt like doing, in honor of our wedding. (nine months ago) But there were so many things that we had to do that we kept busy until far into the night.

I worked on the Xmas cards this morning while Ray went to the Mission to plan the pictures. He got lost on the way, the Boy Scout sense of direction is very poor, and didn't get back till nearly dinner time.

Went to take pictures in the church this afternoon. We got a shot outside but found the light too bad indoors to take any movies. Bishop Springer preached in English [using an interpreter] so we went. At four, after the service, we shot a meeting of the many workers here in the mining camps and native city. By the time we were ready to go back to our hotel it was dark and we found it overrun with beer drinkers! There was even an ochestra and all the couples in town seemed to be there. We had dinner, at reserved tables, and saw the Lambeth walk for the first time.

Packed all our bags in a great rush so Mr. Booth could take most of them to his house tonight. We can check out in the morning and go to Jadotville with just the cameras and a suitcase. Went to the Methodist service for white people and were surprized to find twenty five or more, all of whom are English or speak English very well.

Monday, November 28 [Elizabethville—Jadotville]

Got up about five AM and ready to go to Jadotville. I asked one of the boys what time it was, in my best French, and he brought me a cup of coffee! Just after I downed that, Dr. Moutoule arrived. We could hardly keep awake during the seventy mile drive. Had breakfast at the Union Miniere Mess Hall—private dining room for mucky-mucks like the Dr. Then we met the Director and arranged to see everything and photograph whatever we wish. The cobalt furnaces are not working until around Dec. 10 on account of the lack of rain and consequently water power. So we will have to come back here later and take the train from here to Lobito. This is seventy miles nearer so it is allright with us.

Went all through the concentration plant where the copper ore is crushed until it is almost like sand. Then to the floatation plant where the ore is mixed with water and beat up, then with an oil and beat into a froth, and finally it is removed by floatation, leaving a wet green sand which is about 50—65% copper. In some cases even more. All this took us two hours to see and was very complicated and involved a terrific amount of machinery. We saw the foundry and machine shop before going back to the mission for lunch. We are staying with Mr. Brastrup who is one of our missionaries. He is a Dane and a bachelor so that he has all the work here alone. It is a terrific job in a center like this and almost impossible for one man.

This afternoon the chief geologist called for us. He is our Dutch friend that came to Congo with us on the boat and played Palet with us. He is swell fun and speaks English beautifully. We saw his museum first which was real interesting and in the swellest offices we have seen, on top of a high hill. Then Mr. Schuiling left us at the Electrolitical plant where the concentrated copper is made into sheets of 99.95 % copper. It took a couple of hours for us to look at this complicated process. Then back to the Mission where we had a hasty supper and drove ten miles to an out village.

Mr. Brastrup has a projector which runs with a dinamo attached to his car engine. He shows movies to the natives and has a good bit of "The King of Kings" which is by far the best religious picture ever made. We took pictures of him showing pictures, using flares to light up the scene. Unfortunately the flares were so bright that the pictures on the screen dissolved into it. Ray took a closeup though, by reducing the movie to about 4 by 6 inches. This will fill the screen in our pictures and will be a movie of a movie.

Tuesday, November 29 [Jadotville]

Mr. Schuiling called for us early this morning and drove us out to Kambove, the largest copper producing mine in the world. It is a big open cut and looked just like I've always imagined the Grand Canyon! There is an underground mine too, and with a little persuasion we managed to get down in it. It was quite a thrill to go down so far into the ground. We had to walk as the bucket elevator is a wet and muddy trip. Personally we would like to have tried it anyway.

We took some stills with flash bulbs, of the natives working in the mine, and of me crawling through passages on my hands and knees. Coming up again was the most fun. We had to climb 24 high ladders, one above the other [in the dark]. My little lamp kept getting in the way and I felt as if I would fall down on Ray's head any minute. But we got safely to the surface again and arranged to come back and take movies some other day.

Drove to a cobalt mine before coming home for lunch about 1 PM. We must have gone seventy miles in all and were pretty tired. But Mr. Schuiling called for us right after lunch and left us at the foundry to take some pictures. We had trouble with our lights again even tho Ross supposedly had them fixed for us in Elizabethville. But we got a few shots without them before the plant shut down for the day.

Ray gave Mr. Brastrup a lesson in making movies tonight as he has borrowed a camera and wants to make a picture.

Wednesday, November 30

Someone else called for us this morning and we went to the hospital to take some pictures to show what the company does for the worker. We had some help with the lights and managed to get three sequences. We showed the children of the workers, young girls, learning to sew on machines, the babies getting their daily baths in hospital tubs, and a worker being examined by the doctor with a Floroscope.

Tonight we went to meet the train from Elizabethville as Mr. & Mrs. Springer were on it, on their way to Lobito. Everybody in the town comes to the station when this train comes through at 8:30 PM. It is like a social gathering and even if you aren't seeing anyone off, one of your friends may so you go just in case.

We dashed off to the movies as soon as the train pulled out. We were a little late but as they were showing "Gold Diggers of 1937" we didn't care very much. They showed a French picture too which was really very good and put our American picture to shame. They don't usually have double features here but they were trying to get an audience tonight.

Thursday, December 1 [Jadotville—Elizabethville]

Packed again and Mr. Schuiling came for us about nine. He has a native chauffer for long trips like this so he can just sit in the back and relax. The native is an excellent driver and the car rides so beautifully, Buick, that it puts us to sleep.

About half way Ray let out a yell and we stopped and saw 14 great Sable Antelope just off the road. They just stood and looked at us for a full minute and we were as dazed as they and just stood and looked back. They were beautiful, as big as horses and with straight horns about two feet long. We have been kicking ourselves ever since that we didn't come to enough to take a movie shot. We even had the telephoto lens on the camera. But the antelope trotted off before we thought of it.

Mr. Schuiling took us to lunch in another private dining room at Union Miniere, here in Elizabethville. We had an elegant meal with real [beef] steak. Then he left us at the Mission where we unpacked once more. It looked too cloudy to take pictures so we went shopping again. Before we were through though it began to rain a little and we rushed back to the house to keep our packages dry.

Friday, December 2 [Elizabethville]

Mr. Schuiling called for us this morning and we drove out to the cobalt mine. It is an open cut and very good, photographically. The sun wouldn't come out long enough for us to take a few shots. We waited around but as it was nearly 12 when the men stop for the day, we decided to come back tomorrow. Went on a little further to see a new bore hole [for locating vein of ore] and then came back to the mission for lunch.

Mr. Booth took us to the native city to see if we could find some slums. We need them for one of our scenarios but the natives have little brick huts here and they don't even look as slumy as their ordinary houses. So we have to let the slums go—maybe we can find them somewhere else.

We got a sequence of some natives looking in a store window at shoes, with a closeup of their bare feet. The sun went in after that so we had to go home. The tax collector saw us taking pictures though and told us to come see him in the morning. Uh, oh, we need that letter Mr. Ross didn't get from the Governor-General.

Saturday, December 3

It was too cloudy this morning to go out and do the things we planned. Mr. Schuiling came at ten and took us to meet his geologist here. Mr. Briant will take us out to the mine when we get a sunny day. Mr. Schuiling has to go back to Jadotville this afternoon so we will be without our guide and chauffer for awhile. We showed him our scenarios and had quite a talk before he left.

Mr. Booth and Newell went to Kipushi to a native conference and to baptise some babies, so we had the house to ourselves. They didn't get back till late so we waited supper for them. Then we went to the movies again. We saw Laurel and Hardy in Victor Herbet's Toy Shop operetta. It was in French but the songs were all English and we just loved it. It was really beautiful as well as funny with Mother Goose and all her characters. We also saw two comedies and a cartoon all American pictures, and an English news reel. It couldn't have been so very old because it showed Corrigan in N.Y. with his tons of ticker tape.

Sunday, December 4

Today we had a real holiday. Mr. Booth and Newell left early to drive to Rhodesia and meet Mrs. Booth and Esma Marie. They won't be home till tomorrow afternoon sometime. We had a grand day just being together and feel a little rested for all the work we must do this next week. Here's hoping the sun shines!

Monday, December 5

Got up at 6 AM to hear the Methodist broadcast. We were hoping there would be a message for us but we only heard two and then the radio buzzed and went on so that we couldn't hear another thing. So we ate breakfast and went back to bed again. I slept until 9.30 and just as we were getting up the sun came out.

Ray went to the Post Office and telephoned M. Briant to come and take us out to the cobalt mine again. We got out there and the sun went in! After a two hour wait we came home [about 2:30], starved to death. The men blasted before they laid off work so we at least got something out of the trip. It was an awful bang and before the sound could reach us we saw the earth shoot up in the air. We were a long way off, at the end of the cut, but could feel the ground shake and the wind from the explosion.

Tuesday, December 6

M. Briart called for us again this morning. The sun was shining but by the time we got out to the cobalt mine [bad luck] it had gone in. So we went on to Kipushi which is the largest underground copper mine. We met one of the men that came out on the boat with us and he took us into the mine to take pictures.

First they dressed us up in trousers, jackets, and helmets, and gave a a little miner's lamp to carry. We got in a bucket elevator that was all dripping wet from going through the water table, and went down and down to about 500 feet. Our ears were buzzing loudly when we got off and started to walk through the tunnels. We reached another shaft, where we had to walk, and went down 14 long flights of steps, to a depth of 1000 feet. We sure had a lot over our heads and there didn't seem to be much holding it up either.

We walked way into the mine to where the natives are taking out the ore. As they were about to blast we had to retreat a little. It was quite scary standing in a narrow tunnel with not a sound around and waiting for the explosion. We waited for ages it seemed, and then instead of one explosion, there were 15! We could hear stuff falling all around us and expected the beams over our heads to come down any minute. But they didn't and we went in to see the damage that had been done. We had to wait a long time before the smoke cleared and we could set up for the movies.

But it finally did and we got a separate extention cable for our lights and got them connected up. We blew out the lights and all the drills and pumps stopped, no less than twice. And then we took the pictures. After getting a sequence with the Special we tried to get another with the 35 mm. But the darn thing jammed again after three feet. ???? Took a few stills before starting the climb back to earth again. During all the picture taking we had to keep wiping and wiping the lenses as moisture kept coating them over.

Changed our clothes in a rush as it was after twelve and M. Briart took us back to the cobalt mine. The sun was shining brightly and we thought sure we would get the sequence at last. But when we looked down in the cut we found the men had gone home for the day!

Went home for lunch and then took a sequence on natives registering with the state man and one on natives of different denominations coming to join this church, bringing their letters of transfer. It was 6 PM by the time we were through so we went home to eat, wash, and sleep.

Wednesday, December 7 [Elizabethville—Jadotville]

Found a lovely clear day awaiting us at last. I took some stills of the school before 8 AM when M. Briart was supposed to call for us. But he took so long in coming that we drove down to the plant thinking there had been a misunderstanding, as his English is not too good. By the time we fussed around trying to locate him he came back from the Mission where he had been looking for us.

Drove out to Kasomba [the cobalt mine] again and when we arrived darn if the sun didn't go in! We managed to get our sequence in between clouds though and then we rushed back to the company compound. We got our scene organized there and it began to look so much like rain that we shot it without the sunlight. And the last shot was taken in the rain with me holding my hat over Ray's camera!

About three we got our actors together again and took the last shots to complete the sequence we started this morn. Then we took the car and went to the pool—they were just refilling it so we couldn't swim. Went home and packed, ate supper, and got the train for Jadot at nine o'clock.

Thursday, December 8 [Jadotville]

After dinner when it cleared we drove up the highest hill to take some shots of the plant. We just got through and another rainstorm descended on us. It was swell watching it come and the wind blew and blew. We ran down to the car just as it started to pour.

Mr. Brastrup has borrowed Sarah's camera and has 1000 feet of film he wants us to help him shoot. We started to write a scenario for it tonight from an outline Mr. Brastrup wrote of what he'd like to have. We won't have much shooting time left however when we are through at Union Miniere.

Friday, December 9

This morning Mr. Brastrup left us [& equipment] at the plant and we started photographing the Gravity Concentration process. The director of the whole works gave us the chief electrical engineer to help with the lights. Ray also had a couple of boys to carry cameras and hold lights, and me to keep records. So all he to do was choose camera angles (usually on top of the highest machine or frame work) and take the pictures.

We worked until 1:30 and then got a car to bring us home for lunch. [I] Drove back in Brastrup's car and set to work on the Floatation process and the concentration plant. We worked until six and got a lot done. It was pouring rain when we came home but we had accomplished a whole lot.

After supper we finished the scenario for Mr. Brastrup. It took a long time to get it all straightened out but now we feel he can go ahead with it when we are not here. Ray even made up a shooting schedule for him. He has never taken any movies so we are hoping for the best. He has more equipment than we ever saw one person have. He's always buying some new machine or gadjet and must spend all his small salary on them. We hope to shoot some color film for him and a little black and white so he will learn how to use the camera. Ray went over the whole story with the three boys who will play the main parts and [they] clapped when he was through!

Saturday, December 10

At eleven a car came for us and we went to the plant. M. Marshal had been waiting for us and the native chauffer couldn't find the Mission! It is an awful out of the way place but he might have gone back and told Marshal, instead of making us all wait three hours. We photographed the filtration process as the men only work in the other plant in the morning.

We had to use our lights for a few scenes and got through about 1:30 and went home for dinner. This afternoon we drove back and took a few outdoor scenes as the weather was good and clear.

Ray drove one of the natives home to the native city tonight and got lost. Then he ran out of gas and didn't come back for so long that Mr. Brastrup was worried to death. He kept trying to get me to help him worry but I told him Ray could always walk home—and he was horrified.

Tonight we started to look at some of Brastrup's films but found them in such a mess that Ray undertook to straighten them out. He even typed new labels for the film cans and stayed up till eleven o'clock doing it.

Sunday, December 11

Mr. Brastrup went out to one of his out station chapels this morning and stayed most of the day. We slept late and after breakfast I sewed on my gray suit and helped Ray do some writing.

A Mr. Martin called about three and we had coffee and cake. He is one of the few Protestant Belgians and he helps Brastrup by holding meetings with the natives. We talked cameras and every thing under the sun—he was so interested.

Went back to our sewing and writing until five when Ray took me to the movies. He showed me Mr. Brastrup's version of King of Kings. The original Hollywood picture has been cut so that it no longer is really good. And they have stuck things in from other pictures and from present day Jeruselum so that sometimes the whole point of the story is lost. We hope the prints the Harmon Foundation are putting out now are not like this.

Got a letter from Mother and our article that was in News Week so we were really thrilled.

Worked with Mr. Brastrup tonight and went to bed rather late. We hope we have time and sun, to shoot a little of his picture before we go.

Monday, December 12

It was so cloudy this morning that we put our trip out to Kambove off. We started work in the electrolytical plant instead. About 10:30 Mr. Schuiling came for us as it seemed to be clearing up. Ray was out on a girder six inches wide and very high, so he finished his picture there before we went.

Kambove (like the Grand Canyon) had beautiful light on it when we got there so we hiked through the canyon taking pictures. We got a train to go where we wanted it in one shot, holes drilled in another, and a big blasting in another. We climbed all over and got good and tired and dirty and some good pictures, we hope.

By three o'clock when we got back to the mission for dinner we were pretty well played out. Fortunately it rained so we didn't have to do any more work today.

Tuesday, December 13

Mr. Schuiling had to be at a meeting all day today so we got our electrical engineer to come for us again. We went back to finish the electrolytical plant and the furnace for making ingots. The furnace wasn't working though so that has to wait till tomorrow.

After lunch we went out to a native village to help Mr. Brastrup with his picture. We got a few scenes but about four o'clock the sun went in and we had to come home.

Ray and I went shopping then for some things to eat on our train trip and a few other things we need. I had an awful time trying to get some gray material to line the collar and belt of my suit and use for facing on the skirt. No one seems to speak English here and shopping is the hardest of all with our meagre French.

The Ellis left this afternoon. A good thing because Ray was making them quite mad by saying things about Kings.

Wednesday, December 14 [Jadotville—RR]

Mr. Schuiling came for us this morning and we went to his office and museum to get some shots of pitchblende. (radium ore) The Congo now leads the world in radium production and no one is allowed to visit the mines for fear of diplomatic complications.

Then we went to the hospital and took a few outdoor shots to finish the sequence we started there before. We still couldn't get the furnace but Mr. Schuiling has made arrangements for someone to call for us when they are about ready to pour.

After dinner we went to another native village with Brastrup to do some more of his picture. We had a storm about four and waited awhile for it to clear. But the sky was too dark to do anything and we had to go home to pack and get ready to leave.

After supper Mr. Marshall came and told us we could not get the furnace working until nine o'clock. So that's out, as our train leaves at eight thirty.

Thursday, December 15 [Aboard Angola Train]

Rode through miles and miles of bush and late this afternoon stopped at Dilolo on the border of Congo and Angola. We had to have our passports and matriculation cards checked through and then our baggage. As we are going right back into Congo we didn't expect any trouble. But they fussed about the little ivory we have so we paid duty on it. Taking ivory out of the country costs 75 francs a kilo. We paid eighty on our four pieces that cost only fifty! An English lady missionary came along and helped us out with the French. She is stationed here and comes looking for English and American people when the train comes through every two weeks. Fortunately Ray didn't wax eloquent on the King subject and she helped us a good deal.

A little further in Angola we all had to get off the train and show our passports again. We were put back in 2ⁿᵈ class at Dilolo and are at the very back of the train now. There is a platform we can stand on and see all around. They hooked a baggage car on though and we considered letting it loose so it wouldn't spoil the view—but our baggage might be in it!

Early this afternoon while we were still in the Katanga we saw a baby Civet in a natives arms. He was trying to sell it so we bought it for five francs! It's only about as big as Ray's hand and can't be more than three weeks old. When we got to Dilolo we had to get it through customs so we put it in a tin cracker box that is only as big as the animal. He was very good and slept the whole time, all curled up in a ball. Tonight we took an envelope to the dining car with us and I swiped some meat and fish for him. He wouldn't eat much and is so little that he can't hardly chew. We gave him a drink with my enama tube. We had to fasten a piece of sponge on the end so the water doesn't flow through too fast. We have a lot of fun fussing with our animal and have decided to call him Katanga.

Friday, December 16

Today I managed to get some letters written and a few records done. Most of the time we spent out on the platform looking at the scenery though. This country is wilder looking than any we have seen. It is full of rocks, which are seldom seen at all in Congo.

This afternoon we went out over a vast plain and for miles and miles saw nothing but a few huts scattered here and there. A huge mountain was skirting the edge of the plain and we kept hoping we would go by it. We did and then into a series of pretty vallies. One of them had quite a town in it and the natives came to the train selling great baskets of strawberries for five francs (15 cents) They were wonderful but when we went in to supper what should they have but—strawberries. And they heaped our plates so full, at least a quart. We haven't had any in so long that we enjoyed every one anyhow.

We saw a great waterfall early this evening. It was as big as I always imagined Niagara to be and quite a surprize to find it in this kind of country. Just rolling hills now.

Went to bed right after supper so we can get up early in the morning when we get near Lobito.

Saturday, December 17 [RR—Lobito Bay]

I woke up at 5:30 and looked out and saw mountains all around us. Ray got up without a murmur to see them and we went out on the platform. Great jagged rock mountains were all around us and we had on an extra engine to pull the train up and down the hills. This is the wildest and most beautiful country I have ever seen in my life. Ray says its very much like our west.

The hills are covered with short grass and the trees and bushes are scattered so that it looks like a park. The trees are the funniest we have ever seen. The trunk is about 12 feet in diameter and the whole tree only twice as high as it. The leaves look like any ordinary bush because there are no branches.

In one place we took on an engine with its front pushing toward us and went down a long steep hill. There was a track for a cog wheel too so that we wouldn't run away. At the bottom we got a regular engine on again and went over a valley and some gently rolling hills. Finally we caught a glimpse of our own Atlantic ocean and we jumped and cheered just as if it were Coney Island.

Arrived at Lobito at 11 AM and after much difficulty found an agent of the SS Line that could speak English and tell us what to do with our baggage. Then a taxi out to the Mission Americano.

Our room is on the second floor with a porch in front looking out on the ocean and one in back looking out on the bay. Lobito is no more than a block wide and its swell. After dinner we went down to see the steamer that came in today. Mr. Neipp is a Swiss and speaks French like one of them so he got us on a French submarine that had just docked in the bay.

We climbed down ladders into it and then went from one end to the other and had it all explained to us. It is very long and narrow and the bunks slide into drawers so that they will be out of the way. This one can stay under water eight days and it is mostly intricate apparatus and torpedo shooters. Hisssss! Back at the house we put our suits on and went in the ocean. It sure was glorious and so cold. Oh boy! And no one else was swimming so we had three miles of beautiful beach to ourselves.

Monday, December 19 [Lobito—"SS Thysville"]

Our boat was due at 6 AM and at exactly that time it went passed our window and its waves breaking in the bay woke me up. We jumped up to see it and then were so excited that we packed and were all ready to go by breakfast time.

Mr. Neippe took us down at eight o'clock and we found our luggage safe and ready to go on board. One of the first people we saw on the boat was our steward that we had on the 'Annversville'. He told us that she is in dry dock and most of the officers and men are on this boat. So we felt quite at home. We checked in with the Purser and got a nice cabin, 1st class for missionaries with 2nd class fare, and a cabin next door for all our luggage.

As soon as we sailed at 9 AM on the dot (the Maritime Belge steamers are the only ones out here that always arrive and leave on the minute) we looked the ship over. This is the sister ship of the 'Annversville" and very much like it—so we feel even more at home. We met the Captain, who remembered us and even knew our name. After talking a few minutes he went and got a young American who is traveling on the ship. (the only one) This young man looks so much like Lawrence Tibbet that we wonder it it's his son traveling incognito? He says he is a dentist and is making a study of African teeth in the Congo. He looks about 30 and I imagine he has just graduated and is going to write a book on the subject and so get his PHD.

We have a table and waiter to ourselves and so much food that we are in heaven. We each had two ice creams and three cakes after an enormous dinner. Our waiter is young and handsome and seems to understand our need of such things, having just come out of the Congo where many of them are lacking.

Tuesday, December 20 ["SS Thysville"]

This afternoon we entered the mouth of the Congo and the little steamer loaded up with natives and a pilot to take us up to Matadi, which is about 200 miles. The pilot sat at our table tonight and we had great fun with him. He used to be with the Red Star Line going to N.Y. so he speaks good English. And he has had some of the funniest experiences I ever heard of.

Anchored for the night just off Boma and it wasn't as hot as last night, thank goodness. Played our last game of Palet this afternoon. I lost, so Ray could sleep nights.

Wednesday, December 21 ["SS Thysville"—Matadi]

The first day of winter and it sure was a scorcher. We got off the ship at Boma and went to visit the mission. The people sure were surprized to see us as we told them we'd be back in N.Y. by Christmas when we went through in May. Had a nice visit with them and got back to the boat just at 12 when it was ready to sail.

After our last dinner we packed and went on deck to see the Devil's Cauldron. Now that it is rainy season it is boiling at a great rate. We hoped the ship would turn around once, at least, but it went through very nicely.

Docked at Matadi about 3 and found a troop of soldiers, boy scouts, and flags waiting for us. The Bishop of Matadi was on the boat and got a band out. There were loads of priests and nuns too—quite a turn out for Africa.

The Swedish Missioary met us again and got us through customs and into the hotel as they have a full house for Christmas. The hotel is real elegant, roof dining room and all. And we had a balcony overlooking the river and hills. It was so hot that we wanted to go swimming. Our friend took us to meet an English lady who belonged to the club and she very kindly took us to the pool. It's the only way of getting in so we were very lucky.

After a long swim we had to get our baggage to the station and then we had dinner in our roof garden.

We wanted to get our money's worth so we sat on our balcony a long time before going to bed. It was nice and cool for a change. African summer is beginning to show us how hot it can be.

Thursday, December 22 [Matadi—RR—Kimpese]

Got up before seven and went to all the native stores trying to buy Ray a hat. He wants a pith one, made in India, like he got in the Cameroons, but there just don't seem to be any.

At eight the missionarry took us to the train and after we got our baggage on we looked some more for the hat. Left Matadi at nine on the last lap of the way to Kimpese. Ate breakfast on the train to help kill the time. We had to sit with the lady doctor as the train was crowded and she just talked us the rest of the way.

We are staying with the Engwalls who have four daughters. (one away at Lubondai) They are eight, twelve, and thirteen, and Ray is already moaning because they are going to Sona Bata from Sunday to Monday and won't be with us. Seems to me he takes quite a shine to other girls!

We aren't going to think of pictures or anything connected with them until after Christmas. Ray won't even want to think of them then because right out the front door, about three Kilometers away, stands a mountain. It has rock faces showing all the way round and we hear of a waterfall that starts at the top and cuts a deep chasm through the mountain to the floor of the valley. And no one has ever been able to go more than a short way down this deep fissure. So we are looking up a rope and hoping to get over there soon.

We started right in on our presents as we have to make sixteen now. We didn't expect as many people as that but are glad they are here. The American, British, and Swedish Baptists, cooperate in maintaining this station and the Bible Training school, which is the only one in lower Congo. That's the reason for so many missionaries at this station, and so many languages. We wonder why they don't mix up their English, Swedish, French, and Kikongo. Every time they speak to another person they have to use another language.

Friday, December 23 [Kimpese]

Because the Engwalls are going away tomorrow afternoon the Christmas party is tonight. We had a great rush to finish all our presents and then help with the decorations.

I made six sachet baskets for the ladies and luckily had just six hankies to put with them. We wrapped them in blue paper with gold ribbon and a blue bell tied on. The twenty apples we got on the boat came in very handy at this point as we had to have presents for five kids and five men.

We had just ten lollypops left and made Santy Clauses out of them, using the apples as stomachs. I found presents to put in Santy's sack, for the kids. Two packages of chewing gum, a toy car, a little dog, and a bottle of perfume. It was the perfume Mrs. Beasley [the lady next door] gave me to wear on my wedding night and I never even opened it. If it affected my husband like it did hers I'm glad to get rid of it.

We put up streamers, made of green shade for the dining room light, made crepe paper bells, and lettered the place cards. We made nut baskets too and set a long long table so that it looks like a banquet.

After a swell American dinner with duck, potatoes, string beans, salad, and plum pudding with hard sauce, Santy Claus came. I helped paint up the younger Stenstrom and paste whiskers on him and they had a regular Santy Claus suit. We took pictures of him giving presents to the kids. Everybody got presents and it was almost like Christmas eve at home, except that we were sweating. We got some fudge, an enamel sewing box, and a box of chocolates.

Saturday, December 24

This morning the Christmas pageant was held in front of the church. The large entrance with an arch over it made a lovely place for the manger. The shepherds field was by the side of the church and the audience sat on the grass in front of the church.

The natives put on a beautiful pageant and sang the Christmas songs in places in Kikongo. It didn't seem funny at all to have a black Mary and Joseph and a black Christ child. In fact it was more thrilling to see them and the black wise men and shepherds come to worship. And then a group of black children with the Engwall girls mixed in among them came and sang before the manger. The costumes were lovely and I felt so moved by it all that I could hardly keep from crying. One of the fishermen mending a net saved me. He had a machete, to make it look more natural he said, and during the pageant a fly began biting him in the middle of the back. It must have been quite a nip because without thinking at all he picked up the machete and thumped himself on the back, with three resounding whacks. It was the funniest thing I've ever seen happen in the middle of a pageant.

Sunday, December 25

Woke up at 3:30 with the Christmas bells ringing in our ears. Ray got up very nicely for once for the Candle Light service. It is a Swedish custom to have it at the ungodly hour of 4 AM. But it was certainly worth getting up for.

The church was lighted with 106 candles, I counted them myself. The little wee children sat in the front on the floor and the church was full to over-flowing. We sat just outside the door and could see it all beautifully. How wonderful it is to see the faith of these people. It seems greater than ours and just shines from their faces.

We opened our presents for each other at 5 AM and had our own Christmas prayer. Ray gave me Van Loon's Wide World game and a bracelet and ring to match. They are made of elefant hair and gold and are simply swell. I gave him a Monopoly game, English version with pounds instead of dollars, and two Snow White jig saw puzzles. Also a tie, garters, and shoe laces, which don't count as real presents.

Then we went back to bed again and slept until 10 AM. We raided the kitchen and found some cookies for breakfast. And made up for our loss at dinner with Dr. Mabie. She had another Christmas dinner and we got some more candy and a picture. The Reynolds and Watkins were there too so we had quite a party.

Monday, December 26

We got to work photographing the Christmas pageant with Dr. Mabie's help. We weren't scheduled to do this here but feel it can be used.

This is the first real bright day we have had and we are hoping Sona Bata will have better weather. This is the hottest season of the year and the sun is due to shine.

Tuesday, December 27

We've been married for ten months today! A package arrived and we thought we'd have a real celebration but it turned out to be the Photoflood lamps. But we had a very nice day anyway.

We started with a game of Croquet and then worked on our records and scenarios till dinner time. We have a long table out on the porch where there is a breeze at times and it makes a lovely office.

Wednesday, December 28

I went over all the scenarios and typed up all the things we still have to take in Congo. Then we had a meeting with the Stenstroms, Engwalls, and Dr. Mabie to plan the pictures we are to take here. If we don't get some sun soon I don't know when we'll take them though. There are black clouds threatening us with rain, all the time, but it doesn't rain.

Ray and I were initiated into a Missionary Society that is really too silly for missionaries. We aren't allowed to even tell the name of it to anyone who isn't a member. So we'll have to initiate all our friends in order to tell them.

Thursday, December 29

We were engaged just three years ago and we sure are glad for this day. We have had such happy times ever since and life has been so full of love-liness.

This morning it was still cloudy so we went to the school and set up our lights to take indoor pictures. Still we couldn't get enough light. The daylight seems to absorb all of our artificial light. So we left them up and went back after dark to take the pictures. We worked until ten o'clock then, until we blew the fuse.

The sun didn't show itself all day so we wrote letters again and an account of the poison cup sequence we shot at Mushenge. We wrote all the informa-tion down so that the Committee can select their own titles.

Tonight the three girls went out to play in the moonlight tonight, with the native children. They play native games because they like them the best. And they all go barefooted.

We got a letter from Loomis "Dear Ray and Virginia" and he says that when we get back maybe we can take pictures for the National Park Ser-vice—if our price isn't too high. That would be swell!

Friday, December 30

Another cloudy day. This seems to be a short dry season in the midst of the rainy one and it should end any day now. They say that January and February are very sunshiny and hot months—so we still have hopes.

Tonight we took more pictures in the classrooms. Indoor pictures are so long in the making and we don't feel that we accomplish much in one evening. Our lights are so inadequate that we can't light up a whole room and get a really good scene. Next time we will bring better lights and more of them.

Saturday, December 31

The last day of 1938 was swell fun—a fitting close to a wonderful year. Ray and I packed a lunch, found a rope, and set off for the Bangu, early this morning. We took two native boys with us, one to carry the lunch basket and water, and a smaller one to keep him company while we were climbing.

Two hours of hard walking, over a river and through grass higher than our heads, around a pond and through a marsh, brought us to the foot of the Bangu. We started up the side of this great range of mountains from the western end. It looks like just one mountain but when we got to the top we found a long chain of hills and vales stretching eastward for miles.

It was a tough pull up the hogback leading to the cliffs that rise straight up to the top. I never saw a grassy slope as steep as this one. At home grass just wouldn't grow on ground so nearly perpendicular.

We left our boys and climbed around the base of the rock to find a way up. Much to our joy we found a cave instead! We had to go up on an overhanging ledge to reach one of the entrances and then we cautiously creeped into the side of the mountain. There was a low noise like a snake or young eagle might make so we hastily backed out again. After throwing stones in and not being attacked, we tried again. Every once in awhile we'd hear the sound again. And then I discovered that it was the water squshing in one of Ray's shoes!

We found five entrances and they let a little light in so that we could explore the passages. My mirror helped too as we used it to throw a beam into the dark corridors. We found five corridors and one seemed to go deep into the mountain. It was too black for us to explore but we hope to return and find a great inner chamber and a cave that really is something. No one here knows anything about it and very probably we are the first people to ever set foot in this cave. It is so hard to get to that a native would never attempt it.

After this adventure we went back to eat lunch on a rock ledge, looking out over the valley and mountains on the horizon. Then we climbed 300 feet to the top of the Bangu. It was a hard climb but Ray led it beautifully and I got safely to the top with his careful belays. The view was wonderful and a cool breeze was blowing. There wasn't any sun all day but we got very hot climbing. Going down was bad as we could find only a few trees to rappel down from. And our rope was never long enough to reach down to the next rappel place. I went down over an overhang for the first time and it wasn't bad at all. The two boys watched us every minute but I'm sure they think we are crazy.

Africa Diary:
1939

Sunday, January 1 [Kimpese]

The sun hasn't appeared yet. Fooey! We have come to the conclusion that Africa just isn't photographicable. But we like it here very much—Ray says better than anywhere else. I think the girls are the main attraction for both of us and of course, the Bangu.

Monday, January 2

Took advantage of the 'unusual' weather by getting all the Engwalls (except Mother) to go on an expedition up the Bangu. We packed great quantities of food, found all the bathing suits, decided to take Carol's native playmates, two of them, and the little boy who went with us before—just because he begged to go, and then we all piled in the car.

Then we started up the steepest, highest and hottest mountain I ever encountered, all at once. But at the top a cool breeze was blowing and in every direction we could see plenty of compensation.

Tuesday, January 3

This afternoon we took two sequences and got sunburned again. The sun sure is hot here now. We had to take more showers before supper and they sure felt good.

Wednesday, January 4

Ray worked on his records this morning and I tried to straighten out my expense accounts. I have lost 700 francs somewhere and it is too much to just stick on some day's expenses. So I am in a dither as to where and how I can find it.

This afternoon the Ericksons and Esther Ehnbom stopped here on their way back to Sona Bata. They are just staying for the night. The sun came out unexpectedly so we dashed out to take pictures. We got two sequences and did a lot of walking around in order to get them. I was quite worn out but Ray wanted to play Croquet so bad that we had a game before supper. We got Mrs. Engwall and the girls to play too. I won, Ray says on a fluke. The Bum!

We had quite a discussion on Chamberlain and the war situation at supper. Ray and I are for and Mr. Engwall very much against. Of course, none of us really know very much about the situation. We are just beginning to read detailed accounts now.

Thursday, January 5

This morning it got very dark and then began to rain in a big way. We had to have the lights on in order to see at all. Ray got busy on his records and worked at them most of the day. I wrote letters but gave it up as a bad job on Engwall's typewriter.

We were going to take indoor pictures tonight, just so we could say we did something today. But the power was so low we couldn't get enough light. A beautiful full moon came up so we walked around a bit. Everybody is busy with school work and Chapel services now so we have no one to play with. All the missionaries here are really just school teachers as no other work is carried on but the school. They have some very interesting classes and teach the natives everything under the sun.

Friday, January 6

After lunch it looked promising so we spent an hour and a half getting ready for a woman's cooking class and a child care class. The sun was shining brightly until we were ready to shoot. Then it went in for the rest of the afternoon.

After supper we went to school and got three sequences. The Hygiene class for the women was the most interesting. Dr. Mabie had big malarial mosquitos drawn on the board and a tiny bed with a net over it. One woman came up and put her baby in the bed and arranged the net—to show the others how to protect their children. It was the sweetest baby, just like a doll, and how I wish it was mine. Even as black as it is.

Saturday, January 7

This afternoon the sun came out just as we were beggining to enjoy a nice lazy afternoon. We went to the family gardens for pictures and then took outdoor classes in sewing and child care, for women. We just about roasted it was so hot and my tan that was so faded is beginning to make a come back.

Sunday, January 8

Ray and I both wrote to Sherm today and then spent most of the day reading. Mr. Reynolds took us out to a village in the bush this afternoon to see if it would do for a few scenes we need. He held a meeting there in the stuffiest little chapel and everybody was falling asleep. At least we were and all the children too. After the meeting one of the women shook hands with me and that got them all started.

Monday, January 9

Cloudy all day today. If we had only known we could have gone to the Bangu. But the weather has become more changeable than ever and we didn't want to miss any sunshine.

Tuesday, January 10

Went to a nearby village this morning for a sequence. We had an awful time trying to get the men to take off their shirts and wear cloths instead of pants. They are all leaning backwards now and are embaressed to expose their chests. We finally got three to do it and a couple of women to tie cloths under their arms. They didn't like it at all though. We took a worker bidding his family good-bye and going off over the valley. We wanted to get him at the RR station as the train came in. But Mr. Engwall tried and tried to get the car started and by the time he found he couldn't it was too late for us to walk. We made arrangements to take it tomorrow—if the sun shines.

Took the rest of our indoor pictures tonight. We have used all the teachers now, Swedish, British, and American. There are nine in all as the wives teach as well as the husbands. Too bad we had to use Mr. Reynolds, British, because he's a prune-puss if there ever was one.

Wednesday, January 11

Ray got a letter off to Bob this morning and then the sun came out just before eleven. We dashed down to the RR station with our actor to show him getting on the train. He came with the wrong cloth around his bundle and by the time he got the right one the train was pulling in. We got him in position and took the shot just in time—then we discovered that we forgot to set the exposure. So we'll have to go back another day—if the sun shines. Came back to take a class but the woman who is the star had washed the clothes she is supposed to wear! We contented ourselves with eating and then prepared to shoot the school scenes, general with everyone in them. When it was time to ring the bell and get the people together the sky was as black as the Africans. It didn't clear until the moon came up.

Thursday, January 12

Got up early again as the sun was shining right in on our bed and calling us to work. After breakfast we took a lot of men, women, and children, over to a nearby village, and set up a church scene. When we were all ready the sun went in and we all sat and craned our necks in order to see when it was coming out again. It finally did, when our necks were all stiff and taking and acting in pictures was such a pain in the neck that we could hardly get the scene. But Ray's sticktoitiveness held everyone until it was all down in black and white.

Went home for lunch and then went to the one o'clock train to reshoot the scene we missed yesterday. Today we did very well and even got a shot of the engine wheels as the train started up.

When we got back to the station we got all the people together for the school scenes. We had them changing classes and had to make them practice about six times too many in the hot sun. Then we kept the women, almost by force, and shot the last class scenes. Everybody was standing in a pool of perspiration by the time we were through with that and our interpreters all ran for cold drinks and showers. But we, true photographic geniuses walked a mile to the gardens for our last shot. By the time we got back to the cold drinks we were so elated at having finished that we went out to play Crolf. They all say, "Don't you ever get tired?" Of course, we do but somehow we have gotten used to this climate and 'unusual weather' and are cramming all the fun we can into each day.

Friday, January 13

Got Ray up at 6 AM and got myself all tired out before the day began. But we packed and ate and got off for the Bangu by 7.30. Again over miles of rough country to the base of the cliff where Garner Caves are located. We found the grass much higher this week, way over our heads in some places, and each blade a fat two inches wide. We kicked and fought our way through it, up and down hill, under a broiling hot sun, of course.

This time we did some real exploring in the caves with flashlights. We took the two native boys with us just to give them a thrill. They were scared at first and didn't want to go but then they remembered that Ray can make airoplanes, trains, telephones, and all other articles of civilization, that white men make. Ray crawled on his stummick through one little opening and I thought sure he'd get stuck in there. But he got through and found more passageways and a way out to the face of the cliff.

Great black clouds were blowing up all around us and it was so late, and the sole was off Ray's shoe, so we gave up going to the gorge and started home. The sun beat down on us unmercifully and I thought I was melting away to a shadow of my former self. (I didn't though, according to the scales) It got blacker and blacker all around us. We could see rain in the distance and hear the thunder roaring. And the sun kept on shining. When we don't want it it burns us up. Fooey. When we got in the house the sun went in and it began to rain. Who has put the curse on us???? The Africans usually blame their ancestors and I suppose Ray has had a number of blackguards in his family.

Saturday, January 14 [Kimpese—Sona Bata]

Packed and packed and finally got our 23 pieces ready to go. After the boys took them off to the station I found Ray's white coat, a map, book, and some shoe polish, that we left out. But we carried them along with a box of sandwiches, another of cake, a bottle of water, and a pineapple, feeling well prepared for a trip around the world.

We said goodbye all around the station. Each one brought a groan, as I realized it meant another thank you note, and there have been so many already.

After much luggage fuss we got on the train at eleven, in the third class section. It was chock a block full of natives but we squeezed all our stuff in and got a seat at the rear of the car. This afforded a first hand view of 'How an African Travels'. Most of the five hour ride I spent torn between the scenery on one hand and native life on the other.

The scenery was really something—hills greatly assorted and covered with green velvet. But the natives! They say they only have one meal a day and I believe it now. The meal simply lasts all day. Great stalks of sugar cane, 12 feet long, disappeared like an albino on a white horse in a snow storm. Stink fish couldn't go down fast enough for us and still the memory lingered. Loaves of bread and bundles of manioc were nibbled on until our jaws ached from watching. And we couldn't seem to feel hungry ourselves we were so satiated by noontime. We did manage to eat our pineapple and a little cake before we got to Sona Bata.

This time we not only have a house all to ourselves but a cook and houseboy too. So we have started housekeeping in style, for the first time in our lives, and feel quite worried because we just don't know what to do with servants. Ray carried me over the door step of all three doors in the house— just to make sure we start off right. Some kettles, pots, and pans, of water arrived so we curled up in the tub and took a bath, or something. Then we got unpacked and switched half the furniture around to suit our needs. By the time we were able to walk without tripping over more than three things, we had to go to Freases to eat. She is a Bryn Mawr graduate and not of the missionary cut.

Sunday, January 15 [Sona Bata]

Found a package from Ed full of funny sheets [newspapers] so we stayed in bed late and read some of them. Ngonda had breakfast for us about nine and Davide waited on the table. They sat us at either end of our dining room table and we were so far apart that we had to stand up to pass things to one another. At Engwalls everyone recites grace "God bless our food and make us good, for Jesus' sake, Amen. Now that we have our own house Ray has revised it and insists on saying, "God bless our food and make *it* good, etc." But it was good—we had waffles.

At ten the primary Sunday School class met on our front porch with Mrs. Erickson. Little Ruth Tuttle is in it with all the natives. Their singing was a treat and we were sorry when it was time for church. There was no getting out of it as Mrs. Lanoue called for us and we had to get introduced. We enjoyed the sermon especially because it was given by a bearded gentleman who is to be the witch doctor in our picture. After the sermon he gave, using the whole front of the church in which to illustrate it, we are sure he will do very well.

Had supper with the Ericksons and then the rest of the folks came for Prayer Meeting. We met Mr. Lanoue, who is just back from a ten day trip in the bush, and who looks a lot like Bob. He is young and will be the one to help us with most of the pictures.

Dr. Freas is all het up about some medical pictures he wants us to take for him. We would like to but have so much to do here wonder if it will be possible. We are going to concentrate on "Bwamba" first, at any rate, and then clean up our little odds and ends that are hangovers from the Katanga. We hate hangovers and can't cure them by a raw egg or any other pick-me-up. We hope to clean them up once and for all before we go up river though.

Monday, January 16

After breakfast we went with the Ericksons to look at the village Carpenter selected when he was here working on our picture. We were disappointed that he didn't do a little better—it's only advantage is that is in within walking distance. There are so many trees that it would be impossible to get a camera angle that included more than a hut or two.

This afternoon we went out alone, with two native guides, and looked at two more villages. One has definite possibilities but we had hoped for something better for "Bwamba". It has been decided that the Ericksons will help us for the first part of the picture. The doctors will take over the the medical work, one as director, the other as actor. Mr. Lanoue must have backed out all of a sudden. He has been away a lot though and has to make out all kinds of reports at the begginning of a new year.

A gang of little boys met on our front porch this morning and we chose 14 for the hunting scene that we shot before. We are keeping the same boys for Bwamba and Kimbu that we used before. I am a little worried about Bwamba though because he isn't as cute as he was. He has grown some and is as thin as burnt match sticks.

Tuesday, January 17

When we got up for breakfast this morning we found a note from our cook. It said, "Please have breakfast ready at nine o'clock because I have gone to market." We didn't really think he meant for us to cook it though so we went off with Mr. Erickson to look at some boys for the cast. We chose five hospital boys and arranged to meet and talk with them so that we can get someone real good for Bwamba as a man. The boy we selected before doesn't look very good to us now. He has rather odd features and is not good looking or typical enough.

After breakfast we walked out to see two more villages. One has definite possibilities. We were late getting back to meet with the boys but they were waiting on our porch. We chose one who really has a bright look and we hope he will do well in the part. He has two little brothers, in his village about a days walk from here, and we have sent for them. We hope the little one will do for Bwamba as a boy.

This afternoon we went in the car to still another village. This one is further away but we had to walk a good bit as a bridge was too far gone to attempt driving over. The trail is really only a native footpath anyway. This village was rather spread out but had its good points so we talked to the Kapita about it. He says, "I am only one" but he will call the people together tonight and discuss the picture with them.

Wednesday, January 18

This morning we stayed home and wrote a scenario for the pictures we took at Kimpese. Much to our horror we find we took about 500 feet on the training school. That was over shooting a little as we were only supposed to use 150!

Wrote to Engwalls and sent them the scenario for titling. Ray got all the films ready to send to Leo. to be checked thru customs. We took them over to Freas to get our things mailed but no one was home but the Tuttle children. We had a grand time playing with them before we came home to dinner.

This afternoon Mr. Erickson took us to see the state administrator of this section. We got our matriculation cards signed and talked pictures with him as we want to take a few scenes with him for "How an African Tribe is Ruled." It was nearly supper time by the time we got home so we read on the porch.

We hope to get all our cast together tomorrow and give them a pep talk. Here's hoping the boys arrive so we can start with the little Bwamba in the afternoon.

The weather has been fairly good ever since we arrived. It rained a little tonight which is a good sign because then perhaps the short dry season is over. When we get the cameras out I suppose the sun will go in.

Ray says it is a good thing we did use the extra film at Kimpese as we are approaching a dead line. The film we brought out with us is to be developed by March and we still have about 800 feet to use in a hurry.

Thursday, January 19

We received word from the selected village this morning—the people will not be in our picture as they think it will bewitch their village to play the parts we want! And this is the most civilized part of Africa we have been in! I suppose they are afraid because a witch doctor plays an important part in the picture.

We went off to another village that we liked fairly well and there was another big palaver there. We got an answer from them this afternoon. They won't do it because the white people have already taken their land and they don't want to have anything to do with any of them for fear they will take more. They say all the villages around have joined a pact and will not help the white man in any way. ?????

We went off in the car this afternoon to a village that has one of the church deacons in it. It isn't ideal but we were so royally received that we think it best to use this village. The natives explained what we wanted to do and then our Ngonda translated for us. They would love to have us use their village. And he used the word love, too. They presented us with a duck and some eggs and we came home quite happy about the village.

Friday, January 20

Went out to our chosen village again with Mr. Erickson. After much pala- ver about which huts should be fixed over etc. we found that there are only ten adults in the whole village! We understood yesterday that there were sixty and can't do much with only ten. So we had to give up using the village as it will be impossible to import people and have them all come the same day and when the sun shines.

It was lunch time when we got back to the station and we had to wait till 2 o'clock before we could look any further. Everyone here is dead to the world until 2 so we usually stay home and read or sew. Then we went back to the first village we saw and decided to use it if the people will agree. It isn't ideal but the natives said they would be in the picture when Carpenter was here. So if they don't go back on their word the village will have to do. Ray is rather dissappointed as he wants one that is just ideal—but that is impossible in this section.

Our little Bwamba arrived today and he does look like his older brother that we chose. But he is all covered with itch and to further complicate matters we will have to wait four or five days before we can use him

Saturday, January 21

Got up early to see about our village and found Mr. Erickson had gone to see the medal chief of this section. He is over all the villages in this immediate area and he has the say about whether or not we can use Ndimba, the village we selected yesterday afternoon.

Ray and I went to try out the little boy, with the itch, to see if he can play the part of Bwamba. He is awfully small but seems bright and he is so cute looking that we want to use him. We had Mfienge, who understands English and helped us before, translate for us. The boy seems intelligent enough although naturally a little shy right now.

Mr. Erickson got back and said the Chief was hesitant—he too thinks there is something behind all this. But he was finally convinced that it is just a movie and wants us to use his village. Ray and I went right over to see it and found it the one we preferred when we were here before! But we were told then that it was pretty Catholic and so probably we would get little or no cooperation. But now the Chief has gone over to the Salvation Army (which is a third religion out here) and he has promised us the help of the people. He also has soldiers in his village who can keep order and hold back the curiosity seekers. And the village is really the best we've seen as there are lots of palms and the houses are not too modern. Hurrah! its settled at last.

Made arrangements to have some props made and others gathered together. We hope everything will be ready by Monday so we can go right ahead and shoot. Saw Dr. Freas about Bwamba's medical training and arranged to take that Monday and Tuesday. During those two days we hope little Bwamba will be completely cured of the itch and then we can go right ahead.

After supper played 42 and then went to see a baby get born. But it was a bad case and would hang on most of the night. Then it might have to be a Ceasarean and we wouldn't want to see that the first time. At any rate we wouldn't want to stay up all night for it. I much prefer to see a nice normal birth anyway.

Sunday, January 22

Got up latish for breakfast and then ready for church. We can't get out of going because Mrs. Lanoue calls for us. We can't imagine why unless someone at Kimpeses told her we didn't attend and she has taken us under her wing to see that we do.

We heard that Mother and baby died after an all night struggle. Are we glad we weren't there for that one. Haven't heard any of the details except that the Mother had a hemmorage. It was Dr. Tuttles case, poor guy, and a good thing his own baby was born last week.

We tinted a map and fixed it for our picture. The dispensary stations are supposed to be marked on it and we just put them where they look good. I got some letters written and Ray unpacked some of our curios to use in the picture. We'll have them all worn out before we get home! But we do want some real African looking things in the old time village.

Monday, January 23

Got up early, had breakfast at seven, and went to the hospital. We had an awful lot of fuss with the lights. Dr. Freas got out some extra ones with reflectors so that we can take pictures in the day time. Finally when they were all connected we blew the fuse. Dr. Freas had to keep going back and forth on his bicycle between the plant and the hospital. A mile trip each time. Finally everything was ready and we got the medical boys in and the tribal markings on Bwamba's face. He didn't like that much.

But there wasn't enough light! We found that one light read as high on the meter as all six! The other five were just cutting down on the voltage. I thought there just couldn't be any more light delays but they fussed until twelve o'clock without getting them fixed.

Had dinner with Freas as we are so far off and Ray ate so much I was embarressed. He even told them we only have a little bitty meat so might as well eat theirs, as long as its free. I came home this afternoon and let them fuss as I didn't feel good and they weren't getting any pictures taken anyway. Ray finally brought Bwamba over so I could paint the tribal marks on again. He was so upset about going back to the hospital again like that that I put some on Ray too!

Later Ray found they ran off when Bwamba perspired so he sent a note saying he couldn't do a thing without me. They hadn't either. Dr. Freas decided he could mix ether, menthol blue, etc. and make a sticky paint that wouldn't run. I came home and let them experiment and they finally produced a waterproof stuff that can only come off with an alchohol and ether solution. Bwamba started really kicking up about it then and had to be taken aside and reasoned with. No one can discover why he is so sensitive about them. He says it isn't pride or shame but just his thoughts. Finally they took him to Mr. Erickson and let him try too. In the end he said he thought God would tell him to do it but his thoughts still wouldn't let him. So he went home to "drink water over it." That's their expression for thinking it over!

Ray came home for supper and acted as though he hadn't seen me in a week. Said he just couldn't wait to get home and was so impatient all the time they were talking to Bwamba. Imagine him still feeling like that!

Tuesday, January 24

This morning Ray went over to the village with Mr. Erickson to see about the necessary changes and the building of a burial ground. I stayed home and did my sewing and was glad of the chance to relax.

Bwamba finally gave in and said he would go ahead with the pictures without further objections. Personally I think they used a little force to get him to do it. We would rather not have had that as he may be a little resentful and not do as well as he might.

After dinner we went to the hospital and set up for a class room scene. It was four o'clock by the time we got the lights working and everything set. I painted the marks on Bwamba with the menthol blue, alcohol, ether, and collodian mixture. When we got him in the class we found a boy right behind him with the same marks on his face! They were a little smaller but very permanent and yet Bwamba was so touchy about it.

Shot the class room scene with Dr. Freas and some bones and a skull.

Wednesday, January 25

Got to the hospital at eight AM and tried to get ready for an operating scene. The sun gave us enough light so we blocked off one of the windows and got ready to shoot without lights. By the time we got Dr. Tuttle ready and Dr. Freas to help direct the sun was under a big black cloud and we had to run for the lights. We got started pretty late and couldn't finish the scene till 1:30. But no one complained and we got some very good shots.

After lunch we went right back to go on with the next scene. We had to rig up an office in one of the classrooms and Dr. Tuttle had his desk, bookcase,

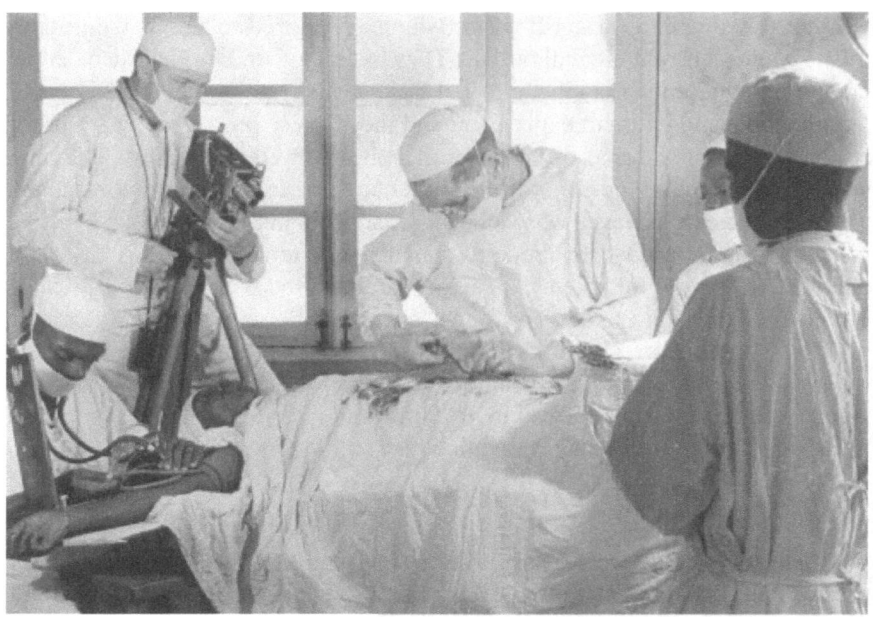

and all kinds of paraphanalia brought from his house this morning. So we moved in and established a very nice looking office for a few scenes with Dr. Tuttle and Bwamba.

After one sequence was finished we had to make everything look like two years later for another one. It was 5:30 and really to late to start but we wanted to take it so the doctors would be free tomorrow. The poor patients have all been dying for the last couple of days. At 7:00 we were nearly through, on the last shot, and Ray discovered the shutter had been closed ever since he put in a new film. So we had to go back and retake three shots.

Thursday, January 26

This morning I let Ray go ahead to set up a scene while I wrote some business letters. He and Doc. Freas take so long to get ready that there isn't any sense in my being there. I only pester them by being efficient and showing them how to get things done in a hurry.

When I did get there they weren't quite ready for the shots of Bwamba dispensing medicines. When that was finished we went on to a microscope scene and didn't get home for lunch till 1 o'clock again.

I took a cat nap after we had our lunch and then we went back for a scene in a ward. We pestered all the poor patients to death by changing pillows or borrowing them for the scene. And Ray consistently dropped lights plugs, books, pencils, etc. on the feet of one man who had just had an operation. When he got through and I was ready for some stills our socket burned out and we had to call it a day.

Friday, January 27

This morning we went back to the hospital to shoot an operation for Dr. Freas. He wanted the whole thing, insides and all, so we took the whole process of removing tumors from the uterus. We took the Dr. washing up, getting into his gown and gloves, giving the spinal aneasthetic, and cutting open the abdomin. He had to dig down under the intestines and pull the uterus out and then he cut the tumors off and sewed up the holes. One tumor, about the size of an egg, shot out of his hand and right across the room.

Ray and the Dr. fussed around so much about the pictures that the anaesthetic wore off when the woman's stomach was still wide open. She began moaning and going on something awful. That did me in and I got sicker and sicker. Who wouldn't seeing a perfectly conscious person lying there with her stomach gaping and all kinds of tools sticking in her. Dr. Freas tried to get her sewed up without giving her any chloroform, because its safer, but she went on so that they had to put her to sleep. Was I furious at Ray and Dr. Freas for doing that to the poor woman! I was so mad I don't see how I could still feel sick.

This afternoon we planned the school scenes with Ericksons. These show Bwamba, as a little boy, in the Mission boarding school. We selected the boys to be in class with him and got uniforms to fit them all. They wear striped blue shorts and shirt that look like baseball suits.

Saturday, January 28

Took our last pictures with the pesky lights. Little Bwamba played his first part in a class room scene. We think he is adorable and one of the best actors we've ever had. After we tell him what to do and then turn to our cameras and lights, we look back and find him rehearsing over and over again. When he tried to frown over his studying, he was so cute I felt like hugging him. He tries harder than anyone we have worked with and is the only one who ever rehearsed himself.

This afternoon we intended to finish with the school boys but the sun didn't come out. Ray and I tramped through a couple of valleys looking for a setting for our forest scenes. We didn't find one though and got too hot to go on.

Sunday, January 29

Had breakfast at eight o'clock and then wrote letters until the children came for Sunday School. I couldn't pound the typewriter then so we read in bed. After S.S. we selected a few more little boys from the group to be in the hunting scene. We had to drop some of the boys we selected last week as they are bigger than Bwamba.

Went to church and nearly had fits laughing at the preacher [native]. They have a different one most every week and this one carried on so that even the congregation were giggling. We sit right at the side of the pulpit and have to be on good behavior as we are in full view of the whole church. But it sure was hard today.

Went to prayer meeting at Lanoues and thought about what we would be doing if we were home. Going to the movies, we decided.

Monday, January 30

Got up early hoping to take pictures but it was much too cloudy. The little boys came at 8 o'clock anyway so we fitted them out with loin cloths, spears, and bows and arrows. They looked awfully cute—some of them are so little. We told them what we wanted to do in the forest and they showed us how. They were darling—creeping along, peering behind bushes, and looking as if they really were hunting. We gave them all a piece of candy before they left and they loved it.

Mr. Erickson went with us to find a forest scene. We tramped through some more valleys and got all hot and tired. We finally found two places that will do nicely. One for morning sun and another for afternoon sun. We stopped at the village to see how the graveyard is coming along. They have made a lot of graves for us and are going to decorate it with all sorts of fetishes. We chose a place for an entrance to the village and arranged to have a path cut. Now if we can only get some sun!

This afternoon we started the outdoor scenes with the schoolboys. The sun didn't stay out long enough for us to finish up though.

Tuesday, January 31

Woke up to find it pouring rain and almost as dark as night. We ate breakfast by lamp light and then wrote letters. It let up a little around noon and by two o'clock the sun was out. We got all the schoolboys out again and finished the shots of them.

As it was too late to get the people together for another scene this afternoon we walked down to the market place. We found just three native stores mostly full of stink fish. Managed to buy Ray a pair of tennis shoes and felt like we were shopping—even though it wasn't very Fifth Avenue.

After supper I was just about to take a bath when Mrs. Tuttle called from her back porch that somebody was having a baby. We ran and ran all the way to the hospital—over half a mile.

But we were in plenty of time and an hour later saw a darling little black boy come to life. It was like a miracle and so much simpler than I'd imagined. As it was the mother's first child she had rather a hard time of it. But it was all so easy that I'm sure I won't mind having seven. And I could certainly deliver one myself now. Dr. Tuttle was swell about explaining everything to us during the birth and answering a million questions. I am convinced that this should be part of every girls education. And husbands too!

Wednesday, February 1

Mr. Lanoue is helping us with the pictures now—when we are able to take some. This morning was dull again and we got our witch doctor, chief, and poison cup victim, together to see about costumes. We are apparently going to have trouble with them too as they cannot lower themselves to remove their shirts unless they can wear a cloth draped around them. We decided not to press the point until we are actually shooting the pictures.

This afternoon all the little boys came and got ready for their hunting scene. We took them down into the valley to one of the places we selected the other day. But by the time we were ready to shoot the sun was down behind a tree! The valley is so deep that there is no sun in it after 3.30. We had an awful time with the monkey who kept getting away, but we managed to rehearse a little. The little boys love their bows and arrows and are constantly shooting them. Our two little spears are popular too—especially with Ray. He has the art of spear throwing done to a T and can hit a small leaf at 25 yards. He's got Lanoue doing it too so that they are constantly spear throwing if there is a delay due to sun, etc.

Thursday, February 2

Received a letter from Miss Bentley and she says Dr. Ross is lecturing with our Leper picture. She heard it was very good but hadn't seen it to tell us anything definite. We are a little mad that everybody forgets about us and that we are more interested in the results of our labor than anyone else. We hope someone will get around to writing us soon.

At twelve o'clock the sun appeared and we ate lunch and got the kids together for the picture. Three of them didn't appear until 2 and the clouds were very good so we worked on the opening shot of the picture. I got the kids dressed and painted up and then went to the spot and found Ray and Mr. Lanoue spear throwing! They are worse than the kids who are always shooting their arrows and getting them stuck up in trees etc. We took one shot and then waited till 4 o'clock for another. But by that time a rainstorm was approaching and we had to let the kids go home.

Friday, February 3 [Sona Bata—Banza Manteke]

This morning when we found it cloudy again we decided to go to Banza Manteke with Dr. Freas. He has been asking us to go ever since we arrived and has had invitations from the folks there who seem very anxious for us to pay them a short visit.

Left about 11.00 o'clock in "Freas' Folly". It's an old Ford, small truck, 1928 model. We had the back of it full of baggage, medicine, three native women and a baby. We just managed to squeeze our cameras and suitcase in.

What a ride! 270 kilometers over a bumpy curving road with a driver who goes as fast as he can without turning over. It was sure wild—but lots of fun. We stopped at Kimpese for some cake which they luckily had. The Engwalls were delighted to see us again and we wish we might have stayed longer.

On to Banza Manteke! I got used to the bumping and actually fell asleep for awhile. That's a record as most people just hang on and grit their teeth all the time they are riding with Freas. It has been so cloudy all day that we are sure the couldn't have been shining at Sona Bata and we're very glad we came.

Arrived just at suppertime and met the Geils and the two single girls. They have three nice houses. One belongs to the Carpenters and still has their furniture in it. Their beds are marvelous—the first thing we look at when we arrive somewhere. So many of them have been so terrible.

Saturday, February 4 [Banza Manteke]

After breakfast Mr. Geil took us up on the water tower to see the country. The station is built on a ridge in the middle of a great area that is hemmed in by mountains all the way around. There are gently rolling hills and clumps of forest here and there that make this station one of the most scenic. Some people might call the surrounding country barren but it has the wild rugged beauty that we love.

We were to see a little more of the station but it began to rain and kept it up all day.

We really expected to take some pictures but of course couldn't on account of the rain. Dr. Freas got a lot of his operations done anyway. There is a sizeable hospital here but only a nurse to run it and Dr. Freas has to come down every month.

Sunday, February 5 [Banza Manteke—Sona Bata]

We read until time for church. After the singing I had time to plan my summer and fall wardrobe and going home costume. Had dinner with the Geils and then went down to see the famous power plant that Carpenter put in this last year. It is supposed to be a great engineering feat and it supplies the station with more electricity than they can use. They have electric refrigerators (others burn Kerosene) toasters, waffle irons, and a great water pump that gives them running water all the time. But I still think my Ray could do it too. He's just as smart as Carpenter any day, and could study up on it and maybe make a prettier power house.

Started home quite late, about 3, and after 50 kilometers something went wrong with the rear wheels. After taking it off, putting it on, taking it off, and putting it on, we proceeded on our way. This time of year everything is so green and lovely. The grass grows and grows and some of it, elephant grass, is twenty feet high!

On again! A full moon lit up the country side beautifully and we saw a number of animals. One we got very close to. It was some kind of lynx or something belonging to the cat family. Others we didn't get very close to but could see eyes shining in the darkness.

Monday, February 6 [Sona Bata]

Got out of bed this morning and was overcome by a dizzy spell. The sun was shining brightly, it would, so Ray went off with the kids and Mr. Lanoue. Ray was quite dissappointed at how the kids walk all over Lanoue and don't do what they are supposed to. They weren't able to finish the valley scene as the kids were so unruly they had to let them go home. Now a beautiful sunny afternoon is wasted because Lanoue says the kids are too tired and we can't get them back this afternoon. He and Ray went to the village to see about things and I slept most of the afternoon.

Tuesday, February 7

Mr. Lanoue said he couldn't give us any time today. We hoped to start in the village tomorrow but he has some boys coming in to register and can't help us then either. We feel that we just can't make a picture this way. The weather has been discouraging enough but now the missionaries are going back on us. Lanoue thinks we can get everything set up and ready and then just call him when we need an interpreter. But we just can't make a good picture that way. We can't ask for props or even get the people together, when we can't speak the language.

Wednesday, February 8

Dr. Freas and the four natives who have come in to play main parts in the picture went with us. The Chief tried to call the people for a meeting but they just wouldn't come. They went right on with their work and some even went off to the gardens. Some say that we are going to bury one of them in the graveyard we made! Others say that if we take pictures we will take their spirits home with us and they will die! Why did we ever have that graveyard built so near the village? The more civilized natives in the village go to the other extreme and say we will make a lot of money while they will get practically nothing. Now we are in a pickle!

The sun didn't appear all day and we waited impatiently to go back to the village at six when the people are eating. We were supposed to have supper at Freas but the picture is more important. We managed to get the men together but the women just wouldn't come. Erickson talked and talked to them and they finally agreed to help us. But they don't know about their wives and will tell us tomorrow. It doesn't sound very encouraging.

Everybody came to Freas then for regular prayer meeting. We left afterward as they are having a monthly business meeting. Its an important one to us and we would like to have stayed, as they are going over this picture business again and deciding who should help us. We wrote an outline of the things that remain to be done and asked for one man to help us throughout. Here's hoping we get one and that it isn't Lanoue. He can't very well be any help to us when he just isn't interested.

Went to bed wondering what the answers would be to these two momentous decisions. We've had more trouble and fuss here than anywhere but we still vow to make this our best picture!

Thursday, February 9

Got up early this morning and waited for someone to come and tell us the answers. Erickson finally arrived and started out with very bad news. The villagers all went off to their gardens this morning and obviously won't cooperate at all in the making of this picture. It doesn't speak very well for this mission—we just can't find a single village with enough Christians to help. We can't blame the Catholics, Salvation Armyists, and heathens for not being interested.

The next choice bit of news was that the missionarries decided we weren't cooperating! Imagine them deciding that without us there. And this is our life's work that we are more interested in than anything else. We can't very well cooperate all by ourselves. Later today we found that Lanoue is the one who thinks we aren't cooperating. Evidently his idea is that we should have done everything and then just called him when we were ready to shoot. He and Ray didn't make out very well the other day when I was sick and there were a number of misunderstandings on Lanoue's part.

But Dr. Freas has been freed to some extent and will help us! Thank goodness he at least, is interested in the picture and realizes how helpless we are without someone to translate. Dr. Tuttle has taken over all the hospital work and will play the part of the doctor in the picture as well. We gather from what Freas said that no one else is interested enough to give up any of their regular work. We think most of this is due to the fact that Carpenter and others of this mission wrote a scenario and sent it home, hoping to have the Committee accept it, in place of "Bwamba". But the Committee didn't and all their hard work was in vain.

Dr. Freas drove us out to a large village this afternoon, that has a powerful medal chief. We were delighted to find that it was Boko, the village where we were so royally welcomed last May. The Chief is a Christian and has quite a group of church members living around his house. He was enthusiastic about the picture and said we could live in the house next to his. It is a brick one, better than the house we have at the mission! The Chief has been a trader for years and is very wealthy. In fact he has two trucks and a passenger car! Despite this we found a section of the village that looks nice and old. And there are lovely palms all around. We planned to move in tomorrow and came home all pepped up again.

Now we find Dr. Freas has been called to Matadi by the state, to investigate an epidemic of spinal mengitis. He has to go tomorrow and won't get back out to the village till Tuesday. But we can get everything set in the meantime. Nfienge, who speaks English, has been released from hospital work to help us. He is a swell character and we should get along fine. Dr. Freas is going to travel back and forth as we have so many punk days (haven't seen the sun since Monday) and he might as well be doing his work at the hospital. Boko is twenty kilometers and he should make that in half an hour.

Miss Enbohm had Freas, Ericksons, and us to supper. Helped Freas show movies to Medical Boys and their wives. Were they terrible!!!

Friday, February 10 [Sona Bata—Boko]

Packed twice as much as usual in preparation for three weeks or a month at Boko. Beds, bedding, food, cooking utensils, etc. were added to our already heavy luggage.

Dr. Freas went off on his job and Ray chased down to the train after him with a copy of the scenario. Fortunately he got there in time. We finally got everything packed and ready to go in the truck.

Ray went over for the monkey and Mrs. Erickson said she wouldn't dream of letting him go with us! He would turn wild if he lived in a native village, we never paid any attention to him at Kimpese, and a lot of other childish reasons. This tops all for cooperation. We finally decided that we'd have to take the grown monkey even though he is so big that the kids can't hold him and so strong that we can't keep him in the trap we had made. It is going to be almost impossible to use him in the picture but what else can we do?

After a quick lunch Nfienge went around the village with us. We explained all the changes we want and he started right in on some of them. We also walked out aways and selected a site for our graveyard. The people here make fun of the others when we tell them how scared they were. But there is no telling what is going on inside these people anyway. We found a forest trail that we like too. Tomorrow we will get some workmen to help make the changes and build the graveyard.

Saturday, February 11 [Boko]

It rained off and on all morning so we couldn't do all the things we had planned. We spent a good part of the time out at the burial ground, choosing camera angles and seeing that the graves were put in the right places. Everybody who went by on the path stopped and joked about it. We were glad to see that they are enjoying it.

This afternoon we selected the little boys to be in the hunting scene. They seem even brighter than the ones we got at Sona Bata. We told them all about it and they are real interested. Here's hoping we can soon get that scene once and for all.

Had a real hard rain that lasted till after dark. We hope this means the end of this short dry season and indefinite weather. There has been no sun at all since the early part of this week.

Sunday, February 12

Church was supposed to be at nine but the gong didn't ring till eleven. And then the people staggled in until twelve. Ray told them all about us, the picture, and what we want them to do. Then there was a sermon and just as we thought we'd get out they started a communion service.

We sat right by the pastor in the very front as he poured the pink water into the glasses. When he got to the end of the row he kept right on pouring even though the last glass was missing. It spilled all over the floor and almost on us and I got giggling. It was awful and I didn't have a pillow or anything to stuff in my mouth. Just as I'd get myself under control Ray would give a snigger and start me off again. None of the natives thought it was a bit funny! Finally got out at two o'clock and we laughed and laughed all the way back to our house.

Monday, February 13

Woke up real early and saw the sun coming up. We jumped right up but by the time we were dressed the sky was all clouded over. We got all the people together and selected men and women to live in the old village. Some of them kicked a little about the clothes they can't wear but we think they'll do it allright. Mfienge got us three workmen and they built us a "John" and a shower room out of palm branches.

Wrote some letters and helped the men get everything ready for tomorrow when Dr. Freas is coming out. We will be ready to shoot in the village when he arrives. We have decided to do the hunting scenes a little later so that the villagers don't get tired of seeing us around.

The sun came out a little while this morning but didn't stay long enough to be of any use. We looked around again for settings and found one elegant place that looks like a stage. But we don't know what to use it for!

Tuesday, February 14

A package and note came from Sona Bata and Dr. Freas can't come out today! We were awfully disappointed at first but had only a little weak sunlight this afternoon. The note said Dr. Freas had to get off the train at Banza Manteke when he was on his way home yesterday. One of the girls is sick and as it is the one that is a nurse it must be serious or she wouldn't call for a doctor.

This afternoon we helped the men make a setting for the monkey scene. We pulled up bushes, planted banana trees, hung vines, and have a lovely setting.

Wednesday, February 15

Saw a little blue sky at 6 Am and had hopes of some sun. But it didn't shine all day. Bwamba got a bite on the eye anyway and it is so puffed up that we can't possibly use him till tomorrow.

Ngonda went off to market this morning so I made the beds. It sure was good to have something to do. Ray had the men build a hut interior outdoors so we can take pictures without lights. We will do it on one of these dark days. The only trouble is that we can't do them now as we need Dr. Tuttle and the grown up Bwamba. The workmen we hire built a bed and then spent most of the morning trying it out. We went over with the camera and found them all sitting in a row on it. They spend half the day sitting and at 3:30 or so Mfienge tells us they are tired and want to go home. That seems to settle it—they go home. There is no pushing the African. They work in their own slow way and quit when they feel like it. They usually feel like it three quarters of the time. Here in the village we can look in any direction at any time and see a man sitting. Ray might have made a good African but I am as far removed from them as the Eskimo.

Thursday, February 16

Wrote letters this morning and was interrupted by three women from another village. They came to see a young white woman! I never expected to be an oddity in this section of the country. White people have been through here for a hundred years. The Portugese traders came from Angola and many settled here in the lower Congo as it is a thickly populated area. I suppose there weren't any women in Africa in those days. My visitors were amazed at my height. I am taller than any of the missionaries and I suppose being young I should be small, according to the African. The natives here are all quite small and the women average not more than 5 feet 2 or 3. The women said "How wide & how high she is!"

This afternoon the sun fooled us again by appearing for half an hour. We hastily got the kids together and into their cloths. By then the sun was in so we just took them to stage 1 and rehearsed them a little. We gathered quite a crowd to see the first cinema taken and they were a very appreciative audience. When the two boys fought they all yelled and cheered as if they were in the picture too.

Friday, February 17

Today is the day of the fete in Leo. But Mrs. Coxill wrote saying that the troops do not parade. There is no sense of us going just for the school children.

Ray has been reading a book of literature and was quite impressed by Thoreau who walked at least four hours a day in order to do his thinking. So Ray went off this morning (he could only think for two hours) and came back with some good ideas. One is an introduction to a series of pictures for Loomis. We are going to write up a short scenario and send it with his letter. Just to show him we're really interested.

Every morning the chief has a lot of peanuts spread out on mats to dry out. One bedraggled looking man sits by them with a long stick to chase the pigeons, pigs, and chickens away. He gets sleepier and sleepier, while the animals are eating, and finally gives in and rolls over on his back fast asleep. Somebody yells, he jumps, gets slowly to his feet, walks slowly to the peanuts, chases the animals to one side, and drags himself to the shade of the tree. By the time he is seated the peanuts are being devoured again. He sits and looks at them. Then he starts falling asleep again and the whole process is repeated. He is a typical example of the African at work. We sit and watch him just for the laugh and wish we could get a movie of him just as he is.

The sun came out at 3:30 and we got the kids together again. This time we really managed to shoot a scene! It was a short one but nevertheless encouraging. The kids were very cute and I got a still of the tiniest boy peering into Ray's camera. It is awfully cute and I should think Eastman could use it.

Saturday, February 18

Dr. Freas came out early this morning and he and Ray hitched up an engine, wires, projector, and screen, so we can show movies tonight. After dinner the sun really shone again! We took the little boys hunting scene again and we hope this is the last time. It is our most difficult sequence as it all has to be done in one afternoon's shooting and the kids get so hot and tired. I spent most of the time washing their faces and giving them drinks. Our littlest hunter fell sound asleep when I was resting him on my lap for a minute. We left him out of a couple of scenes and then I had to wake him up again and make him run after the other little hunters. He did it but plodded along like a little old man—he was sooo sleepy. Kimbu got hurt in the fight scene and then we had an awful time with him and Bwamba. Kimbu cried eventually and all our native helpers wanted to let him go right home. But Ray is a slave driver and took pictures of him crying. He was supposed to lose the fight anyway. And the monkey bit Bwamba so that his finger bled a lot. We had to spend ten minutes consoling him and then he sulked. But it was finally finished and we put a beautiful bandage on Bwamba and made him and Kimbu beautiful pinwheels with fancy designs.

Had our movie show tonight and it was a roaring success. The natives howl and cheer at everything and how they love it.

Sunday, February 19

Suffered through another church service for the sake of our actors. Not so many of them were present though. Ray gave another movie talk. This time he used Dr. Freas movies as an example of why we can't take pictures unless the sun in out! Almost all of his pictures are badly underexposed so that the faces hardly show. The people got the point.

Monday, February 20 [Boko—Sona Bata]

Got really sick this morning and even a hot water bottle didn't help. I have been taking quinine because I have no more Atabrin and Dr. Freas says that is probably the cause. He came out this morning and decided to take me in to Sona Bata. We were thinking of going there anyway to shoot the little boys in two settings that we have been unable to find here. We had a storm then that lasted most of the afternoon. So there were no pictures at all. Ray wanted to go back to Boko tonight as we told the people to be ready early in the morning to have the first village pictures taken. But I wouldn't let him go without me and it seemed pretty late and stormy to be starting out.

Tuesday, February 21 [Sona Bata—Boko]

Got up at 5 AM to come back to Boko. Everybody wanted me to stay in bed and come out tomorrow but I felt allright and knew Ray would need me. Besides I haven't been away from him for a single day or night in almost a year and I'm not going to start now.

Got back about 6:30 and tried to get the people together. We had some difficulty with the men—they just don't want to be in the pictures without shirts. We finally took down all their names and promised to buy two yards of cloth for each one to wear in the picture. This will be good pay for them and will induce them to come.

Had breakfast about nine and then went to Madimba for the cloth. I also got a little food—we have been running short of vegetables. The sun wasn't out this morning anyway so we didn't lose much. After dinner we got the village ready and the people and were finally able to shoot. I set gourds, mortars, and fires, around in the village and made a sketch so that we can put them back the next time. Took a rather long sequence and hoped to take the graveyard scene too. But we had to wait for the sun a good bit and didn't have time to go out to the graveyard at all. But we got some really beautiful scenes and the people did very well.

Wednesday, February 22 [Boko]

Felt better this morning and helped Ray decorate our hut interior. It was cloudy so we had dinner without Dr. Freas even though he said he'd come. He did arrive about 1:30 and we got the people and went out to the graveyard. But by the time everybody and everything was ready the sun went in again. It looked very black and threatening so we gave up and let everyone go home. I wasn't a bit sorry to get home myself.

After supper Ray and I read awhile before going to sleep. The men were all having a confab on the porch and the noise was as bad as the goats. At least four men always talk at once and the sounds they produce are like an enormous cat and dog fight.

Thursday, February 23

Ray and I made some fetishes for the graveyard this morning. We didn't think it looked quite African enough when we were out there yesterday. Then we fixed up our hut interior again and took one sequence in there. Bwamba was supposed to be sick and during the shooting he fell asleep! Finished just at dinner time.

We expected the sun and Dr. Freas this afternoon but neither appeared. It gave me a chance to rest and get rid of my headache and Ray time to fill out the Consul Invoice and write a letter to go with it. This is all because we sent film home valued at over 100 dollars. Miss Bentley had to post a bond in order to get the film out of customs and then write to the American Consulate here for an invoice. Too bad nobody told us about the $100 limit. We could have sent our film in smaller lots.

Had one of our chickens for supper as we wanted to use the feathers for our fetishes. Played games on the porch and all the little boys in the vicinity gathered around. In the light of our little lamp they were all teeth and eyes smiling at us. But some arrived who had been eating stink fish and we had to chase them all away. Went to bed at nine so I will be sure to feel really well tomorrow.

Friday, February 24

Cloudy again! We did some writing this morning along with our cursing and wondered if it was at all worthwhile. After dinner the sun began to peek through so we went out to dress up the burial ground. We waited and waited for Dr. Freas without daring to call all the villagers together for fear he wouldn't show up. We have given up the idea of trying to shoot any scenes with Mfienge directing. He tends to confuse rather than help the actors. Finally 'Kipula' arrived at nearly 3 o'clock.

We got the people together very quickly and started right in. And then the clouds began getting in the way of the sun. We tried very hard to finish but the sun went down into a haze and it was impossible. The weather certainly has been discouraging and Ray is almost in despair.

After showers and supper we all felt better and got ready to show movies again. The natives have been asking to see the same ones they saw last week "because they went so fast". We showed two new reels and the snow pictures again. We didn't mind seeing them ourselves.

Saturday, February 25

For once the sun came out early so we All got up and had breakfast thinking we could start right in on a long scene and really accomplish something. But by the time we got the village ready at 7 AM the sky was all hazy again. We sat over there most of the morning waiting for it to clear and took one shot of the witch doctor going into his hut. This was for a prelude to the interior shots we took the other day.

By the time the sun came out it was so high in the sky that we couldn't do anything. Went home and helped Ngonda get dinner ready.

This afternoon we chose a site for the modern native village and made arrangements to have trees trimmed or cut down and a house fixed up for Ngoma.

Then we got our villagers together again and went out to finish the burial ground pictures. We tried to get all the fetishes and people back in the same places from a little sketch. By the time this was done the sun was lower— about the same as when we took the pictures yesterday. After the first few shots the darn sun went into some more haze. Ray just had enough light to finish his sequence and I got stuck with hardly any stills again. My camera isn't fast enough to take pictures when the actors are moving unless it happens to be a very bright day.

Sunday, February 26

We decided to celebrate our wedding anniversary today because we were married on Sunday and because we could be alone and together all day without pictures or anything to fuss with.

I gave Ray his first present after dinner. An itinerary map showing where we have stayed in Africa and the number of days in each place. He was tickled with it and put it in his record book for safe keeping.

Monday, February 27 [Boko –Sona Bata]

Dr. Freas arrived as we were eating breakfast and I hastily got a little more together for him. We hoped to do the long village scene but the sun was not shining brightly at all. Instead we had Dr. Freas take movies of us and a few stills. We spent the whole morning doing it and I sure am glad I'm not in the pictures. Its much nicer to be directing them.

After dinner we got the little boys and went to Sona Bata again. We got set up for a distance shot of the village there with the boys approaching. But the sky was too dull to shoot. We want clouds and lovely ones for this shot. Took the kids fighting again instead. Ray wasn't satisfied with what he got before. We had trouble with them again as they didn't want to do it and when we thought we were through we found the shutter closed! We had to bribe the boys to get them to do it again. But we got the pictures!

Tuesday, February 28 [Sona Bata—Boko]

Got up at 5:30 as the sun was rising and the sky was clear. Dashed around collecting the paper and the real cakes and getting ready to rush back to Boko for a morning scene. Then all of a sudden we looked out and found the whole sky overcast! We could have sat down and cried but sat down and had breakfast instead.

Then we had a meeting with Dr. Tuttle and Mr. Erickson to decide what to do about Dr. Freas trip to Banza Manteke this week end. Erickson says he isn't anxious to get into this picture business now and Tuttle can't leave the hospital very well with Freas away. And next week end Freas has to go to Leo. to the dentist as he is going home and they will be without one for a year! We have more interruptions with this picture than I ever thought possible. Erickson finally agreed to come out to Boko one morning, only one as he has a class at 8:30. I made out schedules for Freas, Tuttle, and Erickson, showing who should come when, if the sun shines. It is awfully discouraging to have things like this happen but what can we do?

After dinner we took the boys out and tried to get the scene we want. But the sky got worse all the time and we finally packed up for Boko. Joshua, the native chauffer brought us out.

Wednesday, March 1 [Boko]

When the sun saw us getting ready to shoot it promptly went in! We had an interior to shoot with Dr. Tuttle in it anyway so went ahead with that. A little hazy light leaked through when we finished the interior but it just didn't seem good enough to start a scene with. We were glad we didn't as a little later the thin light dissolved into nothing.

Walked out to see the sunset after supper and wondered if we should have a tower built so that we can see the sun in all its glory. Even though it thwarts us all day it goes down in a beautiful array of colors—more glorious than it ever does at home.

Thursday, March 2

Spent the morning finishing my records and writing a letter to Rogers that will certainly knock him or somebody dead. Ray told him just what I am doing for this project and in no uncertain terms that it would have failed without me. All this leading up to the fact that we want a credit title that reads "Mr. & Mrs. Ray Garner" and a little publicity as well. In the four pieces of publicity that we have seen we were mentioned only once and then hardly. "… Garner is combining the trip with his honeymoon." Here's hoping the letter has an effect.

This afternoon Dr. Tuttle came out again and the sun was really out. We shot two scenes with him in them and might have done a third if we hadn't had a number of waits for clouds that were shutting off our light. But its a good bit accomplished.

Friday, March 3

No pictures today. Erickson drove out this afternoon because he said it looked good when he left Sona Bata. But there wasn't a spot of sunlight when he arrived so he turned around and went home again.

The chief's court met again today out under the big mangoe tree by our house. We heard a commotion this afternoon and turned to see a man walloping his wife, who had a baby in her arms. Of course the whole court saw it too, a policeman rushed over and dragged the man into the court. They stood him up at the bar (which is for the accused to lean on) and had a noisy palaver then and there. That was quick justice all right.

Saturday, March 4

Clouds! Sat out on the porch all day working on letters, expense accounts, and records. Every once in awhile a lot of birds fly up under the porch roof and create such a wind that all our papers blow away.

Sunday, March 5

Spent the morning reading and just as we were ready for dinner it was time for church again. We voted in favor of the dinner and then got films, mail, etc. ready to go to Sona Bata. As the ticket will expire April 5th we have no time to lose. So we borrowed the Chief's car and son, for a chauffer, and went to Sona Bata ourselves. We went to Freas first and found six letters waiting for us. So we sat and read them and Mr. Watkins went off to the Leper camp in the meantime. Drove home by moonlight as the car lights went out.

Monday, March 6

Clouds all day! I wrote to Miss Brady who has long been neglected and Ray to Mr. Easson. The rest of the morning I spent gargling because I suspicion a sore throat coming on. Dr. Freas has had it and many of the natives are sick. It seems to be the time of year for it. I find it so hot in the middle of the day, or all day if the sun is out, and then in the evening I get real cold.

Tuesday, March 7

Got up at 6 AM as the sun was actually shining. We ate a hasty breakfast and then tried to get the villagers together. I rushed around getting props and setting up the village scene. Dr. Tuttle and Mr. Erickson arrived about 7:45 and we had high hopes of getting one of our big scenes. The men didn't appear however and not all of the women. And before we knew it the sun was gone! The whole sky clouded over and looked so hopeless that the men went back to Sona Bata.

We got a letter from the Cameroun saying that they had to close the Industrial School and there is so little else for us to photograph that there is no sense in our coming! Of course the 35 MM would make it worthwhile but we must have another camera. We wonder if the Committee will have us shoot the 35 in Congo or if we won't do it at all???

This afternoon Mr. Erickson came back and we took two sequences. Little "Bwamba" was sick and felt so badly that we didn't dare do a third even though the sun was good. Took stills of our helpers and Ngonda's family who came from his village especially for them. We are going to have them developed in Leo. and give them prints to hold their interest until we can finish this picture.

Wednesday, March 8

Clouds and market day made it impossible for us to do any thing this morning. This afternoon the sun came out and Mr. Erickson arrived about 1:30. He sat and read a newspaper until we said we were ready to shoot! By then a storm was approaching from the south and it looked as if we wouldn't get any pictures. We had a rehearsal and then it looked too dark to do anything. Mr. Erickson went home as he didn't want to get wet.

Later the storm went by and we took more stills for our helpers and the couple whose house we are living in.

Thursday, March 9

It was so cloudy and cool this morning that we thought it a good time to develope some of our films. Ray did two before it got too hot while I got some of my mending done. This afternoon there were a few holes in the clouds but not enough to do any shooting.

Friday, March 10

Got up early to develope more films while it was cool. I did two and got Ray to do another. He suddenly discovered that we have been living with a microscope this last week and not using it. I dragged him away from it for one film but after that he kept his eye on it all day. It is lots of fun looking at butterfly's wings, ants, feathers, copper, and any thing we can find, at close range.

Saturday, March 11

Got a surprize this morning when Ngonda told us that the natives do not like Erickson and do not want him to come out to help with the picture! This is supposed to be the stronghold of the mission. The chief is a medal chief and is over other villages and he is very much of a christian. We are working with the christians that have known Erickson for years. We don't consider this a real drawback as Dr. Freas will be back soon and we have a good reason to keep him working with us—as a last resort of course.

Freas had to go to Leo. this week end and we do hope when he comes back this time he won't have to dash off somewhere else.

This afternoon I was making fudge and heard a kid yelling and yelling. When the fudge got to the beating point I went to investigate and found a witch doctor (not in regalia) cutting a little girls arms and legs to let her rheumatism out! They were rubbing some black acid in the cuts, also to help the rheumatism. Ngonda told me all about it and as the process was about finished I couldn't do' a thing. The little girl belongs to a christian family whose brick house we live in, who own a typewriter, sewing machine, and still camera better than ours, and whoese Mother had her last baby in comfort at Sona Bata hospital. There's no telling what the African will do next!

A woman from Sona Bata brought us a letter from Don and a cable from New York. "Travel budget exceeded. Cameroun cancelled. Mailing 35 scenario involving Bolenge. Cable if backtracking required. If Eyemo unusable, unborrowable, use 16."

Monday, March 13

The sun appeared about ten o'clock this morning but as we had no one here to help us we couldn't do even a short scene.

Mr. Erickson came out this afternoon bringing his wife but not our meat, for which we could have choked him. They visited with the monkey while we got our scene ready. We shot it without any trouble as it was a short one and there was plenty of sun. Unfortunately Erickson didn't bring the older "Bwamba" so we couldn't do anything else. He sent for him but as he didn't come to his house by One o'clock Erickson left without him. Too bad because the one small scene we took wasn't worth the expense of bringing the car out here. We are about thru with afternoon scenes and will have to get some morning light in order to finish. In the afternoon the huts in the village are all in shadow so we have to do the important scenes in the morning.

Tuesday, March 14

We found that the chief's truck was going to Madimba with a load of smelly cassava so we had dinner early and went with it. I felt as if I was going on a real shopping expedition even in the handful of native stores. We had little Minsoto [Bwamba] with us and were going to buy him a shirt. But we found a little coat that fit him exactly and couldn't resist it. Then we bought him a belt and a whistle. We looked in every store before we found a shirt that would fit him. He was tickled pink and felt very rich I'm sure.

Wednesday, March 15

The sun came out about nine o'clock this morning and it shone brightly all day. But we had no one to help us and our villagers were all off to market. We felt like kicking everything and everybody.

Ray did two more films this morning and I did some mending. (Not sewing—I can't leave myself open to that 'So what!) After dinner it got so hot that we had absolutely no energy left and it was an effort to hold a book up. I fell asleep on the bed but a group of men came over to look at the negatives that were hung in the window right over my head.

Thursday, March 16

The sun came out at nine o'clock again but we had no one to help us. I fixed two of Ray's shirts and he cut out an automobile and mounted it for a picture for little "Bwamba". Then I told him that the two men in the car were Tata Garner and Tata Freas, which he very gullible swallowed. I made a mask for the kids out of a paper plate and it looks a lot like Freas with eye glasses and all.

A boy on a bicycle came from Sona Bata with our meat and a note from Freas. He wanted to know who he should bring for the pictures. Imagine our surprize when at two o'clock Erickson drove up! The main purpose of the trip was to play the radio for the natives tonight and the one scene we could take in the afternoon was incidental. We told Erickson all this the other day but he came out anyway. Dr. Tuttle has been putting up a kick about Freas leaving the hospital so much (most of it hasn't been for us though) and he says Erickson promised to help with the afternoon scenes. We took the one scene and were pleased with it as the natives did very well.

Last week we let our witchdoctor and his boy, who is Kimbu in the picture, go to Sona Bat for a vacation. Erickson brought them back today, the kid with all his hair shaved off, and Nsiata with his clipped very short. We could choke them. We have been saying "No haircuts" to them for a month. Now what can we do?

We have taken one scene allready that is followed by another that is supposed to be the same day. And we have three other scenes that the witchdoctor is the chief actor in, all taking place within three days time. And he looks terrible with his haircut where he looked very distinguished before. I gave the barber a can and told him to collect as much hair for us as we can. We'll have to try pasting it on.

Friday, March 17

We have written to Mr. Coxill asking if it is possible to borrow a 35 camera from someone in Leo.

This afternoon Ray started to help the man next door take some pictures. He has a good plate camera but doesn't know much about using it. But just as they were ready the sun went in! I guess every camera is a fetish against the sun—not just ours.

Saturday, March 18

Today I passed another milestone. I'm getting entirely too old I'd say. I had Ray fooled for awhile—he thought I was only 23 today.

You'd think there might have been sun on my birthday. But the clouds were as black as ever this morning. Dr. Freas sent a note saying he would come out at 5 o'clock this afternoon and give a radio and movie show tonight.

Were very glad to see 'Kipula' after 19 days and had lots to talk about. Heard that Germany had taken the rest of Checko-Slavakia. We aren't quite as late hearing this I hope, as we were in hearing about the Pope's death. We were just reading about Chamberlain's visit to him two weeks after he was dead!

Freas gave the people a pep talk along with the show and we hope it works.

Sunday, March 19

We had quite a rain last night and woke up this morning to find the sun shining! But it is Sunday and the day is lost so far as our pictures are concerned.

Ray developed the stills of me that he took yesterday before we went to church. It wasn't so long today for which we were very thankful. We feel that we have to go in order to keep the good will of the Christians that are in our movies.

After dinner I read some more of "The Fool Hath Said" to Ray. We think it is swell and it is certainly teaching us a lot about the New Testament. It is beautifully written and puts down all the facts both for and against Christianity. A modern search for God it is called and it is indeed modern.

Dr. Freas brought us some contact paper so we got set up for printing this afternoon. We borrowed a gasoline lamp in order to expose the prints properly. Ray rigged up a bottle, basin, and pail, so that we could wash the pictures with running water. He's really very smart. After supper we started printing and let "Bwamba" and the favored few watch the prints come up. We worked until we were so tired we were ready to drop.

Monday, March 20

Were really disappointed this morning when we woke up and found no sun. This picture is going to take six months at this rate and the Committee will be having a fit.

We mounted the pictures this morning in little folders of matstock. Then Ray put a line around them with india ink which made them look real elegant. I lettered the names and the date on them and all the recipients were delighted.

This afternoon the sun came out and we took some more stills for the natives. The old Chief dressed up in his uniform and state medals. And Mongongo wore my shoes. I took them off and gave them to him this morning because he liked them so much, by sign language.

Tuesday, March 21

Ray wrote to the Ka-na-da-his today and I worked on my article a bit. I wonder if anything will ever come of my efforts. We hope to take a few stills to go with it and so increase its value.

Wednesday, March 22

Some men were sitting in the court this afternoon and they gave Ray a name. It is Mpangala—which means one who jumps all around doing things and playing with the little boys. The Africans are so slow and lazy that they think he is energetic and I think he is slow and lazy.

Tonight there were stars and we looked at a few. A sliver of new moon showed just after the sun went down and all the kids sang and danced when they saw it. I thought it was something really exciting the way they went on but it is just because they like to play in the moonlight so much.

Thursday, March 23

Looked out at 6 AM and saw blue sky and a few wisps of pink cloud. I got Ray up in two minutes this morning and we danced and sang all the time we were getting dressed. While waiting for Freas we got out all the props and went to see about getting the village set up. Freas collected most of the people and then we sat down to breakfast. But some clouds were moving over head and we were not quite so optimistic.

We rehearsed two scenes this morning and told the people to come back at two o'clock. We decided to do the poison cup scene if it cleared. It looked as if it would so after dinner we got all set up again. But the sun didn't come out. As fast as one layer of clouds moved away we'd find another layer underneath, still obscuring it. At 3:30 we gave up as it was too late to start any scene. A whole day wasted! Our time doesn't matter so much but the people are so impatient and Dr. Tuttle is having a fit because Freas has already had to give us so much time.

Friday, March 24

Heard it raining in the night and woke up to find the morning wet and drippy. It wasn't actually raining but every tree and every bit of air was dripping moisture. It was just like we imagined African rainy seasons.

The people have taken to calling me Mama Mpangala so the name must fit me too. They usually give people different names even if they are married. The wife out here doesn't take the husband's name when they marry either. I am getting use to the Mama although it does seem funny to have men, women, and children, calling you that.

Saturday, March 25 [Boko—Sona Bata]

Got all ready to shoot again this morning. The sky was very blue at 6 AM but by 7:30 when Dr. Freas arrived it was getting very cloudy. Again we had to let the villagers go and collect all the props etc. We had a palaver with our witch doctor too who refused to let us stick the hair on him. He was afraid it was dirty and he would get sick. We said we'd sterilize it—then that we'd cut some fresh hair off of Ngonda. He refused flatly and he and Dr. Freas argued at length. I was furious and to think that a pastor, who is supposed to be an outstanding Christian, would do this. There are superstitions connected with hair and nails and an African can have nothing to do with those of anyone else without bringing the wrath of the ancestors down on his head. This seemed to be back of Nsiata's refusal but when Freas got thru talking I guess he was more afraid of being kicked out of the church and his job. Why did he ever get his hair cut in the first place? When asked that he said, "Oh, let them get somebody else if they don't like it." And this is what we get for treating these people like whites, playing with them, making stills for them, etc. It is too bad that Nsiata has such a terrifically large and important part in the picture.

Decided to go to Sona Bata this afternoon with the little boys. The sky was cloudless when we left Boko with 11 kids, 4 adults, the monkey, and a great load of stuff and things. The car was crammed just about as full as it could be. We arrived about 2:30 and set up for a shot immediately. We got one and then some dopey Belgians came along and had to see Dr. Freas for ten minutes. A storm blew up out of the West and covered the area of sky we were using that had nice clouds in it so we let the kids go.

Rogers sent two scenario outlines—The 'Saga of the River' and 'What a Missionary Does in Africa.' He thinks we can do both on the small amount of 35 MM film we have, if we can fix our camera or borrow another. We can't do either. Or he figures we have enough 16 MM film left to do them both. We have just about enough to finish the scenarios we now hold. The dope! We'll have to send a cable asking for both film and camera.

We don't approve of the two outlines. The first covers too great a story and will take months, and money, to do properly. The second is, after all, what we have already done with Washburn in a different form. And it seems a little amateurish to us. Of course, we have only an outline—the scenario may be better.

Sunday, March 26 [Sona Bata]

Decided to send a letter instead of the cable so that Rogers will understand the whole story and make plans accordingly. Ray worked on the letter all afternoon and I made out a list of all the sequences we still have to shoot for our original scenarios.

The Freas told us today that they knew nothing of "The Story of Bwamba" until two days before we arrived last May. Then the station said it was impossible to film such a story at Sona Bata. The Ericksons had approved a different scenario in N.Y. and said they weren't at all interested in this one. Ross apparently heard all this last summer as he approved the writing of another scenario, "Tulanda". A number of missionaries spent a lot of time on it and sent it to Rogers for approval. They got the characters chosen, village etc. and were ready to help us with it. Then Rogers refused the story and left us to make "Bwamba" in the most civilized section of Africa. No wonder there have been so many difficulties.

Monday, March 27

Dr. Freas woke us up about seven to say that it was clearing. We looked out and didn't think it was particularly promising and decided to stay and finish with the little boys. Had breakfast and by nine o'clock the whole sky was clear. We could have kicked ourselves. Why is the sun always out at the wrong time.

We rode over to the village to see if the light would be good enough for a morning scene. Decided it wasn't and went to our little house to hang all our clothes out to air. Then back to Freas and the letter. Had to stop and go to Tuttle's for dinner.

Dashed back to Freas and got the kids ready for the pictures. Ray and I set up and we were all ready to shoot when the clouds were just right. But Dr. Freas didn't come and didn't come. He arrived too late because another car with some state people came. We waited and waited for it to be right again. I wrote the rest of the letter while Ray dictated and then rushed home to type it. It was so long I thought I'd never finish. The mail boy had to leave and the train was in the station as I sent the letter off with a boy on a bike. He made it but I was a wreck from rushing so long. Went back to Ray and found him having an awful time with the kids. They wanted to eat and wouldn't keep their costumes on and kept wandering away. We sent for Freas, who was off at the hospital, and decided to shoot this and the village scene even though the clouds were messy. It was nearly five and we had to rush to get through before the sun went down. Ray was disgusted because he didn't get the beautiful scenes he wanted for the opening of the picture and I was completely exhausted. Went back to showers and food and felt better. Freases went to a medical meeting and we were left to play the Victrola to our hearts content.

Tuesday, March 28 [Sona Bata—Boko]

Got up early and off for Boko as it looked promising again this morning. But we got a flat tire! There was no spare so it meant a patching job that held us up a good while. When we got to Boko it was 8:30 and two of our main characters had gone off as well as most of the villagers. The clouds behind the village were not good and Ray was afraid it would be too late to do anything by the time we got the people all here. He is wary of shooting now because he doesn't want to spoil any more scenes. I feel sure that all the scenes we have are very good but he always feels that the clouds or lighting or something is wrong.

Wednesday, March 29 [Boko]

Another day of clouds and intermittent rains. We couldn't even get the few stills we wanted.

It looks as if we won't finish by the end of next week when we are due at Leo for the parade. We shall hate traipsing back here again and dragging the people out for the few remaining scenes. I don't think we should miss that parade though as there is no telling when there will be another one. I'll be glad of the change from here and Sona Bata though. We have been here as long as I used to be in camp, nearly two months, with almost nothing to do.

Saturday, April 1

I woke Ray up this morning telling him that the sun was shining. When I said "April Fool" he went back to bed again. Then the sun fooled me by coming out! We got up and had breakfast because I was afraid it would go in again. It did too so we let the people go and didn't bother setting up the village. About 8:30 it came out again and Freas arrived. Much to our horror we discovered the Chief had gone to another village. As he plays an important part we had to get him.

I went off in the car leaving Ray and Freas to get the village ready. The road was terrific and I hit a stump once that stopped the car dead. But I got Bangu and somehow limped back to Boko.

Started our scene much too late and Ray was ready to die because he had to do it. The people were all gathered again and even Freas said his time was valuable and pushed us into it. I helped push Ray too because we have had so little morning light and the dry season starts in May and there are no clear mornings then. Its just impossible to get [beautiful] clouds, sun, people, and interpreter all at the same time.

Worked hard for three hours and didn't finish till 1 o'clock. The shadows were very short but I guess it can't be helped.

Sunday, April 2

I went on strike today and refused to attend another church service that doesn't mean a thing. Ray was only too glad to join me and we spent the day writing letters.

Ray worked on George's photography report and a long letter to go with it. He started at 8 o'clock this morning, took time out only for meals and to see the sunset, and didn't get through till 9 o'clock tonight! He sure can work when he wants to.

Tuesday, April 4

This morning it was fairly clear so we got up and started to get things ready. Dr. Freas arrived at seven and we were thrilled at the idea of getting an early start. Then we discovered that our chief and the poison cup victim had gone to Kifwa! Ngonda swore they had started walking when he left on his bike so we went ahead with preparations and hoped they would come. Then we found that our drummer had gone off in another direction to a funereal! Dr. Freas had to go after him in the car and by the time he got back the other two wanderers had come and we were ready to shoot.

I spent a very hectic morning taking movies of Ray as he photographed the poison cup scene, and stills of him besides my regular stills. In between I kept records of every shot and wondered if I was coming or going. We had a few waits for sun and didn't get through till 12:30. Had dinner and Dr. Freas left us both so tired I wonder how we did anything else. But we took more stills of the chief actors—for them—and I took some portraits of Ray.

Wednesday, April 5

Woke up early and found it cloudy so gave up hope of doing anything to-day. I developed a film before breakfast and another one after. Then it began to clear and we had just sent all the people off to market. I was getting ready to do a third film when Dr. Tuttle drove up at 9 o'clock. We never expected to see him so late but decided to split a scene and start with him arriving in the deserted village and finding Bwamba. We had an awful lot of waits for sun as the clouds seemed to be moving in every direction. Finally we finished at 12 just as a thunder storm came up.

After dinner and the rain we got ready to take a forest scene. The sun went in again just as we were ready and we had to wait for another shower to pass by. Finally got the shot—it was only one—and dashed to the modern native village for the last scene that Dr. Tuttle and little Bwamba are in. It was 4:30 by then and I thought we couldn't do it. But it suddenly cleared and we actually finished. What a break! We were so glad to get rid of Bwamba who has been beefing and belly aching for two weeks or more. After all we've given him too. I am afraid we spoiled him.

Thursday, April 6

Ate breakfast early as we were not expecting Dr. Freas it was so cloudy. But he came, arriving at seven, because there were a few blue holes. The parade is off! The celebration of King Albert's birth has been dropped in

Belgium so it will be dropped here too—even though we did plan to photograph it.

Got a swell letter from Rogers in answer to Ray's 'knock em dead' one. He said we would both be mentioned in all future credit titles and that we will be given publicity but they are saving most of it till we reach N.Y. He even agreed that the Project should have been planned more carefully in the beginning! And he will try to sell any articles I might write for us. I'm thrilled over this as there will be no trouble over having pictures to accompany them and we may be able to make a little money.

We found ourselves with no food because we planned to go to Leo. and didn't even order meat and butter. So we decided to have the Chief's son drive us to Inkisi so we could go on a spending spree.

It is quite a town, about 20 miles away, but in the opposite direction from Sona Bata. We bought all kinds of things to eat that we haven't been able to get. Jam, chocolat, canned fruit, spaghetti, and of all things fresh pears. They taste marvelous to us even though they are rather green—having come from Belgium on the streamer. Got Mongongo a shirt—his has been falling off—and a penknife. Found an elegant pair of brown and white canvas shoes that Ngonda liked. I think it better to buy them presents than tip them at the end and they seem to like the idea too. Ray found seven pith helmets for the Kanadahi like his. They only cost 33 francs, $1.12, and are really swell. We hope to find three more so there will surely be enough. We hope there will even be two left over for us when we get home.

We hoped to take the hats home with us but Rogers has sent us the new 35 MM camera and enough 16 MM film for another picture. So we will be doing the two extra pictures and will never get home by August. We hope to find a missionary who will take them for us.

Friday, April 7

Just as we were about to eat breakfast Dr. Tuttle arrived. He says he wants to help some now as Freas has so much work to catch up. We dashed to the village, even though it wasn't very clear, and got ready to shoot the scene of the people fleeing. We skipped breakfast entirely because there was so much to do.

Between each shot we had long waits for the sun. Swift moving clouds would come over it as fast as a clear area formed. But we got some swell pictures! The people did very well and we think this will be one of our best and most dramatic scenes.

Didn't finish until noon because of the long waits, which nearly drove us frantic. It is awful to have to shoot under such poor conditions.

Read awhile this afternoon and then took close-ups of the monkey and little Lemba as they were supposedly watching the boys fight. We never got these scenes when we took the rest of the hunt. When we were all through at five o'clock Ray decided he might have had the shutter closed all the time. And here I am all scratched up from holding the darn monkey in position. Went home and rigged up a red flag on the fade-in lever so that he can't leave it shut without our knowing it. Its very clever—but why didn't we do it before?

Saturday, April 8

It looked pretty dull this morning but Dr. Tuttle came and insisted we ought to get something. We set up and rehearsed the scene hoping the sun wouldn't come out because it was too late to start an important scene. By nine it did appear but there were clouds all around and so few holes that it would have taken hours to shoot the scene. Tuttle was pretty hot and bothered but we did our best to console him. They seem to be trying to rush us through this picture now in order to get rid of us in a hurry. But we are more anxious to get away than they are to get rid of us.

I got supper tonight as Ngonda had to work on his house. The state has decreed that the grass for fifty yards around each house must be cleared. We are having a time keeping our village intact. As soon as we get one more scene there will be another lapse in time, of two years this time, and they can cut all the grass they want to. There usually isn't much anyway in front of a house. I suppose the State wants to get the trash cleared out of the back yards.

Sunday, April 9

Woke up to find the sun rising, as it should on Easter morning. It was a beautiful day although not at all like Easter in New York.

We went to church and partook of the dirty bread and burned water again. But we thought it was even more symbolical than communion at home. The church was crowded with people, dressed in their best for the occasion, and happy to have us to share their communion. The church was decorated with arches of palm and great yellow flowers for the occasion.

Monday, April 10

The sky was pretty clear this morning and when Dr. Freas arrived at 7:15 we were all ready to shoot. The sun went in a bit then but by 8:00 the sky was actually cloudless! The first time we have seen this phenomenon and we took advantage of it and finished our scene by 10 o'clock!

Dr. Freas left then with instructions about tomorrow and we ate breakfast. It seemed funny to have the pictures finished for the day so early in the morning. But it got pretty cloudy and we were thrilled that for once the gods were on our side.

Planned a feast for all our helpers and actors with Mfienge. We gave them 300 francs, which is a small fortune to them, to buy all kinds of stuff. The date has been set for Thursday night and we hope to finish by then. There are two long sequences still to be shot.

Tuesday, April 11

Didn't see a sunbeam all day. We hoped to finish "Bwamba" by Thursday when the big feed is scheduled. If we don't we wonder if the people will come after they've had their pay or if they will find it more convenient to go off and work in their gardens. There's no telling what these folks will decide to do. But we still can finish Thursday if we get some sun.

Wednesday, April 12

This morning the sky was banked with clouds and it looked absolutely hopeless. But by 8:30 the sky had miraculously cleared. If only someone had been out here we might have finished one of our scenes.

Wrote two letters this morning. Ngonda went to Madimba and got a new typewriter ribbon and some carbon for us. Ours were so worn we could hardly type the new "Bwamba" scenario and our records with them.

Mfienge and the actors were gripeing again today. Ray says they tell him they want to go home about every day. Its a wonder they wouldn't realize that we do too and how helpless we are until the sun comes out. We long and long for a movie to while away a little of our time.

Thursday, April 13

Clouds all morning. It cleared nicely this afternoon and when we got the monkey all ready to shoot, about four, it got cloudy again. The monkey got away and led us a merry chase all over the village. Everybody had grand fun running away from him—they are all afraid of being bitten—and we got some exercise chasing him.

A note came from Sona Bata saying that there is to be a parade on Sunday! We wrote saying we would go to it even if we do not finish "Bwamba". We need the pictures for two of our scenarios and native troops are of particular interest now to the war minded public. The fare to Leo. third class, is so cheap that it will pay us to make the trip and leave some of our baggage there. Otherwise we pay high rates on all our excess stuff.

The contact printing paper arrived at last and we made 84 prints tonight. We were awful tired but wanted to finish up the paper and developer as we will not do any more developing in Africa.

Friday, April 14

Still clouds. Our last hope of finishing before we go to Leo. tomorrow, is buried under a blanket of clouds. Spent the morning trimming pictures and mounting them for the natives. The few we finished, with black line border and lettering, were received with great delight. We have some very good prints this time.

Our yard was full of preparations for the feast today. The little boys killed, plucked, and cut up chickens. When they were all through the meat was pretty feathery, here and there, and Mfienge made them do them over. The men butchered goats, and cut up every bit of them for cooking. The big feed was supposed to be at 3 PM which would have been ideal for me to take stills. But the weather was very unusual and it rained so hard that the big event did not start till 4:30. Little Lemba was waiting the whole time with a big bowl and a spoon! He was the first on the spot when the time came.

All the tables in the village were put in a row and the church benches brought out to sit on. The women all came with their babies on their backs and their bowls or basins balanced on their heads. A big spoon was usually sticking out of the bowl as it would get more than fingers. The men sat on one side of the table and the women on the other. The little hunters felt very proud to have a place at one table as all the other kids had to squat on the ground in circles and lick the empty pots.

We counted 85 people in all and when their plates were heaped they sang a hymn and had a prayer. Then the fun began and chicken, goat, rice, beans, rolls, manioc, and coffee began to disappear like cake in our house.

Ray and I then retired to do our act. I dressed up in my native dress, tied a borrowed black baby on my back, and carried our plates and glasses on my head. Ray wore the witch doctor's cloth, fetishes, and headress. When we appeared the natives went wild! We walked all around the table amid their howls of delight. Our supper was ready on the end table and we sat there to eat it. My bare feet attracted the most attention of all! They just never had seen white feet before! All the kids, and many of the women, came and peered under the table.

When we first arrived they had begun their sing song and hand clapping—(the one they change the words to fit any occasion.) This time it was "Oh, we used to be sad about the pictures but now our troubles are over, only two more times!"

Saturday, April 15 [Boko—Sona Bata—Leopoldville]

More clouds. We found a break big enough to shoot a few close-ups of the monkey but that was all. We got all ready to leave but by ten o'clock Joshua still hadn't come and we were beginning to wonder if Dr. Freas had forgotten us. Just before eleven who should drive up but Lanoue, with Mr. & Mrs. Hall. They are down from Leo. for the week end. Piled everything in, Mr. Lanoue, Ray and the Monkey in the back. Ray sat on a box with the monkey underneath.

Got to Sona Bata just in time for lunch and then packed our clothes and films etc. Had a little while to read before dressing and going to the train.

Lutete met our train. When we got outside the station and were getting ready to get in the car a woman came up and shook hands with me. She said "Kiambote, Jinny." and I nearly fell over. It was One of the women from Boko.

We felt like hicks in a big city after our native village. Got slicked up for supper—the U.M.H. is crowded with folks on their way home.

Sunday, April 16 [Leopoldville]

After breakfast Ray called Mr. Coxill and found that the parade was to be the biggest military review ever held in Congo with the troops in full war regalia. We decided to try to get it with the 35 mm camera as it seemed so newsworthy.

Lutete took us and Mr. Engwall down to reviewing stand where we set up three movie cameras and made the two other photographers look cheap. The GG arrived at 9 o'clock and the review began on the dot. We took pictures furiously and were horrified that the parade was over so soon. We felt that we didn't have half enough and no close-ups of the GG. I suggested dashing to the GG's house before he got his plumed hat off and asking him to pose. Everybody laughed but when we asked Mr. Coxill what he thought he said sure, go ahead. So Ray ordered the GG around and had him salute Mr. Engwall who was supposed to be the troops. He got a big kick out of it and went around telling everybody that the GG saluted him three times. It was fun but I didn't like photographing troops. When I saw them coming down the street with band playing and war paraphanalia strapped all over them, I almost burst into tears. I really had to keep swallowing hard so that I could take the pictures!

Monday, April 17

Decided to stay over today as we couldn't get anything done yesterday with stores and everything closed.

Mr. Watkins helped us get our films ready and took us to customs. It took us all morning to renew our sheet and get the films sent off.

Watkins brought a young American photographer to meet us this morning, Bill Bonsor. He was with the Gatti expedition but seems to have had some difficulties with Gatti and was eased out because of the low finances. Gatti hasn't even given him fare home and he didn't put up the bond with the Government, as he was supposed to. Consequently Bill is living with the Halls and Watkins free of charge and waiting for the Gov. to send him home or collect the money from Gatti.

We went over to Watkins tonight to see him but got into a game of Monopoly. Then we went to Bill's room and gabbed our heads off. He is a New Yorker, has worked with society photographers taking stills in night clubs, etc. and has done adds for merchandise in McCreery's and Peck and Peck's. The ones we saw were'nt much. He showed us a few of the stills he was able to get without Gatti's knowledge (he counts every piece of enlarging paper) and without being at all predjudiced we think they weren't much. The subjects were interesting of course but the pictures were not artistic in any sense of the word.

Learned that reflectors of gold metallic paper are the best. If we had only had them instead of our ineffectual white cloth, we might have lit up the front of our huts. And our interiors would be vastly improved.

Gatti does not wait for sun! We can't agree with this—he must be getting just pictures. He is way behind schedule anyway and hasn't started a picture he is supposed to have at the World's Fair.

Bill was surprized that we won't shoot unless we have good lighting conditions. The chief photographer for Gatti, Harry Squires, shoots at almost any time.

Tuesday, April 18 [Leopoldville—Sona Bata—Boko]

Got up at 6 AM and had breakfast. Lutete sent a boy to buy meat and vegetables for us and we were off to the train in the pouring rain. It left at 7 so we didn't have time to think before we were on our way back to Boko.

Were so sleepy we nearly rode by Sona Bata. Erickson met us and we went to Freas' to pick up some things. Drove right out to Boko. The sun was shining by this time and we saw some of the bluest sky Africa has yet produced.

Wednesday, April 19 [Boko]

Got up very early as we woke up and found the sun shining in our window. We got ready to shoot but Dr. Freas didn't come. There were some clouds over Sona Bata way but we thought sure he'd be along. Had breakfast and still he didn't arrive. By 8:30 there wasn't a cloud in the sky but it was too late for him to leave Sona Bata then. We suffered all morning because it was so beautifully clear and we might have done most of our remaining work. Hell and damn!

Worked on our scenario today and got it done except for the scenes we still have to shoot. I got a few of my still records done too. They have been piling up as usual so that there are a lot of them to do. Ray's movie records are way behind again too.

Thursday, April 20

Had breakfast very early as the sun was shining. Dr. Freas came this time but the sky was all clouded over when he arrived. Gave him his breakfast while we continued preparations for the scene. When it still looked hopeless at 8:30 we let the villagers go. Then the sun came out!

We divided our scenes again and took one sequence with Bwamba and his caravan and a family who were running away from the village. Then we fixed up our hut interior and got ready to shoot the last of it. The sun was shining very brightly by this time and we had to pin sheets up over the interior to shut out the sunlight! If we had only known and kept the people and if Dr. Freas had only been here yesterday we might be finished today instead of fooling around with short sequences. All this extra delay means we will miss the H.C.B. boat and have to wait eons for another.

Dr. Freas left after dinner with many instructions for the state administrator. We hope to get him out here tomorrow afternoon and shoot the taking of taxes etc. for 'How an African Tribe is Ruled." We can't do a thing on "Bwamba" in the afternoons and might as well catch up on some of our other work.

Friday, April 21

Rain most of the day. Our hopes of getting the H.C.B. boat are now wetted down to a soggy mass. Are we ever ever going to finish this x%#xx$ picture! The Chief called in a mob of men today so we could take our pictures with the state man. Dr. Freas saw him about it yesterday and we hoped to shoot a few scenes with him for "How an African Tribe is Ruled". We sent a boy to

Madimba to tell him to come at 2 o'clock if it cleared. We even got all slicked up, but it didn't clear.

Mungongo came and asked Ray, by signs, why he had a tie on and his face clean. That shows how native we've been getting.

Got Ray's records nearly up to date. Now if I can get him to help with mine we'll be all ready for our next picture.

Saturday, April 22

At one pm the sun came out and we decided to send a note to the state man. Ngonda went with it but the state man didn't arrive till about 3:30. We had about 400 natives, that the chief called in, but couldn't do a thing with them until we had some one to talk to them. We had fits because we heard that the guy didn't speak any English and thought we'd have to talk to Ngonda and have him talk to the state man.

But he recalled school day English and as time went on talked quite fluently. The sun went in as soon as we set our camera up and then it poured rain. I sat the men on the porch and tried to locate some tea. But there was none in Boko and I finally had to squeeze our last two oranges. That wasn't enough so we added some pineapple, scraped, and some water. Had some crackers to serve with the drinks but what a way to entertain these formal Belgians.

Monsieur Godisiabois came in a car but it went on to Inkisi leaving him here. He is from an outpost above Leo. where there are no roads, no shirts, and the Africans still look like Africans.

Sunday, April 23

By the time we had breakfast together this morning we were pretty good friends and had decided to take our state pictures in the Bamfununga country. M. Godisiabois is going back there in a week or so and will be traveling by hammock through the country. The people sound so wonderful to us that we are determined to go with him, or meet him up there.

Godi's car finally arrived this morning and we parted with good intentions of meeting soon and planning our safari. Ray and I are all excited about it—at last we will see some real Africa.

Skipped church today and talked about our expedition. Ngonda and Mungongo will come with us and they are all pepped up about it too. We have to have Ngonda as we will certainly be traveling alone some of the time.

I took pictures of hairdressing this afternoon and the women wanted to fix mine. They were surprized when I let them and only spent an hour giving me

an African hair-do. They spend hours doing theirs in a very intricate fashion. Mine is the same style but not divided into such very fine sguares. I attracted quite a crowd and had about six women working on me.

Monday, April 24

The sun was shining and we tried very hard to get every thing ready before Dr. Freas came. But we couldn't get any of the people! They had all gone for water or some such thing. We didn't even have Mfienge which further complicated matters. Finally Freas arrived but it took him until 8:30 to get enough people and at that he had to get the Chief.

The woman that starred in the last scene was missing so we had to skip the work we planned and go on to the grand finale. We worked very hard on it and at ten thirty the sun went in when we had only four shots to take! We just couldn't take the last concluding shots of the picture in the dark and had to let the people go. If this picture is good it will be a miracle.

Tuesday, April 25

Got up at 5:30 hoping to shoot the last of "Bwamba" today. Dr. Freas got here by seven and we were all ready to shoot. But the blue sky we'd been counting on lay buried under a pall of gray by this time.

Had breakfast and Ray and Dr. Freas played with the microscope for a couple of hours. I let them do all the fussing and then enjoyed looking at the bugs. "Wretched beasties" they were called by the first microbe hunter.

At ten thirty we had a little sun and shot the microscope scene in the village. This will cut down on our last day's work and we hope will fit smoothly in with the rest of the scene.

Took some stills this afternoon of Mama Maketa and baby and a very pretty little girl we discovered. She looks like a white child, her features are so regular.

Wednesday, April 26

Clouds all day. It rained a bit but not enough to clear the sky. Every day we wake up hoping that it will be our last day here. But alas, it never is.

Thursday, April 27

Dr. Tuttle came out this morning. It was rather late and so cloudy that we weren't expecting anyone. We decided to do one of the sequences we have left although it would have saved on expenses if we could have done everything in one clear morning.

Fast moving clouds kept hiding the sun and sometimes we had a half hour wait. In two and a half hours we took six shots! Then the sky was completely gray and we had to leave two medical shots—till the next time. The people are having fits and how can we blame them when we are having fits ourselves.

Friday, April 28

Dr. Tuttle did come about 9:30 as there was a bit of sunlight. But the sky was clouded over again before anything could be done. Ray drove to Madimba with him to see Godisiabois, as he is leaving for Leo. on Monday. He got some information and ordered tepoys to be made at Maluku. Now we'll have to go!

Saturday, April 29 [Boko—Sona Bata—Leopoldville]

Got up very early but found the sky all overcast. Our witch doctor threatened to leave today whether we finished the picture or not, and seemed to mean it. We ate breakfast and saw a little hole in the haze. It grew and we rejoiced. I began furiously getting stuff packed, beds down, etc. Ray paid water carriers etc. But Dr. Freas didn't come. We waited and swore and waited while the sun shone. All our helpers were packed and ready to leave and we were in a dither. Finally at 9:30 we gave up hope and sunk to our lowest depth of despair.

But after twenty minutes of suffering we heard the kids yelling 'Kipula' and we tore into our last shots like a cyclone. Mrs. Lanoue was having her baby—hence the delay. But thank goodness her little girl didn't arrive any later or we would have had a real rebellion on our hands.

Worked hard on the pictures and served big fried manioc and rice cakes to the actors. Then I dashed to finish all my packing of dishes etc. Ngonda helped but he is an awful packer and leaves so many holes that I have to go back and fill them in. While I was working like a demon Ray and Dr. Freas paid off the people. We planned with Mfienge to give the faithful women each 8 francs and the others a little less to equal the cloths we gave the men in the beginning. This seemed fair enough as when we first came the Chief said the people would be very happy if they got a big feed. All the people, even kids, who had appeared in the pictures even once, crowded up on the porch. Then the fun began. They all hollered and talked at once because everyone wanted to collect as many francs as possible. These the cooperative Christians of the Baptist mission. Boko is the stronghold of the field, they tell us. First the women bellyached about the 8 francs. Freas paid 21 of them, many of whom came once or twice and others appeared at ten o'clock instead of eight. The men then began hollering for pay even though they already had had more than the women—ten francs worth of cloth. Then Mfienge, who is supposedly fair but always over generous to Bokoites because his daughter is marrying the Chief's son, said to give the men each 5 francs. This they flatly refused! They demanded 10 and Freas immediately gave it to them with no argument. One man objected to this because he was a 'Kapita' in the village even though he did no more than the others. Freas gave him an extra 5 then after more bellyaching another 5. And we had made him two excellent pictures, mounted, that he couldn't have gotten for any amount of money out here. That's gratitude. Seeing the money flowing the women began griping for their filthy lucre. So they each got 2 francs more. The crowning point was that the men now said some of them got cloths of a cheaper quality than others so they should get extra money. This was the straw that broke the camels back.

Eight of the eleven men demanded and got 2.50 francs. There was almost no difference in the cloth we bought. It is hard for us to believe that men who have been accepted into the Bapyist church could stoop as low as this. The Baptist are so strict and so fussy about their Christians not smoking etc. (which we have seen even the pastors do) The people here have been under the influence of white men for many more years than others we've worked with. (Maybe that's why their money grabbers) But they are supposed to be more civilized and more Christian than other tribes. The kids mothers and the kids all yelled at this point. We remined them of innumerable balls, aeroplanes, pinwheels, candies, cookies, cake, and hours and hours of play with them. Some got a franc as well and some had been paid long ago.

They all seemed to forget the four movie shows and the radio. These cost plenty because of the engine and the people were crazy about them. They even forgot the big feed we gave them, at 5 francs a head, in their desire to get all they could out of us.

Ray and I couldn't help but get mad. This picture has cost a terrific amount. We even shot way over our film allowance—4,000 feet in all. And how we have suffered for three and a half months trying to make it good. I hope we can enjoy the picture after all the difficulties it's involved. Freas says the missionaries have to live with the people so we must satisfy them. But we can't believe in paying people to keep them liking you and in your church. After we got in the car there were more complaints from water carriers, who wanted a tip, and the Chief who wanted a 100 francs for the measly room we slept in. And we gave him a gift of six pictures and 70 francs. We went with a pretty bitter taste in our mouths.

At Sona Bata we had to pack curios, clothes, books, and everything we own. It was so late we didn't have time to eat. The Tuttles, who are the best of the lot—she is tops, helped us. Without them we never would have made the train. We didn't have time to even see the Lanoues or Esther Ehnbom before leaving. When we got on the train I ached all over I was so tired. The two and a half hours to Leo. seemed like an eternity. What a day and night!! But "Bwamba" is finished!!!!! We can't really believe it yet.

On the way to Leo, we picked out cloud formations. God shaking both fists at Boko. A gorilla threatening the people. Another God pointing a finger & admonishing. An angry looking figure sweeping down on Boko.

Sunday, April 30 [Leopoldville]

Walked to the Baptist church near the U.M.H. It was very hot and I promptly wore a blister on my heel with my new shoes. We arrived fifteen minutes late but were that much less bored. These English preachers are not much. Saw all our Leo. friends and Mr. Lovell from Wembo Nyama and Mr. Morrison from Loebo. It was fun talking to them again after all these months.

Had supper and went to bed again! We really have lots of things to do but the let down after "Bwamba" is very down.

Monday, May 1

Got up early and had breakfast before seven o'clock when Lutete came to take us to the U.M.H. We went over to Salmon's house, which is now empty, and set up for the C.P.C. meeting. We had to fix curtains hang a map, fill a bookcase, arrange table and chairs, and worst of all, fix our lights. We could only get two of them working in one stand which wasn't very much light. As the meeting had started we took Mr. Coxill's car and went to the B.M.S. church in the native city. There we got two gasoline lamps. They seemed to give no light and a great deal of heat so we had to do without them.

Shot the meeting in an hour. There were eight present and we got close-ups of all as well as the long shots. When Ray was taking a reading on the English minister's face he remarked at how much brighter it was. I said without thinking "Maybe his face is cleaner." At this everyone howled and Mr. Coxill laughed. Then he thought a minute and started all over again. He almost burst something. I hope the dignified old gentleman pastor didn't mind.

Wednesday, May 3

This morning we walked down to the A.B.C. to the dentist. I only had to have my teeth cleaned and then Ray took his turn. He had five fillings and had them all done so I had a long wait. Bill came in and we talked a bit. I felt headachy and wanted to go home. At twelve Ray was ready and we tried to get a taxi so we wouldn't be late for dinner. We ambled along but couldn't find any and had to walk all the way. The sun was not out but it was hot and I felt very tired. We were not late for dinner after all.

Friday, May 5

Slept right through breakfast and by the time we got up I felt swell. We finished our "Bwamba" scenario before dinner and sure were glad to kiss it goodbye.

In all the excitement I forgot to say that we received a cable last night from N.Y. It says,

Garner Bwamba material superb
Congratulations! Lerrigo

Well, now we do feel set up. Lerrigo is Chairman of the Committee and the mucky-muck of the Baptist board. What a thrill to at last have someone agree with us.

Saturday, May 6

After breakfast Ray started his letter to Rogers and I did some of the dirty work—typing the list of the cast, figuring how many reels we ought to have left, finishing up my records, etc.

After dinner I claimed a short rest and then stuck the gold paper on one of our reflectors. We took it out to try it and find we can shoot light 100 feet or more and its almost as bright as sunlight!

Ray didn't get his five page letter done until just before it had to get in the mail. I had to type like mad to get it off. It went air mail with the scenario and records and we put $3.00 worth of stamps on it.

Monday, May 8

Went over to Brazzaville in the launch at nine o'clock. We went to the Swedish mission and had cake and coffee—so we got our calories after all.

Drove out to the industrial school near the rapids. There the mission boys make beautiful things of wood. We spent some more money, that we haven't got, because the things were so ridiculously cheap.

Got a letter from Rogers and have been dancing a jig ever since. He says, "Let me warn you if you do anything better than this you are in danger of being stuffed, mounted, and stood in the museum. It is beautiful. (Underlined twice) This in regard to the first 12 reels of "Bwamba". Goody, goody, goody, goody!!!

Tuesday, May 9

Spent the morning, washing, mending, and making a belt for one of my cotton dresses. After dinner Ray wrote a letter, only one page, to Rogers to check the film speed of the Dupont film and the filter factor. Rogers sent figures that are different from ours and we want to be sure.

Wednesday, May 10

Photographed Mr. and Mrs. Coxill working in the C.P.C. office. We had been invited for lunch so didn't hurry. The Coxills think Ray is marvelous because he knows exactly what he wants to take and directs the action so beautifully.

We intended to photograph the mail plane coming in from Europe this afternoon. But the weather is so 'unusual' that we will have to wait till the next time.

Thursday, May 11

The anniversary of our arrival in Congo! We didn't celebrate but got a letter from Mother which was a present in itself.

Walked to the H.C.B. place and found that a boat will leave either Sunday or Tuesday. Met Bill in the Consul's car so we got a ride back. Just in time as it started to pour when we reached the U.M.H. It has been threatening all day. If anything the weather is worse than at Boko!

Saturday, May 13

Got all our curios packed this morning and also the helmets for the Ka-na-da-his. We hope we can find someone to take them home for us now.

This afternoon the Russells and Miss McCrackin arrived from Bolenge. They are the three people who were to have worked with us the most. And they are all so swell that we are kicking ourselves for not having gotten to Bolenge earlier. We are especially crazy about the Russells who are in their thirties and just grand. Darn the luck!

Monday, May 15

Just before dinner we learned that our boat is to leave tomorrow morning and they would like us to get our luggage aboard this afternoon. So I spent the afternoon madly packing everything under the sun. We are leaving four pieces of luggage behind but the other nineteen must go with us.

Ray went down to the customs with Miss Miller, A.P.C.M. Loebo, whom we prevailed upon to take the hats as far as Antwerp.

At 5 o'clock Ray still hadn't come back and as Lutete and the car were with him I had no way of transporting all our stuff to the dock. They went to visit the Captain however and it is allright for us to load the ship tomorrow.

Tuesday, May 16 [Leopoldville—Congo River]

Were all ready to leave at seven A.M. when the folks were starting breakfast. We went to say goodbye to them all and then to the "Lukula" to put our stuff aboard. We were delighted to find that we have the de luxe cabin—it has windows on three sides. There is only one other and as there are no other passengers we have that one too.

The Captain is Portugese and the nicest one we've met. He speaks only French, Portugese, and Lingala, so we use French—the little we have of it. The Captain is swell, very good natured, and very patient with our struggling, half drowned vocabulary.

We are towing seven barges and wonder if we ever will reach Bolenge????
Strange to say we don't seem to be moving slowly. The strong current moving against us probably gives the illusion that we are moving fairly rapidly.

Wednesday, May 17 [Congo River]

A terrific racket woke us up at 4:30 AM and there was no sleeping after that.
The boys were cleaning the decks just over our heads. Whoever said swabbing
must have been either deaf or 'foo' because they never just swab. They scrape,
scour, and scrub, very loudly on all the boats we've ever been on.

Got up at 5 as we seemed to be having trouble. Just last night the Captain
was telling us that he never got stuck on the sand and neither did his barges.
But one was very much stuck this morning, and it took three hours to get it
free.

After breakfast I made the sketches to go with my article. There is no India
ink aboard so I cannot finish them until we get to Bolenge. This afternoon
I started retyping the article leaving spaces for the sketches. I only did five
pages before so don't feel too badly about doing it over.

The river is not so wide now and the hills on either side are very much like
those around Bear Mountain. We could almost believe we are traveling up
the Hudson if there weren't so many palm trees and natives. It cleared beautifully this afternoon and we sat out in front and enjoyed the changing scenery.
We were amazed at the many shades of green at this time of year. The trees
do change color and although they don't take on the brilliant hues they do
at home they are quite colorful. Africa isn't just all one shade of green but a
whole range all the way from pale yellow green to deep blue greens.

Thursday, May 18

The river is still narrow—about like the Hudson—and there are few islands
and sand bars so that we are following a very straight course. Passed a little
colony of shelters built on logs. The natives are transporting valuable wood
from Stanleyville and they live on the logs with their families and just drift
downstream. It takes a month for them to reach Leopoldville then they go
back on a streamer—deck passage. Whole families live like this all the time.
Ray says they're amphibians.

Friday, May 19

Slept till eight o'clock this morning and then had breakfast alone as the
Captain wasn't up. I guess the wood-chucking keeps him awake too and then
he gets up at 4:30 to get the boat off.

Its swell being the only passengers because we do anything we want and are waited on hand and foot. The boys run our baths, clean our shoes, and wash our clothes without even being asked. We feel as if we are traveling on a private yacht!

I finished typing my article today and then Ray went over it and pulled it to pieces. Sometimes I think it would be better not to have a critic. I have to write a number of pages over again and am getting sick of the thing.

Took a few pictures this afternoon as the lighting was beautiful about 4:30. Saw the sunset from the front of the boat tonight. The river bends so that we are traveling west now. Are at the mouth of the Kasai tonight.

Saturday, May 20

Got up to find that we were still in port just off the Kasai river. A metal dory had been sunk by some native who didn't know what he was about and as it was an H.C.B. boat we had to salvage it. By nine o'clock it had finally been hoisted up on a cable and after the water ran out set afloat. We started bravely out into the middle of the river but there we couldn't go a bit further. The last two barges were stuck in the sand. They are fastened alongside of each other and as somebody else forgot the anchor they both had their rudders buried in sand. Some fun! Went merrily on our way this afternoon. After passing the Kasai we travel twice as fast because the current has been lessened fifty percent. We now go 6 kilometers an hour!

Sunday, May 21

Went back to my article today and typed most of it again because of mistakes and husbandly criticism. Read a book in between times.

The country has flattened out almost entirely now. The river is therefore wider and there are lots of little islands. Some of them have villages, on stilts, built by nomad fishermen. We hope to get pictures of these up around Bolenge.

Reached Bolobo tonight at midnight. We hoped to buy ivory here as the natives are really skilled craftsmen. But we'll be leaving at 4:30 AM. Ray is as disappointed as a child but maybe we can get some on the way back.

Monday, May 22

Put some of the sketches on my article today but felt generally lazy and spent most of the time reading and gazing at the scenery. There was a real breeze today and we felt real cool and comfortable. Once we went down on the lower deck to see the fires and whew, it was hot then. I took the monkey down and everyone was greatly amused.

Wednesday, May 24

This afternoon we saw some very black clouds ahead and ran into a wind and rain storm that nearly blew us off the river. The wind came first and was so glorious that we stood in the very front of the boat to get the full benefit of it. It slapped our clothes tight against us and whistled through our hair like a good old March wind at home. Chairs blew over, doors banged, and the wood covering blew off the steering engine. Then the boat started blowing sideways. The rudder was absolutely useless and we blew right up against the shore. The captain said we lost twelve hours today—now we won't reach Bolenge until early Friday morning.

Went to bed early—everything was so nice and quite. The captain is still excited about the storm though. It is the worst he's seen and I must say it seemed pretty terrific for Africa. It got positively cold!

Friday, May 26 [Congo River—Bolenge]

Got up early this morning to pack, as we had no idea when we would reach Bolenge. We only stopped long enough for wood last night, about four hours, and then went on upriver. The Captain was asleep this morning so we had breakfast alone and kept wondering when we would reach our destination. But we were ready hours ahead of time—this old boat pokes along so slowly.

Finally at nearly five o'clock we sighted Bolenge. But it was around a bend and no one knew we were coming until we were opposite the first houses. Then we tooted and figures began flying and motioning to tell us where to dock. The Captain very accomodatingly tied up the boat so we could get off and at last we reached Bolenge—only seven months late.

Met a mob of people and were settled in the Russell's house. Its real big and airy and the beds are wonderful. Bless them for suggesting that we might keep house here. We even have a big office with two desks!

Saturday, May 27 [Bolenge]

Mr. Hurt drove down from Coquilhatville this morning to take us to town. He and his wife have the mission there but spend most of their time here as its only about five miles. Went shopping for food and were surprized at all the things we could buy in the few small stores. Coq. is not half as big as I imagined it. Got our camera out of customs and a scorpion along with it. Ray captured the scorpion so we can take pictures of him but I didn't relish sitting in the back of the car with him. (The scorp not Ray)

Tonight was a grand banquet at Smiths with 22 of us, counting two little children. It was the finale of a conference the youngsters have been having and was lots of fun. Ray gave a little speech too—asking when everyone can get together to hear something about the Project. Even though this is the Ross' own mission they know very little about it and practically nothing about us. They seem to have the idea that we are commercial photographers or something.

Got a cable from Ross yesterday when we arrived that surprized us very much. "Garner Saga cancelled postpone Wa mission Does till letter arrives" We can't imagine why he wants us to postpone the 35mm picture. Are glad the 'Saga of the Congo' is cancelled as the scenario was lousy.

Sunday, May 28

All gathered at Edward's tonight for a church service. Then Ray gave a talk on the project, our part in it, purpose of the movies, etc. Mrs. Hurt gave us quite an argument about the shirt question. Some people just can't understand why we can't portray uneducated heathen Africa with the people dressed just like we are.

There is a big work going on here with the Institute for young evangelists as well as all the regular mission work. So many people have gone home this year that they are very short staffed and we wonder how we are going to get all the pictures we need. "What a Missionary Does in Africa" worries us not a little because its got to be good.

Monday, May 29

Arranged to take the night dancing scene on Thursday and talked about all the other pictures. It was dinner time before we were nearly through. Miss Poole, Mr. Byerlee, and Mr. Smith are on the Committee but they are all so busy I wonder when we are going to take any pictures. Arranged to meet tomorrow at ten and went to Byerlee's for lunch.

This afternoon we walked down to a nearby village with Miss Poole to chose some settings. Found one good one by the river for the children's picture. When we got back we decided to shoot our scorpion. The sun has been shining almost constantly and it breaks our heart not to be using it. Fussed with the scorpion a long time to make him walk within the camera angle.

A football team from Coq. came down to play the Bolenge boys at four o'clock. They really play soccer and not real football. Some of the natives are real good and it was quite an exciting game. A lot of Belgians, and priests, came to see the game and it was quite a gala occasion. Some of the onlookers had arguments that grew into fights and Mr. Smith was kept busy squelching them.

Tuesday, May 30

Had another meeting at ten this morning in which we made arrangements for picture taking the rest of this week. This afternoon we scouted around on bikes looking for houses, wells, springs, and gardens, for our rural reconstruction sequence. We found some things and plan to shoot them tomorrow. Visited the 'SS Oregon' which is the mission steamer. Its fairly large and used mostly to bring missionaries down river at conference time. There is a native captain who has entire charge of it.

Wednesday, May 31

Got up about eight and went to Ebinza village to shoot a native hut that is decorated nicely and fixed up cute with curtains and all. We went alone as all the missionaries were at school or eating breakfast. Had a boy carry our cameras down and back but we were broiling by the time we got back home. Just walking is too much exertion for this life on the equator.

Had breakfast and then Ray layed down he felt so bad. I did a few of the sketches for my article and then it was lunch time. Our boy is doing very well but I do have trouble talking to him. He knows some English and a little French and appears to understand me—but he doesn't.

Thursday, June 1

Ray was up and down all night and felt so badly that I was sure he must have dysentery. Miss Bateman made a microscopic examination and said that there were plenty of amoeba. He gets two injections a day which hurt like mad and make your arms all sore. And he has to take two pills with each meal as well as 10 grams of quinine. We had to cancel all the pictures we planned to take today and tonight.

Virginia C. came over tonight and asked us if we didn't want to come over and hear a Music Hall program from England. I thought Ray needed a little air so he got up and wabbled over. The radio was really good but made us feel a little homesick—we haven't heard one in so long. Ray didn't stay very long but I sat and talked to Virginia a while. She must be terrifically lonesome all alone at this end of the station. Her husband died out here only three years ago and I guess it is still pretty tough for her to carry on alone. She teaches a number of classes in the Institute and takes movies for diversion.

Friday, June 2

Ray still felt too weak to get up. The perspiration rolls off of him most of the day because of the weakness and the heat. We bought an ivory carving today and he likes it so much he had it in bed with him. Am I jealous!

Saturday, June 3

Miss Bateman arrives every morning to give Ray his first injection just as we are eating breakfast. Ray is getting so that he hides when he sees her. His arms are all blue and sore and the medicine makes him feel pretty sick. He doesn't feel like doing anything and stayed in bed reading all day.

Sunday, June 4

Ross wrote stressing the importance of our coming home as there is no more money to spend. The cable was all for nothing as we are to do the 35mm picture here. The only change is that we may omit some parts of it and insert scenes from Washburn's picture to make a 16mm picture rather than 35mm. This may be done because of the short staff here at Bolenge but if we can get help we will make the whole picture—still hoping that "March of Time" will use it.

Monday, June 5

Ray felt much better today and we might have done something but it was cloudy all day. Mr. Smith had a meeting with the picture committee and they decided that they would like to make the 35mm picture even though it will mean a lot of extra work. Mr. Hixon will play the part of the new missionary. He will be very good for it—our objection was that he is pretty small. We'll use small natives if we can so he'll look bigger than he is.

Worked on the scenario this afternoon and wrote up a schedule of sequences in order of their importance. We may not have enough film to do the whole picture. If we only get some good weather now we can really go places with this picture.

Got a letter from Rogers that was not sent down from Coq. with the others yesterday. He urges us to shoot regardless of the lighting because the Committee is anxious to have us come home. Unless the lighting is fairly good I'm afraid we will skip some things rather than take them under poor conditions.

Tuesday, June 6

It was cloudy this morning so we made plans for the 35mm picture with Hixon. We selected Byerlee's porch for the language study scene and proceeded to wreck it. We hung mats, sheets, and a blanket to block the light, shoved furniture around, etc. By the time we were through it was noon so we went home to eat.

Went back to take the scene and as Ray started to wind the camera something inside slipped and it wouldn't work! And this is the one Rogers just sent out. It is a secondhand camera and I suppose you never can tell what you will get. I was sick over it but Ray and Hixon took it over to our house and pulled it all apart. The ratchet catch of the wind up handle was broken. So they took the old 35 mm camera apart (both are Eyemos) to get the ratchet out of it.

They had all the parts in dishes all over the room and all the works out of both cameras. Then Hixon accidentally let the spring slip and that rolled out over the floor. At 6.30 they were still putting the last pieces in the good camera. The other one is still laying around.

Ate a quick supper and went to take our night dance around a big fire. We've been planning this for days but rain, Ray's dysentery, or something always put it off. Used flares in the fire and took three movies shots so we should have one very good one. Everybody on the station turned out for this affair. Virginia took movies too and Hixon took stills. We lent our knives and spears to the natives so it looked real wild and terrible. I'm sure no one will know it was taken in the middle of a mission station. Ray had lots of fun dancing around with the natives and showing them the kind of action he wanted. Sometimes I think he should have been black!

Wednesday, June 7

It was cloudy this morning so we worked at home on the scenario, letters, and cameras. Had lunch just after 11 o'clock and then went to Byerlees to set up for the language scene. It all had to be taken in last night on account of rain. Finally got ready and took the scene. Everyone had gone off to see the Edwards off on the steamer at Coq. Mr. Hixon wanted to go too, on his bike, so we couldn't do anything this afternoon.

We rode down to Ebinza and located a place to shoot some village scenes. Now if we can get the villagers to cooperate it will be swell for the caravan shots. Also found two forest trails to use for caravan scenes.

Ray found a plate that he and Hixon forgot to put in the camera yesterday so tonight they had to take it all apart again! We went up to Hixons as they have electric lights at that end of the station. Its nearly a mile from our house though and we don't like the hike. We borrow bikes whenever possible.

When they got the plate in and the camera all together again it wouldn't work! They fussed and fussed with the trigger, shutter, and other parts of the head. But they couldn't fix it. I wanted them to take it apart again as I was sure something was wrong way inside. Finally at 11.30 they took my advice although they said they didn't know why.

When they got it all apart and found everything in order I said that they had put the plate from the other camera in. So Ray ran home for the other plate. They look identically the same in color, size, and everything else, so they scoffed and said that wasn't the trouble. But for want of something better to do they put the other plate in—and it worked! They say there must be something to this women's intuition idea after all and won't give me credit for having any brains.

Hired two boys to carry cameras for us and run errands when we are making pictures. Ray didn't like their names so dubbed them Spike and Butch.
They love it and everyone calls them that now.

Thursday, June 8

Had breakfast very early and got right to work with Hixon. By eleven
o'clock we had finished the three scenes planned for this morning. Went
home to rest and eat until two—and how we needed it.

This afternoon Hixon worked on the tepoys for the caravan scenes and we
took Mr. Byerlee teaching an agriculture class and brick laying. We had long
waits for the sun but finished at five and borrowed bikes to go to Ebinza and
make arrangements to use the people there on Saturday. Mr. Smith and Miss
Poole went with us and he violently objected to using the street we chose
because some of the people are Catholic. Miss Poole told us later she was
surprized at him but some of the older people are that way.

But we found some church members in our village and the chief agreed
to have the people there for us. We have hopes of getting men and women
without any tops. We have seen quite a few people working around only half
clothed but whether they'll do it for the pictures in something else.

Friday, June 9

Got up early to cook breakfast. It was very cloudy but by nine o'clock had
cleared enough for us to shoot the brick making scene we had planned. Went
to Bolenge village where the natives are making them and got them to be in
the picture with Hixon directing. We had a little difficulty because the men
were working in loin cloths and when they saw us coming to take pictures
they put clothes on. We finally got them off and took the scene with some
waits for the sun.

Had a quick lunch, as Ray likes his dinner at night, and then we got the
loads ready for a caravan scene. Mr. Smith got the schoolboys to be carriers
and we took them to a forest trail with Hixon. (We call him Franchot.) Miss
Poole came to help direct and we took a scene showing the mother-inlaw-
taboo. In Congo a native cannot look on his mother-in-law's face. Our native
saw his coming and dropped Hixon's tepoy and jumped in a bush.

Dashed over to Mrs. Clarke's house as soon as we were through to try
to shoot the departure of the caravan before the sun went down. We pulled
blankets, pots and pans, and all kinds of stuff out of Virginia's house so the
boys could be packing. Ray took two shots and then found he didn't have the
filter on. We had a lot of the missionaries there to see the caravan off and the
lighting was perfect to get the scene. But the sun was fast dropping into a haze

just above the horizon and we knew if we retook the two shots there wouldn't be time to do the rest in sunlight. So we had to call it off.

Saturday, June 10

Got up early again and gave Ray only fruit and cookies for breakfast so we could get an early start with the pictures. We got everything ready and the caravan boys and missionaries didn't show up. Finally Ray went over to the jungle trail and set up while I hurried the boys who were straggling in. Had Hixon and Smith both in tepoys and got a beautiful caravan shot although the sun was rather thin.

At 8:30 when we were through we dashed on to Ebinza to get the village scenes with the caravan. Virginia came to take some movies and Miss Poole to help direct. We had a hard time with the villagers as they didn't want to wear loin cloths. The Chief got after them though. Then the women wouldn't take off their blouses. Some of them wear grass skirts here but they look silly with a blouse on top. Had to work in weak sunlight but got some good shots. Before we were through a storm began blowing up and we had to rush and tear to finish with the villagers before the clouds obscured every bit of light. We were told we could never get the villagers again and we just had to finish then. Africans are sure terrible when it comes to taking pictures. Half of them ran off in the middle of the morning because they said "we're tired". We had to chase them up and promise to pay them in order to get them back.

Sunday, June 11

Ray got his old 35mm camera put together so we can take it with us on our trip Tuesday. Decided to wait till then as Mr. Byerlee wants us to shoot the print shop before we go.

Late this afternoon we went down to Hixons to plan the trip. Miss Poole has decided to go with us. We are real glad as Hixons have only been out since November and don't know the language any too well.

Monday, June 12

Got up early to get breakfast and found that Loyenga was back. Ray went down to the print shop to set up lights and take the pictures there. I got a little packing done and then sat down long enough to figure out my expenses and get the balance of our money ready to put in Mr. Byerlee's safe. Found we were 48 francs shorts since the 1st of June and I'd been so so careful about writing everything down! Left fifty francs in an envelope to give the Chief of Ebinza for the people who helped us, and went to the print shop. Ray found he'd forgotten something and went home on a bike. He dashed into the office and saw Loyenga squeezed into a corner in the closet with the door nearly shut. He was obviously hiding! Ray didn't pull him out as he understands so little English but I went home and found 20 of the 50 francs missing. Obviously that's where my 48 francs went and maybe more during the last few days of May.

Ray had an awful time in the print shop and blew 16 dollars worth of our lights. He finally finished about two and we had our lunch. Got ready for our caravan pictures again but the sun didn't come out and about four we let the boys go. When Loyenga came back to get supper I sent him over to Smith and he finally admitted taking the 20 francs today. He went home and got it and after supper Mr. Smith brought him over to our house. I felt very sorry for him because it was just like leaving a cake out before Ray. I should have had more sense than to keep even my small money in the draw without locking it. Mr. Smith kept talking to Loyenga and he finally admitted to taking the 48 francs too. He is supposed to get it for us before we leave Bolenge.

Tuesday, June 13 [Bolenge—Lulungu]

Got up at 5:15 to wash dishes and get everything ready to go by seven. Spike and Butch came to carry our stuff to the launch and I kept rushing to have things ready for them. Left Ray behind as he has to see the Dr. at Coq. this morning and get a temporary filling in his front tooth. Mr. Byerlee will drive him part way in the truck someone left here while they are down river. Then he has to go for miles on a bike through the swamps. Eventually he will end up where we are going.

Had a grand day in the launch. We played Monopoly, saw the most picturesque villages yet, and read magazines. Docked (to a tree) about four o'clock and Franchot went to the village on his bike for carriers. Ray arrived soon after he got back and we walked the two miles to the village and let Miss Poole and Mrs. Hixon ride with the kids hanging on back.

Found the village of Lunggula [Lulungu] on either side of the trail with huts in rows. The heavy jungle background makes this one of the most beautiful places we've been. Ray was so tired from his long ride and so wet that we didn't look at much tonight.

Wednesday, June 14 [Lulungu]

Got up early for breakfast and then went down to the river again. Ray and I had to walk as we didn't bring any bicycles, never dreaming we would live over two miles from the water. Couldn't get the launch running when we arrived so we went into the swamps in two canoes. It was gorgeous in the maze of greenery and we wound in and out among the giant trees on what the natives call a trail. There is water in every direction and nothing to mark the way so we marvel that they know where and how to go.

The sunlight was pretty poor and we didn't have Hixon's canoe fixed up with loads etc. so we took some pictures for us. Ray and I got in a little canoe with two paddlers and rode along under the heavy blanket of green. It went up and up, so far above our heads that we were almost in darkness when the sun went in. The water here on the equator is as black as can be. It looks like black coffee when it splashes up against the side of the boat—a lovely deep amber color and perfectly clear. The decaying vegetaion makes the water black all through this section of the country. Most of the land is under water at certain times of year and the people build temporary villages along the banks of the rivers where they live until the water rises.

Visited three villages and then went upriver, past our landing place, and found a bigger one that is just perfect. We talked with a few men and promised to come back tomorrow before the villagers go off to dig copal. They are all working hard at it now while the water is getting low.

This was one of our most beautiful days. We love traveling on the river with its heavy wall of jungle closing in on either side. The giant trees and dripping vines fulfill our wildest imaginings of jungle. And there are things we never dreamed of like ferns spreading out of treetrunks like hanging baskets, and great trees held up by a network of roots that stand twelve feet out of the water and look as if they couldn't possibly support the tower over them.

Thursday, June 15 [Lulungu—Nteniya]

I had to get up at five o'clock this morning because its my day to be chief cook and bottle washer. We want to get started for our village very early these mornings so there are no late sleepers here. Got to Nteniya and palavered with the people until almost all of them agreed to help us—for three franc today and four tomorrow. The sun didn't come out all morning so we got our canoe and paddlers ready and chose our camera angles. I got lunch about eleven as we were hungry and wanted to get it over with. Had tomato soup and corn beef hash—I had to cook in the end of a canoe—and ate in the launch to keep away from the Tsetses.

The sun came out right after so we started right in. Ray got some beautiful shots of the canoe coming into the village through and archway of trees and vines. Finished one of our long sequences and were all so tired that we jumped in the launch and went home. Stopped at a plantation near the water where we had left our bikes and were inveigled into drinking some tea. The man and are in this God forsaken place just on their own and do everything

from making bricks to buying the copal the natives dig. We will try to get a
sequence on it before leaving here for "The World's Stake in Africa".

Friday, June 16

Got up real early again and started off to Nteniya as soon as we had breakfast. I was so sleepy that I fell asleep in the launch on the way down. When
we got there the sun still hadn't come out so we couldn't do any more than
choose settings. Had lunch early again and kept hoping for sun. The people
all stayed in the village today and we'll have to pay them whether we finish
our pictures or not.

We all read magazines and wished we had brought some games and finally
the sun broke through a little space in the clouds. It was three o'clock by
this time so we didn't waste any time getting started. Shot the first church
service in the village where the people get scared when Hixon is praying to
an unseen spirit and they all duck out. He opens his eyes and finds himself
all alone. Had an awful time as the light was so thin, but finally finished. It
was too late to shoot any more scenes so we bought an eagle that a man had
killed to use in the pictures tomorrow. We are afraid the people will eat it if
we leave it here tonight.

Got home feeling a little discouraged because of the bad weather and ne-
cessity to shoot in weak light. But after those letters from Rogers and Ross
we don't want to spend any more money than we have to. This picture has
already cost a lot—we have to pay the people so much to stay in from their
copal swamps. They get good money for copal—good for them I mean.

Saturday, June 17

It was raining when we woke up this morning so we took our time about
eating and getting ready to go. When it began to look bright in the east we set
off for our village again. Took all our paddlers with us again hoping to finish
in the village and get the rest of our canoe shots. But the sky stayed as black
as could be all day.

Couldn't take even one shot today and our eagle is going to have an awful
stink by Monday. Ray says its allright because the camera can't smell!

Tonight Franchot had to show lantern slides in the chapel here. He is supposed to be having a meeting with all his teachers in this section but hasn't
been able to give any time to it.

Sunday, June 18 [Lulungu]

Would have taken a few pictures here but it was cloudy this morning and
this afternoon we had to let the folks have one meeting. The teachers from our

villages have been waiting all week to have their special conference. We have some of them in the picture now and can't let them go until we are through.

Monday, June 19 [Lulungu –Nteniya]

Had breakfast early again and set off for Nteniya even though it was cloudy. We went into the swamps to choose settings for our canoe shots. Then back to the launch for lunch and the sun finally came out just as we were through eating.

Fussed all afternoon getting lighting and everything right. Got some really beautiful shots even with all the natives gripeing. You'd think they weren't used to paddling canoes. We had a lot of trouble getting the boats in the right place for shooting. Ray took two shots from the top of the launch and one from a tree in the swamp. I held my breath while he was up there above us with nothing but water to catch his camera if he dropped it.

Finally got through with the canoe shots and paid the paddlers off. They worked four or five days. At least they were with us that many, and we had to pay them 16 and 19 francs. It seemed like an awful lot but they are all making money now as the water is low and it is fishing season. They just wouldn't

have stuck with us if we hadn't promised them good pay. Four francs a day
is a lot in comparison to what we've paid others but its really only about
twelve cents.

Tuesday, June 20 [Lulungu—Nteniya—Bolenge]

Woke up and found a sunbeam on our wall. It sneaked through a hole in
our palm thatch roof and got us up faster than anything else in the world could
have. Had breakfast in a hurry and then rode into the forest to a Balumbi village. These people have always been the slaves of other tribes and they are
a poor downtrodden lot. There is as much difference between this tribe and
the others, socially, as there is between the whites and the blacks in our own
South!

The people are very wild and primitive looking, wear practically no
clothes, and were just what we wanted in our village church service. This
one is held by a native pastor (we dressed up our cook to play the part) and
is the finale of the 35mm picture. Finished in no time and then dashed back
to Lulungu where we packed in record time and got down to the launch and
off to Nteniya. We were rushing to finish up and go home as our food was
getting very very scarce.

Skipped lunch entirely and went right to work in the village. Our eagle, that
we bought four days ago and have been saving for a scene, was too dead to
use. He smelled so badly yesterday that we had to take him out of the launch
in order to make it livable. There hasn't been time or light to shoot the scene
and now our elegant looking bird is crawling with ants, maggots, and unknown fauna. We'd use him anyway but they would show in the close-ups.

Finished the third and last scene in a worse rush than ever because a
rainstorm was approaching very loudly. The last shot was taken with the
first drops falling on our actors and reflectors. But we think we got it, so we
jumped in the launch and started home.

Wednesday, June 21 [Bolenge]

The sun was shining this morning but we had to go to Coq. to get our films
through customs and onto the mail boat that leaves this afternoon. There is
only one every two weeks and as it connects with the Belgium steamer we
can get our films right out of the country.

Rushed around making out the customs forms and getting the films ready
to go. Then Franchot drove us to Coq. in the truck that is here for two weeks.
We picked up Mr. Hurt there to help us with French so we could get through
customs and make the Post Office before it closed.

Got the films off without too much fuss but had to pay 157 francs to send them. The 35mm reels weigh about a ton and can't go as printed matter. Went to the Dutch store to buy more food and then back to Bolenge.

Thursday, June 22

Walked down to Ednas, about a mile, and then got bikes and rode to the village. We found a place to use for the scene and gathered some little kids to be in it. Then we had to wait for Franchot and while we were waiting the sun went in. Ray was feeling so tired that we went home again.

After lunch Ray read a bit and then fell asleep. At two o'clock Mr. Smith came over and we decided that the sun wasn't coming out and there was no sense of taking the school boys away from their chores.

The sun came out after a little while but the western sky was heavy with clouds and I was sure it would go right in again. But a little later it cleared more and instead of the sun dropping behind the clouds it dried them up as it went down! So we missed our scene unneccessarily. How I wish the sun would suck up the clouds all the time.

Ray went off to see Mr. Byerlee about fixing the tripod screwin on the camera when he woke up.

Friday, June 23

Today we planned to carry out the program we failed to yesterday. But the sky was as gray as could be. There wasn't enough light all day to take pictures even if we wanted to in order to "endear ourselves to the Committee" as Rogers says. If we don't have light, and plenty of it, on black people the camera won't open wide enough to get anything but a spot.

Ray rewrote his letter to Ross today as we didn't type and mail it last week. He managed to write to Rogers too. They won't have the letters until the 35mm picture is all finished so if they have any objections to doing it they will have to hold them. W figure a little extra time here and a finished picture may earn the $1000 invested in 35mm film and cameras. Then we went off to see Smiths and make arrangements for the rest of the 35mm pictures next week. Now if the sun will shine we'll really finish it and within a month too!

Saturday, June 24

Started out early again this morning but the sun went in before we could do anything. We telephoned Coq. then and found that Captain Lona was in. As we wanted to see him and get a scene with Mr. Hurt we loaded the cameras in the truck and drove down. Captain Lona had 6 small spears and four knives for us and they cost ten francs! For all of them I mean.

Did a little shopping for food and then found three of the ladies who had gone to Coq. on their bikes this morning before we decided to go in the car. We waited for them to finish their shopping and then loaded everything in the car. Part way home Franchot discovered that he'd left the native teacher behind and we had to go back to find him. He wasn't at the native market but a giant seaplane, privately owned, had just landed on the Congo. So we suspected that he was down among the throng who turned out to see it. The natives crowded along the shore to get a good look at it but they were neither surprized or amazed. They have come to regard all white men in such a wonderful light that nothing is impossible for them.

It was two o'clock by the time we got home. Mr. Hurt came down just as we were through eating. The sun didn't appear this morning so we arranged to take the picture here rather than in Coq. We set it up on our porch and got it done in no time. It was a translating scene showing Mr. Hurt and two natives working on the Bible.

Sunday, June 25

Went to church this morning as it was communion Sunday. We were late and arrived just as Mr. Smith was standing and announcing that we wanted everyone to come on Wednesday so that we can photograph a church service. We hid outside because we couldn't walk in and sit by him and the other white folks when he was talking about us. Went in right after; just in time for the collection.

Monday, June 26

There was to be a baptism in the river at noon and we wanted to go. We were late, as usual, and only got there in time for the closing verse of the closing hymn.

Borrowed bikes and went out to the village to take stills for our cook and washboy. We took them and their houses and they were quite delighted. Ray stopped at Franchots to see him about the caravan shots this afternoon. I went home and when two o'clock came around all the boys and missionaries arrived for the pictures. I rushed around getting things ready, expecting Ray to come tearing up any minute. Finally I had everything set and still no Ray. I jumped on a bike and went to find him. Sure enough he and Franchot were playing chess. The bums!

Got the pictures by 4:30 and I went home to flop on the bed.

Tuesday, June 27

The sun really came up this morning. We just ate fruit for breakfast and then dashed out to do some shooting. We got the children writing in the sand and also a carpentry scene before we quit at 11.

We had to get down to the SS Oregon at one o'clock to start the pictures of Hixon's arrival at Bolenge. They got the boat fixed for us even though it was a lot of fuss. Ray and I rode down river on the tip top, taking a few shots as we went. We nearly roasted with the hot sun and the smoke stack both conspiring to raise as much heat as possible. Got the old paddle wheeler turned around and then started back to Bolenge. A mob were waiting on shore to greet Franchot. But when we got near they waved us back and we had to back up a long way to give the rest of the folks more time to get down to the river. This happened three times and I thought we'd never get the picture. But the sun held and we tore around taking shots on the boat, from the boat, and of the boat.

When the welcoming was over we had to fuss a long time to get a shot of the boat traveling along. This was tricky as the sun was shining toward us and as the boat went by it was all in shadow. Finally walked along the shore and found a point we could go out on. The boat squeezed along the shore, which curved way in and we were able to get the shot.

Wednesday, June 28

Ate a hasty breakfast this morning and went over to shoot the advanced school on 35mm. I was in the first shot, marching in to the school building as a teacher. Its the first picture I've been in. I suddenly decided that I wanted to appear in "March of Time" too.

Had to wait for the sun, as we were reflecting it into a large room, but finally finished the women's class. Then it got so black that we were sure it would rain and so we went home.

Thursday, June 29

Went to finish the school shots this morning. The sun was shining brightly so it didn't take long. We were sorry there was nothing else we could shoot. But the sun gets so high in the sky, so early in the morning, that it is better to finish important scenes by 9:30 or 10:00 o'clock.

Right after lunch Mr. Byerlee took us out beyond Coq. to the botanic gardens (Eala). It is an enormous place for experimental purposes, supported by the Belgium government. The director spoke good English and we got along very nicely with him. Took a sequence on cocoa and another on rubber. We went down to the river to get the elephants taking their afternoon bath but it was too late to get any light. We planned a way to shoot both elephants without their trainers and hope we can do it without letting them get away. The elephants are about 23 years old and not full grown by any means. They are very different from the Indian elephants.

Friday, June 30

Were supposed to go back to Eala this morning to get the elephants and a few other things. But it was so foggy and dark that we decided not to go at 6:45, the time we had set to leave here. Then in about half an hour the sun came out and the sky got clearer and clearer.

Planned our "Children of Africa" pictures this morning and at 1:30 went out to Ebinza to shoot. We got the launch, after a terrific palaver because Franchot didn't want to ask the mechanic to take it out for us. He's scared to death the guy will leave him flat and he won't have anyone to take him on trips. Ray got on top and shot a swimming race with the most beautiful village background we've had. The kids were hard to direct—there was such a mob of them—but they did very well. At five we came home completely exhausted. Edna came in for a drink and then invited us to supper. We are getting to be real gallavanters!

Came home at ten and found one of the ebony workers waiting for us. He wanted 150 francs for four pieces. We kept jewing him down and then finally he said he wanted a pair of socks. That started us and in another hour he had an old pair of socks, two pairs of shorts that are too small for Ray, an old tie, and seventy francs. And we had the four pieces of ebony. These guys always ask more than they expect to get. Then you are supposed to name a figure lower than you intend to pay. He comes down five francs, you go up five, he comes down another five, you go up another five, and its a sale. Once we asked how much something was and the guy said, "Fifty francs but I'll take less." And a kid came with a piece of ivory and said, "He told me to ask fifty francs but to take forty". Every time we want to buy something we have to palaver for at least half an hour.

Saturday, July 1

Ray developed a few films today at Hixon's using his tank, developer, etc. Our chemicals are all gone and we left the tank in Leo. He went off to do another after we finished the pictures and I got my dinner ready.

We invited Hixons as they are going away on a trip tomorrow and we will never see them again. Everything turned out very well and we enjoyed our first dinner party very much. This is really the first time we've had company in our own house.

Sunday, July 2

Stayed in bed late this morning and by the time we got breakfast and were dressed we were late for church again. Got there just in time for the collection. This is the day everyone marches up to the front to put their money in. Groups are called such as "schoolboys", "little children", etc. The money is collected in separate boxes and then next Sunday the amounts are read out. Each group tries to get the most, of course. Maybe we ought to do it this way in our church so we could pay off all the debts.

Monday, July 3

A peach of a day. The weather is definitely improving. Now if it will only hold until we can finish our pictures. Started in bright and early on the children's picture. We took them building a relief map in sand under the supervision of a native village teacher.

This afternoon we shot the church scene on 35mm. Burned four flares inside the church and they worked very well. The people sat there very stoically and the smoke rose right up and didn't bother us at all. The flares are so old we expected an explosion but outside of a rain of magnesium powder they were allright.

Finished about 5:30 and went right home for supper. Then to Hixon's to print a few stills. I had to make out all the forms for sending film again and we finally got to bed. The mail boat goes again on Wednesday and we have to send our films through customs tomorrow so they can make it. We are dying to hear how the first few we sent two weeks ago turned out.

Tuesday, July 4

Went off to help Ray get the films all wrapped, weighed, and addressed, and then we went to the school to do an inside picture. Got enough light in the open building to do a class studying malarial mosquitos. I had to draw a couple on the black board and as I had a small sketch to work from they turned out pretty well.

Didn't finish till lunch time so I had to ice my cake after we ate. By the time I got it done it was after two and we dashed off to do more pictures. Got the drum sequence on the 35mm. Ray was drumming for fun and we asked the natives what he was saying. He kept his rythm going and right away they picked up his mesage. "My woman bore twins, my woman bore twins." You have to be mighty careful when you pick up drum sticks in this part of the country. The people have a regular morse code on their 'lukoli'.

Wednesday, July 5

Off again early this morning. Took the mosquito class to a swampy place in the village and had them dig a ditch to drain it off. We messed up the place mightily but Edna says they're not supposed to let water stand like that anyway and the State man would get after them good and proper. Got some really good shots and Ray was the one who fell in the swamp! He got into mud and water up to his knees. The native teacher called to Edna to tell that man that there was water in the grass. But Ray had already discovered it by that time.

After lunch Ray took a nap and I got working on my expense accounts. I got all mixed up and couldn't get them straight. Finally had to leave them in a mess and go out to finish the 35mm. We got a few station shots with schoolboys playing football in one. Went back to my accounts then and looked and looked for the missing money.

Stopped long enough for supper and then struggled some more. Ray wanted me to stop but I just had to get it straight. When I figure out my cash I am about 200 francs short and when I figure the books I'm 900 short! This time I am stuck—afraid Loyenga got away with some of it. We'll just have to hand it in as stolen I guess. Darn it!! That makes me boil. I'm so careful about recording everything and not spending too much money and then we lose all that. Fooey!

Thursday, July 6

Got out early to shoot the girl's games. Edna was busy at her school and we got tired of waiting so went ahead ourselves. Went to the little girl's school and took all the little ones—nearly the whole school. I explained that it was "Cinema' again so the teachers let them come. The kids followed our bikes to the village and there I showed them how we wanted them to dress. Then with singing and dancing I explained to them that we wanted them to play a game. Edna came along just as they were going strong and we went right ahead with the pictures. Near the end of the film Ray put his tripod on a table to shoot down on the finish of a game. Butch held a reflector over his head to shade the camera. There was a lot of fussing to get the girls to do it just right and Butch got very tired. Ray jumped off the table to help with the kids and Butch got tired and tired and finally leaned on the camera! We heard a crash and there was the camera half buried in the ground with its telephoto lens broken off. We were horrified but it still runs. Ray took it apart when we got home but cannot seem to fix the mirror which doesn't flip back the way it should. He has to use two hands to work the camera now and must remember to shove that mirror over or we don't get any pictures. He straightened the lens out pretty well and it seems to be allright. Why did this have to happen at the end of the expedition? We have been priding ourselves on the fact that we have broken no more than the glass in one of the meters. It isn't usable but we really didn't even do that - Franchot was the guilty party.

This afternoon we rode to Coq. on bikes to see Mr. Hurt about the state pictures we need. He didn't have any objections for once and said one of the agents was a friend of theirs. So we arranged to meet him at the state post when we finished shopping. Went to the Dutch house and one of the boys gave us a swell snake skin. Bought enough food for about two weeks and then went to Sedec and found that the only H.C.B. boat before September will be leaving July 16! That gives us less than ten days to finish our pictures.

The agent was very agreeable and although we couldn't talk to him Mrs. Hurt seemes to explain everything. We could understand most of her French. Arranged to come in the morning at 7:30 to take the four sequences we need.

Friday, July 7

Got up early and were ready to go when Mr. Hurt got here at seven o'clock. Went right to the state post and were surprized to find that the state man wasn't there. We waited and waited and finally the police and medal chief came along all dressed up for the pictures. So we tried to set up the first scene of tax collecting that the state man didn't have to appear in. The chief was very unwilling and insisted that we take a picture of him and promise to send it to him. We agreed but wouldn't do it before we got our movies for fear he would leave us in the middle. This made him kind of mad and there was quite a palaver before we got our scene set up.

Then the state man came along on his motorcycle but kept right on going! He must have seen the car if he didn't see us. Mr. Hurt said he didn't think he could give us three or four hours of his time as he is building roads and has 1,000 men working under him. We thought that had all been arranged yesterday and refused to shoot the scene we had set up unless we knew we could carry on with the other three. Hurt was pretty mad about it and the chief stamped off so all the men we'd gathered for the scene did too. We started home then expecting to see the state man and explain just what we wanted. But we found him surrounded by workmen and Hurt didn't want to interrupt him. He probably didn't know what to say to him but if we're not with him he can say plenty. He never has been very nice to us—argues about everything we want to do and Mrs. Hurt is a born complainer and arguer. Hurt seemed so sullen about the whole thing—even when we first tried to set up the scene this morning—that we have decided that we just can't do it here.

Came home and planned the children's picture for this afternoon. Went to the school to select them and felt griped that we'd wasted yesterday afternoon and this morning when we might have finished with the kids.

Went to Ebinza about two and had a lot of fuss setting up and getting the Mother to do her part well. Didn't turn on the camera until four o'clock—much too late. Kept working furiously until nearly six when the last sunlight was fading. It was awfully hard to get the kids to do it right and we were exhausted when it was done.

Saturday, July 8

Got up early but the sun didn't come out. I had plenty to do though and Ray insisted I make some oatmeal cookies in my spare ?? time. By the time I got them done and we had lunch it was one o'clock and we were due at the river to go on a picnic. We tore around gathering cans of soup, beans, bathing suits, dishes, and other equipment.

Arrived at the big canoe just as everybody was getting in. Ray and Mr. Byerlee insisted on playing chess all the way across the river. We stopped at a big sandbar which is out of the water now that it is dry season and the river is so low. Its a nice clean place to swim and only one native was caught by a croc. here.

Sunday, July 9

Read in bed before breakfast and wished for Sunday papers at home. After breakfast I typed Ray's air mail letter to Godisiabois. He is planning the trip to Maluku again as we missed our state pictures here and cannot get an animal for the hunting scene.

Dragged him away to go to church tonight. Planned the rest of the pictures afterward. We have to leave in just a week if the H.C.B. boat is on time.

Monday, July 10

After breakfast we went to Ebinza and when Edna got there with the kids went ahead with our children's pictures. We got some beautiful shots for the finale of the children rushing madly out of school and tearing down to the river where they strip off their clothes on the run and jump into the water.

Went back to the village this afternoon to finish the boy's games. About four, when we were ready to complete a scene we did the other day, we found our baby hadn't arrived. I had to go tearing all the way to Bolenge village to find it. I put it in the basket in back of me and tied a cloth around it to hold it in. The baby's head was the only part showing and it looked so silly that all the natives hooted as I went by. Worked like mad but couldn't finish the scene till 5:30 and it was very nearly dark. The sun was still above the horizon but the sky was so hazy that there was no light to speak of.

Had a quick supper as Bosweswela's wife was waiting for him so they could go out somewhere. Boy! Did he work fast this time—didn't know he had it in him. Went to bed early as we have to get up very early in the morning to go to Eala and shoot the elephants.

Tuesday, July 11

Got up at 5 AM to go to Eala. We had fruit for breakfast, packed the cameras in the bicycle basket on my bike and set out. Went a short way and decided that the sun wasn't going to come up as we expected. We didn't want to go so far unnecessarily so turned around and went home again.

Wednesday, July 12

Got up before dawn again and even though there were no stars got ready to start for Eala again. The sun didn't come up this morning either but we went on as we have only a day or two left and we must get the elephants now or never. Rode about 12 Kilometers up and down hill so that we were exhausted by the time we got to Mr. Couteaux' house. No one was there so we had to ride all over looking for him. Finally located him having breakfast with a State man. They have to go into the swamps today to lay a new road.

But first we could get our elephant pictures if we hurried. Fortunately some weak sunlight was coming through the haze. Had an awful time getting the elephants to behave without their trainers sitting on their backs. When they got off and told the elephants to go on alone they got all nervous and began running in the wrong direction. We had quite a time making them behave and they definitely didn't like our cameras. But we managed to get some very good shots. We were lucky for once.

The Dutch boys arrived with a shield for Ray and two little ebony heads for me. Ray has been hollering about a shield so I'm glad he got one at last. After dinner, which wasn't finished till nearly nine o'clock a car came with a note saying that some Dutchman had arrived and had to see one of the boys immediately. So he had to go off. We pinned the other one down and got him to write a French note to the company at Wendji asking if we may borrow some tusks for a few movie shots.

Thursday, July 13

Tuji weather again this morning prevented us from taking any pictures till about 9:30. Then we went on our bikes and took a few shots of houses for rural reconstruction category in 'Mission Achievements'.

Were invited to Smith's for lunch so I started packing up kitchen stuff to send to it's various owners. Got an answer from Wendji agreeing to our request so Mr. Smith sent some boys down to be in the pictures and we started out on bikes at 2 o'clock. It was cloudy all the way—11 Kilometers with our legs yelling all the way. But when we got the tusks into the forest the western sky cleared and we got some very good shots. We used 20 very big tusks, some weighing as much as 65 lbs. They were all as tall as I am or taller.

Finished at five and started home again. We just about made it after yesterday and then had to take baths and dress to go to Smiths again for supper. They had Edna and Georgia there and we had a grand meal. Played a little 'Chinese Checkers' but Ray and I had to go home to get our films ready for the mail boat. We don't dare leave them to go down with us as the H.C.B. boat may be very late in reaching Leo. and then we will miss the Belgium steamer.

Friday, July 14

Had breakfast at our house and then I got all dishes and other borrowed equipment packed and sent back.

Went to Virginia's for supper and then to Byerlee's to see her pictures. We had to go down to that end of the station as they have electricity and we don't.

The projector was very ancient and Virginia's movies not too good so I had an awful time keeping awake. I was so sleepy I could hardly walk home and was so glad to get to bed. Our last night in the good beds as we heard that our boat has arrived. It won't leave till 5 AM Sunday morning but we will have to get aboard sometime tomorrow.

Edna overheard a conversation between two natives today about us. They said Ray was just the hard workingest man they ever saw. And his wife is just as hard. Why she can take a picture every time he can!! They are so slow themselves that they can't get over us. Glad somebody appreciates us.

Saturday, July 15 [Bolenge—"SS Stanley"]

Got up at dawn to pack as our belongings are spread all over the house and only the curios ready to go. Had a pile of fruit for breakfast when Bosweswele arrived and then worked like mad to be ready when the truck arrived at 9:30.

The captain was on board and he is a round jolly Belgian, speaks English, and looks like no other Belgian we've ever seen. I'm positive there was a dutchman in his family.

Payed the truck off after our stuff was taken off and put aboard and then we walked to the hospital to get our medical passports. The doctor found we didn't have sleeping sickness so my plans to go itinerating with Edna, if we did have it, fell through. Went to Hurt's then and Edna borrowed his car to take us to the State post so we could sign out. Then back to Hurt's to pick him up and go on to Bolenge.

Went back to our own house to rest—I had left the beds made up for this purpose. I had a good nap but Ray read all afternoon. We heard a drum beating on the river in a canoe and wondered what on earth it could be. Found tonight that a croc. took a child from Ebinza village (right where we took all the pictures of the kids in the water) and the people got in canoes and paddled up and down the river beating a message to the croc. "Bring back our child, bring back our child." The loss of a child is a terrible thing to these people. Not because they love them like we do—they don't know love at all—but because there are so few children here. The people are dying out and they know it. It is particularly bad in this part of the country. Many of the women can't have children and that is such a tragedy to a man that he takes another wife—whether he is in the church or not—and then there is trouble. The venereal disease and tropical ailments take their toll too, until there are almost no children left. In the back country there are only a handful in every village.

Went to Byerlee's tonight to a party. The Roberts with two babies arrived today and also Hattie Mitchell. The Roberts are new missionaries and seem like a swell couple. Had swell eats—Ray and Mr. Byerlee played chess all the time we were eating—and then we played games. About ten we said our goodbyes and went back to Coq. with the Hurts. Really hated to leave this time—we've had such a good time here.

Sunday, July 16 [Congo River]

Spent most of the night tossing restlessly on our hard narrow bunks and dreaming of our wonderful beds at Bolenge. At 5AM I heard the boat starting up, made a resolution to get up in time to see Bolenge, and fell asleep again. When I woke up the next time I pulled Ray out of bed and we threw our clothes on as we thought Bolenge was just around the next bend. We were so disappointed to find that it was Wendji! I wanted so much to have a last wave at Bolenge and Bolengeites.

Spent almost all day working on our new 35mm scenario. We got it ready to send home, late this afternoon, and then Ray wrote a letter to Rogers to go with it. He sure was hard working today!

At breakfast this morning the captain told us he had an elephant aboard. We thought he was kidding but noticed an enclosure on the lower deck. Sure enough there was a baby elephant. He is only two years old and about up to my waist. The natives built a heavy timber enclosure and fastened palm branches over it to keep the baby warm. But he's so strong he puts his head through the bars and lifts most of the heavy structure right off the deck.

Monday, July 17

Got up early to work while it is nice and cool. There was a real stiff breeze all morning and it felt swell after seven weeks on the Equator.

Passed the 'Lukula' this morning on her way to Stanleyville again and we waved and shouted our heads off. Captain Lona waved and shouted back but neither of us could understand the other at all. Ray worked on his 35mm records most of the day and got them finished.

Took a nap this afternoon as I wasn't feeling so good in the 'tummo'. Got dressed just as we docked at Bolobo for the night. It was only six o'clock so we walked up to the British mission hoping to find Miss Wilson, whom we met last year in Leo. We not only found her but also a new missionary that we met just the last time we were in Leo.

Tuesday, July 18

Loaded the camera today hoping to get a few stills as we have come into the hilly and most picturesque part of the Congo. But the sun only filtered through at rare intervals so I didn't get a picture. Was really working too hard to care much.

Wednesday, July 19 [Congo River—Leopoldville]

This is our fourth anniversary (of the day we met) and we find it very hard to believe we have only known each other that long.

We woke up this morning to find a real cold wind whipping around our cabin. The boat was pitching a little and we could hear the waves slapping the sides of the boat.

Typed a few letters for Ray in between jumps on account of the wind and got packed up. We were late getting to Leo. as the wind held us back considerably. But Lutete came down for us and even fed us dinner with ice cream! We left the crew all struggling with the baby elephant. They just couldn't get him up the gangplank.

This afternoon we went to town to buy a few things and find out about boats to Europe. We got data on French, Italian, Dutch, and Belgian lines. The young man spoke good English and was swell about looking up prices and everything for us. In the end we decided to take the Belgian boat because it is cheaper than any of the others. We will leave Matadi Aug. 4th on the new liner.

Went to bed very early as tomorrow is bound to be full of big doings. We have only fifteen more days in Congo!!

Thursday, July 20 [Leopoldville]

Woke up early and had breakfast at 6:30 with our English friends. Then we tried to find out if Godi. is still in Maluku or if he is a number of days travel away. After much fuss phoned Madimab and the State official told us that he is now at Maluku. We asked him to send for Ngonda, as he lives not far away, and have him come to Leo. today. The official agreed so we went ahead getting ready to leave the first thing tomorrow morning.

Went shopping with Lutete and down to the Otraco steamer to get tickets on the boat that we take in the morning. After the ticket was all made out we found that it cost 670 francs! Imagine, when we would only be on board a few hours and wouldn't need a cabin. We told the agent to please hold the tickets and we went out to a village to see if we could get a canoe. Had quite a palaver with the old chief and finally left 100 francs and got a promise in exchange—4 paddlers and a canoe to Maluku.

Went home for lunch and spent most of the afternoon packing and borrowing equipment from Lutete and Mr. Guthrie of the B.M.S. About 4:30 the official from Madimba phoned to say that we couldn't go without the Governor-General's permission so he didn't send Ngonda. This from the man who sent Godi. to help us make the pictures at Boko.

I was horrified to think that we were all ready, had all our food bought, and might not be able to go. We were afraid to go without permission as Godi. is one of the rare Belgian Methodists and has been subject to a great deal of persecution out here.

After supper we heard from Coxill that the Commisar of the Province thought it would be allright for us to go. He will look up any correpondence etc. in regard to photographers, spies, etc. and let us know later if it isn't allright—or send official permission. The lemon at Madimba may have trouble for his action. We hope so as he is Godi. chief and treats him like dirt.

I had to type five letters before we went to bed making arrangements for our trip to Scotland, exchange of boat tickets, and other business. Then had to type Ray's letter to Rogers and write a note to Coxill stating exactly what we wish to shoot in the Bamfununga country. Took a bath as I won't see a tub in at least nine days and went to bed quite exhausted at 10:30.

Friday, July 21 [Leopoldville—Maluku]

Arrived at the village and found the chief with our 100 francs in his hand and apparently no paddlers. We palavered around for half an hour and then agreed to pay the 4 men and chief 20 francs each and another 5 if they get us to Maluku tonight. Got our stuff packed in the dugout canoe and then went in the car to the main river. The water is so low that the little stream winding into the village is not deep enough for a heavily loaded canoe. Started out at exactly 7:25, more than an hour later than we wanted to, with the sun shining brightly. It always does when we don't want it to.

Passed a number of women with big baskets on their backs, struggling along the shore in mud nearly to their hips. They were going out to a point of land which apparently provided good fishing—but what a struggle to get there through the heavy clay-like mud.

Traveling along the shore we saw layers of strata sometimes six feet high. We could see layers of leaves—there were no trees nearby so they must have been ages old, pieces of old canoes, and other ancient flora and fauna.

Wound in and out among the many islands in Stanley Pool always keeping close to the shore to avoid strong winds and current. I leaned back on a bedding roll and slept for a bit. The string beans, potatoes, and oranges I'd shoved into the top of the sack weren't too comfortable but I was very sleepy.

Stopped at a fishing village to eat our lunch. The houses were on stilts so that the fisherman can stay awhile after the river begins to rise again. They live in their canoes then and just sleep in their houses. We've even seen them cooking in the end of a canoe. The paddlers ate lunch too, apparently getting food from the few villagers at home. One of them had brought his own cook pot with fish in it and he just put it on a fire to heat and had a regular meal.

Went on until 2:15 when we left the open water of the Pool and entered the narrow mouth of the Congo. Here the river flows between two mountain ranges and is at its narrowest. We had to cross a wide open area to get to the mouth of the river. The wind swept us along and the water was real rough. Some of the waves splashed into the boat, which isn't high above the water anyway. The paddlers call Ray "Mundele' which simply means white man. When the going is hard they sing "Ohhh, Mundele is killing us, Mundele is killing us."

All afternoon the mountains rose on either side of us. They are steeper and higher than the hills of the Hudson but so much like them in general outline that it is hard to believe we are in Africa. But it is a thrill to be paddling up the Congo with no roads or trains or even villages. The few temporary villages are widely scattered and frequently deserted.

Arrived at Maluku after some hard paddling. The wind sweeps through the river gorge and makes the going very difficult. It was just after 4 o'clock and we walked up the hill to the few houses hoping to surprize Godi. Instead we found a Mme. Bentz, who is the wife of the government sanitary agent. We managed very well with our French and found that Godi. is working in a village that we can reach tomorrow. We moved into Mme. Bentz' house—her husband is away now so she was pleased to have company. We tried to locate carriers to take our things in the morning when we go. But there just don't seem to be any. The few men in the village here all cut wood for the steamship companies. Couldn't even get a native to take a note to Godi. In fact they wouldn't even come up here after dark. The lions got a child the day before yesterday so no one will venture out after dusk.

Saturday, July 22 [Maluku—Guma]

Got up at dawn and as soon as we were dressed and packed started for Guma with the one native we were able to get. Didn't have time for breakfast but took two oranges, a few sandwiches and some water, along with us. Our guide had the job of carrying this and our still camera.

Climbed the first mountain behind Maluku just as the sun was coming up. We could look back and see the Congo dividing the great mountains of French and Belgian Congo. Climbed up and up only stopping long enough to take one still of Ray. The view at the top was worth a few minutes but we had to push on after just a glimpse of the beautiful valley. We have to reach Guma in record time so that we can send them back for our loads today. We have to have our beds and food tonight and as the natives are scared to death of the lions we'll have to give them time to make the round trip from Guma before dark.

Dropped down the mountain following the trail into a deep gorge. It was so steep toward the bottom that our feet nearly ran away with us. We crossed a little stream in the jungle valley and then started up onto the plain of the mountain again. We climbed until we were entirely breathless and felt that we couldn't go a step further. Then the trail leveled off a bit—I mean it was no longer perpendicular—and we had to keep pushing and pushing our leaden legs up the mountainside. Stopped only once to take a picture when we found that could see right over the top of our first mountain to the river beyond. There was not a sign of life as far as we could see. The Congo remained our only link with civilization. Farther on we tied the camera to a bush in order to get both of us in the picture. The self timer worked beautifully.

I must be getting very soft because my legs kept crying to stop even after we reached the high level of a plateau. It stretched as far as we could see and was covered with tall grass.

Went through little islands of trees which provided shade and refreshing moist air. Our guide gave us to understand that Guma was on the next hill so we drank the remainder of our pint of water. But we kept on and on for hours.

Finally climbed a hillock to Guma. Godi. nearly collapsed. He hadn't received the letter we sent from Bolenge and had no idea we were coming. For me to walk was almost as shocking. Few white women have ever been in here—Mrs. Bentz probably is the only one and she always travels in a tepoy. The people made quite a fuss over us and the chief dressed up and gave us the double handclasp of friendship. He's been giving it to me ever since!

Sent eleven men for our loads and were surprized when three others arrived with our cameras and beds. Mme. Bentz apparently located them and sent them with the things we wanted most. Had dinner and got right to work on our first sequence as we may not have as much sun again.

The chief arrived in his tepoy with a band and a great cheering crowd accompanying him. He was all dressed up in a feather hat, tooth necklace, fancy grass cloth, and paint on his face. The people are very picturesque and more dignified and fiercer looking than others we've seen. The men wear grass cloth draped like Roman garb. They have fancy haircombs and the elders wear goatees twisted into a ball. Men, women, and children, have rows of scars from the top of their heads to their jaws, covering the whole side of face and head.

Took a long time getting our sequence on the recruiting of laborers because Godi. got his French, English, and Lingala, all mixed up. Finished about 5 when the last ray of sunlight was fading.

The villagers all sat around Godi. hut then and the chief and a young woman danced. They were accompanied by drums and a chorus of voices. Their dancing was reall Hula Hula stuff. When it got real dark the party broke up and we had supper.

Our baggage arrived and we moved into a new hut. The natives have been building it for Godi. but when we arrived were only finishing the roof. The mud wall had not been started so they made grass walls for us in a hurry and we have a real clean and sweet smelling room.

Godi. played his Victrola for us and then we sang while he played his baby organ! Yes he actually carries it all over on his long trips through the wilds.

Sunday, July 23 [Guma]

Woke up at dawn but as the sun wasn't shining took another snooze. Were up and dressed by 7:30 and banging around trying to wake Godi. up. It was 8:30 before he appeared and said his boy didn't wake him because it is Sunday. We wanted to shoot the tax scenes this morning but the sun was so high that we decided to leave it till tomorrow. After breakfast we left Godi to do his work. He has a great deal to do in this village and we want him to finish quickly so that we can see a lot more of the Bamfununga country. He doesn't think he can get through before Tuesday night but we are trying to hurry him. The people have been called in from surrounding villages—all nearly a day's walk from here—to pay their taxes, report for census and public works, so they can't very well be left.

We laid on our cots this morning after we'd made them and both fell asleep. After about an hour I woke up because I was so cold! This plateau is

about 2,000 feet above sea level and three blankets weren't enough for me last night. This is dry season, the African winter, so it is even colder than ordinarily. The natives wear cloths wound around them so that only heads and feet are showing—unless they are in the sun. Even then they are covered pretty well by their cloths draped over a shoulder and I wonder if they won't look silly in the pictures. After all it isn't supposed to be cold in Africa.

After dinner shot the taking of the census. We have an awful time in this village because there are so many trees. The houses are fenced in little groups. All the fences have taken root and grown into trees. They cut out a lot of sunlight and when we are half through a scene the shadows invariably creep up over our actors. Poor Ray is nearly crazy moving them around so they'll be in the sun. It is slow work with Godi as he doesn't understand movie technique at all. Every detail has to be carefully explained and then he asks so many questions that we waste a lot of time in between shots. Finally finished about five and Godi went back to his work while Ray and I took spit baths in our hut.

We hear that six men were eaten by lions near here in just the last week. Maybe I'll get my arm bitten off by one after all!!

Living here is a real thrill—we are so isolated. It is even nicer than Mushenge and the people are almost as interesting. They have intelligent, although wild looking faces and many have features like ours. They say that all Africans mouths protrude farther than their noses—but they don't here. Many have the same jaw structure that we have.

Ray says the people drape their cloths just the way the Ethiopians do. We wonder if they could have come from there generations ago.

This is a real banana village. The trees are thick behind every hut in the village. Got some stills of a darling baby boy today. He was very fat and little but was able to sit up. The children develop very rapidly physically and can sit and walk much sooner than white children.

Some of the houses here are mud and sticks with grass roofs. But many are still entirely made of grass like the houses we used in 'Bwamba'.

Our tepoys are now in progress down the street. The men went a long way to the jungle where they cut straight poles and vines. They have started weaving the seats now and they look so elegant we wish we could take one home. Wouldn't it be fun to have the scouts carry us down Glenwood Rd!!

Monday, July 24

Got up at 6:30 and found Godi already at work and our watch an hour slow. Had breakfast right away and then shot the collecting of taxes. It didn't take so long this time and we launched right into a series of stills of the chief, us, some large tusks, and the construction of our tepoys. The natives are making such elegant looking tepoys that Ray decided to take a movie sequence. Spent the rest of the morning taking shots as the work progressed.

Godi was still at work so I took an hours nap until dinner time—2:30 today. Then back to our tepoys. The seats were all woven, like wicker furniture, and the boys had started a pocket on the side of mine. They said it was for a book and Ray took movies of me telling them to make it big enough for my still camera too.

Godi had a big crowd around his table this afternoon. One wild looking man had a bow and arrow that we borrowed to play with. The natives all began running and hiding behind trees and huts. They were scared to death we'd shoot one of them. Ray put an orange on his head for me to shoot at and the audience nearly died. When I shot the arrow to one side and he spilled the orange everybody went wild with glee. They thought it was just about the funniest thing they'd ever seen.

We almost broke up the census taking when Ray then jumped over five men. One said, "That man is not a man—he is a sorcerer—else he could not fly!!" Later one of the big chiefs came over and said he would like to work for Ray when he has stopped being a chief. We're supposed to reserve a place for him in the heareafter apparently.

Tuesday, July 25

Sat in our tepoys and worked this morning. They make very comfortable chairs even when down on the ground. I wrote a few thank you notes to Bolenge and Ray started to make a cover for the pocket on my tepoy. The vine the natives use is very nice to work with.

We like working with a State man. If we want anything at all we just holler 'soldat' and five or six native soldiers are johnny on the spot.

It was real cold and damp this morning but the sun came out at noon and made it just right. We didn't take any pictures as Godi was so wrapped up in his work we didn't want to disturb him.

The moon is getting brighter every night and about nine o'clock the drums begin their throbbing call. The people dance for an hour or so. I suppose they are just warming up for the time when the moon is full. The drums here have a putt putt sound that is quite different from others we've heard.

Wednesday, July 26

Got up about 7:30 when we woke up and found the sun shining into our hut. As soon as we were awake and dressed we set up a scene out in front. As we were in it we had to take Godi away from his work long enough to shoot it. Took a sequence of us in our tepoys, on the ground and the chief in full regalia visiting with us. Fixed up the interior of our hut then for some stills. We had to pull some of the grass out of the walls in order to let a little light in. Then took time exposures with the self-timer. Ray had to set the timer, dash across the room and freeze into position. As soon as the shutter closed we'd let out our supressed laughter and shrieks.

About 1:30 Godi came and broke the news that we couldn't leave today. He said half of his carriers had gone off hunting an animal for our division of the kill scene. He acted so embarrassed that we suspected the real reason was that he hadn't finished his work. After lunch when he went back to his crowd of natives we knew that was the reason. We were awfully disappointed and felt bad all the time we were putting the grass back in our walls. We are so anxious to see a lot more of the real Africa before we go home.

We haven't been able to find a medal among the scores of natives here so I had to make one, for our movies. Polished a five franc piece, which has Leopold on it, and cut up my old red and blue scarf. A bobby pinned filed short, with my nail file, made a bar at the top, and a safety pin and a little sticky tape finished it off.

Thursday, July 27 ['On the Trail']

I woke up at 5:15 and dragged Ray and myself out of bed so that we could get an early start. Woke Godi up and then packed up our beds and were ready to sail. We didn't have any eggs so ate fruit, potted ham, and jam for breakfast. The carriers arrived by seven and we were raring to start right out. But Godi still had to sign a few tax books and by the time all his stuff was ready to go two hours had fled. Finally set out amid the blood curdling yells of 81 men. They shrieked until we were well out of the village and then settled into their boisterous singing.

Traveled across the level of the plateau marveling at its vastness. The grass is dry and brown now in most places but beautiful in its shades of color. If it were rainy season the thick new growth would shut out all the view. Tassels on tall grasses pat against our faces. Sometimes thick elephant grass closes across the trail and we have to duck our heads as we push through. Its wonderful jogging along with plenty of time to enjoy the scenery. We seem to travel fast and yet see so much more than we would by any other mode of travel.

Our weight is distributed among four men and there are four extras to relieve them. So we don't feel that we are working them to death. They are aclimated and can travel a lot faster and farther in this country than we can. Still as I lean back on a pillow and watch the muscles working in my carriers backs and hear their feet shuffle-patting on the ground, I do feel a little mean.

It doesn't seem right to set ourselves above these people and make slaves out of them.

Ray's tepoy is first in line and mine is just behind. The natives make so much noise that we can hardly get a word in edgewise. We have to shriek to make each other hear but the carriers never take the hint and quiet down a little. This is our year and a half wedding monthiversary so we have all kinds of things to yell at each other. Its nice being able to shout "I love you" or anything we please (Godi is too far behind to hear).

Were traveling along when all of a sudden someone shouted and down went the tepoys. We tumbled out wondering what it was all about. The natives went dashing off pulling their cloths off as they went and splash into a bit of water in a swampy place. After baths they took drinks and then all opened their cloth shoulder bundles and dug out something to eat. Every stop is an excuse to eat it seems. One made a little gras fire with flint and stone and all threw peanuts into it, shells & all. After just a minute they pulled them out, with their tough bare hands. We wondered how they could be good with the shells just blackened a bit but found they were swell.

On again. The plain stretching ahead as far as we could see. In the hazy distance blue silhouettes of trees tried to melt into the sky. When we went down a little slope we stopped for our first caravan pictures. When we were through fussing, arranging, rehearsing, and finally shooting, once was enough for our carriers. They were thoroughly disgusted with this silly cinema stuff. Little did they know what was in store for them during the next three days.

Coming out of the tall grass we found some silky praire grass rippling in the wind. I was hypnotized by the waves of light that flowed through the plain like the waves rolling over the sea. Now I know why the days travel in a covered wagon caused real seasickness among the hardy pioneers. We had to make more movies here even though we'd just finished the others a few minutes before. While we were setting up some of the carriers with our loads sneaked off and went on ahead. We refused to shoot our caravan without all our luggage in it and had to wait for them to be called back.

The country grew increasingly more beautiful. Little rises on the plain affarded long sweeping views, stretching out and out almost to infinity. The grass is like a lovely pieve of velvet as it stretches out around us, shading from light to dark, from shining gold to deepest brown.

The boys sing and shout all the time they are on the move. The one with the loudest voice, who carries the high shrieking call, is right behind my ear. It becomes a little wearing to have such a commotion on this peaceful plateau. Sometimes they stop singing their scrambled songs and get together. Then its, "Ohhhhhhh Mama is so heavy, mama is so heavy." Unfortunately I can understand this. Ray's carriers sing something with Abba Dabba in it but we haven't been able to figure out what it is.

At 3:30 we approached the first village since Guma. Panoka was one of the loveliest we've seen and we longed to stay. We have never seen a village with as many perfect settings as this one has. I took stills of spirit houses and storehouses for maize. While the cook was fixing lunch we scouted around and found that the village was set on the very edge of the great plateau. Looking through the giant trees that spread up and out from the deep valley below us, we saw a magnificent view. When sandwiches were made and eggs boiled we sat in our tepoys in the middle of the village to eat.

Around us grass houses were artistically arranged; palms and bananas formed a perfect background; children wearing no more than a vine around their necks strung with teeth, surrounded us; and the elders looking wild and curious sat in the background. I got a piece of sugar cane to eat along the way.

Just after the sun went down we reached Kingangati, our stopping place. Ray and I had been walking a good bit and were amazed at how soon we reached our destination. Unpacked our beds and things and set up for the night in a tiny hut. Godi was surrounded with natives who'd neglected to pay their tax and worked till nine o'clock.

Friday, July 28 ['On the Trail'—Mokene]

When we got up real early, got all packed, and had breakfast by seven o'clock, we really were annoyed when Godi found some work he just had to do. The sun didn't come out, Godi didn't finish his work, and it got later and later.

Finally we decided to set up for the decorating of the chief and shoot it sun or not. As it isn't important we preferred getting it over with and spending the rest of the day traveling. Certainly we never would reach the village, where we are supposed to stay tonight, in time to shoot it there. With the help of a few policeman we got a mob of people arranged in the chosen spot, the chief in full regalia with wife and henchmen, and then we waited some more for Godi. He kept saying one minute whenever we asked him how long he'd be so we had to amuse the people while the many 'one minutes' dragged. Ray did tricks but eventually the people got tired and all went away. We were furious by this time and I went over and talked hot and hard. He came in his slow way and then it took half an hour to get the annoyed villagers together again. The sun was out by this time so at least we got better pictures. Put the medal in a box I had, with cotton, and it looked so genuine that the chief wanted to keep it. We couldn't do more than let him have the five franc piece. Imagine the trouble if he were found wearing a medal Godi had faked. Finished very quickly and got off with our 26 men regardless of Godi. We just couldn't wait around for him another minute. Left at 11:15 instead of 7:00. At this rate we will never make Leo. Sunday night.

Out on the plain again we found it much hotter than yesterday. The grasses brushing our faces sprayed us with perspiration that had wiped off the carriers faces. We had to duck every one. The grass here was twenty feet high and the trail worn low in the ground made it look even higher.

When we see a few graves on the side of the trail we know we are approaching a village. They have grass sheds over them and are decorated with pots and gourds, some containing food and water for the spirits.

At one division in the trail the caravan stopped and there was a long palaver over which one we should take. Ray finally had to decide—not knowing a thing about it—and we went on amid the cheers of half the men and groans of the rest.

Ray ran ahead of the caravan a lot to take stills. He pesters the carriers to death by continually breaking their pace and insisting that tripod, beds, etc. follow in order.

About two we went up and down some rolling hills that Ray said were perfect for a movie shot. If he were building a set it would look like this. But Godi wasn't in sight and we went ahead hoping to find more hills when he was with us. We'd want the whole caravan in such a spot so Ray couldn't take it and be in it too. We were beginning to wonder if we'd taken the wrong trail when we saw Godi coming to meet us. He had gone another way in order to inspect an emergency landing field. There are five in his territory and the men in the nearest village are supposed to keep them in good condition.

Ray could think of nothing but the hills we'd missed and Godi agreed to go back with us. We walked so the tepoy men wouldn't grumble. Ray said he could forgive Godi everything for this. But not me. I hate waiting and I abhor people who poke. Took a number of shots with the carriers gripeing and continually getting out of order. But the pictures should be worth every bit of it. When we went on again it was after four o'clock. Ray and I walked for a long time. We were in the lead and were surprized to top a small rise and find a deep valley before us. Rows and rows of hills rolled into the gorge beneath us. They were covered with soft brown grass touched with pink highlights from the setting sun. If only we were a little earlier and there was enough light. If only we had not taken the pictures in the village this morning. If only Godi had hurried. If only—that's the trouble with this movie business. We can't enjoy a beautiful place unless we can bring back the memory for others to see. If the light is good we work so hard that we haven't time to feel the beauty—to sit and let it seep through to our very souls. If the light isn't good our souls are full of lamentations and we walk along—if only, if only.

Our trail fell into the valley and wound in and out of the rounds each hill made as it dropped down from its summit. We let the long caravan wind ahead of us and as we tramped saw them, like a long train, stretching and winding before us. After a few miles the valley ended as abruptly as it began. We climbed up the last hill to the plain again, took one long last look behind, and then on across the monotonous level. But our thoughts went up and down with those velvet hills that we weren't bringing back with us, for others to see.

The sun was a red ball far down in the deep haze of the horizon and ahead the moon was riding, nearly full and brighter already than the dying sun.

Soon our carriers began to trot, to hoot and sing with renewed haste and fervor. We were nearing camp, and food, and warmth, and beds.

The village we entered was quite different from the others we've visited in this part of the country. We decided that it was very young; the bananas weren't stretching their long hands high behind the huts; the palms were young and awkward; the huts were so trim and neat. The huts are made entirely of long straight poles, vines, and grass. They are very small and set in neat rows and all through the village the plains grass has been cleared away. At dawn the children sweep the streets with brooms of palm.

Settled ourselves as it got darker and darker and then took spit baths in our tiny little house. It is hardly big enough for two cots, equipment, lantern, and us. We fell over the baggage and each other, bumped our head on the lantern, and hardly had room to open a pack. Our house is very clean and neat. Has palm mats on the floor and every grass in the wall stretches from floor to roof in a trim straight line. They are held in place by stiff vines, split in two, and tied flat along the surface of the wall. The poles of the roof are brown and shiny from the smoke of the family fire. The owner removed his belongings for the sake of these intruders but left his little fetishes hung around the top of the hut. We hope they keep the ever present roaches and rats out.

Saturday, July 29 ['On the Trail'—'In the Jungle']

Woke up at 5:30 freezing cold in spite of three blankets. The fetishes didn't work—we haven't been asleep more than three minutes. The wind was blowing right through our hut, not taking any heed of the thick grass wall. Crawled in bed with Ray and spent ten minutes getting warm and persuading him to get up.

As this is the day we are due to part from Godi we then set about learning a few essential words.

Go	kwenda
stop	Kanga
slowly	malembi
hurry up	nsuala
wait	bika ku nima
back up	vutula ku nima
bring	twala
carry	simba
no good	mbi
yes	inga
no	ve
wait for us	kwenda ku ntuala
what is the name of this village	kumba gata
put on fire	tula kutia
fire	tiya
water	maza
bananas	mankondu
oranges	malala
eggs	maki
table	mesa
chairs	biti

We felt that we could go anywhere and take pictures, eat and sleep, with these words and our every improving sign language.

After breakfast we got all the carriers out and hoped to start off shortly. It was too misty and dark to take the pictures we wanted of the caravan leaving. As usual it took a long time to get away.

The villagers turned out to see us off. They stood huddled together by their huts trying to keep out of the wind. The children are pitifully naked. Some mothers, well wrapped in cloth, hold their naked babies on their hips. When I got my monkey out everybody began running with my tepoy. By the time we were out on the plain they were well warmed up.

I finally had to hide 'Inkima' so the children would go home again. Went down into another valley of soft hills and were most unhappy because it was so dark. Ray ran ahead and took some stills of the whole caravan strung out through the valley. I hope they come out. What a movie shot it would have been.

We intended to make the suspension bridge Godi had been telling us about by lunch time. The carriers palavered about going on a longer trail in order to go to a village where they might by some food. We agreed to this thinking that the sun might come out this afternoon and we'd get better pictures of the bridge. Ate our lunch at Kinkusu where the men got their food. We were so cold that we sat around a fire and toasted our sandwiches. The men weren't a bit happy to leave their fires and cut out into the wind again.

The next village stood on a hillock in silhouette against the sky. With sun and billowy clouds it would have made a lovely picture. The men plunked down their loads here and refused to go any farther. We had quite a palaver but finally got them going again. We must reach Leo. tomorrow night even if we have to walk all the way ourselves.

On the way again they poked along so slowly. When we saw a mountain looming ahead we knew why they wanted to wait till tomorrow to tackle it. Ray and I walked and found that it wasn't a bad climb at all. Found one place for a movie shot and as the sun was looking brighter we stop for a picture. Ray made me peel off my sweater and jacket for the shot and by the time it was finished the sun was hot enough for me to leave them off.

Ray and I led through a jungle trail at the top of a mountain. Suddenly we came out of its tunnel and found ourselves staring for miles at mountains and valleys stretched beneath us, like a giant relief map. We were breathless but when Godi came up behind recovered enough to ask why on earth he hadn't told us. He let us stop half an hour or more for that last picture and so arrive at the most magnificent spot when the sun was fast dying. We took a couple of shots but felt that they couldn't be any good with the little light.

Ray said that this was the most beautiful place he'd ever seen—except the Tetons. And it topped anything I'd ever imagined.

When we started down the sun was a red ball before us. The blue haze hung low over the mountains. Beautiful to behold but treacherous on film. We hope our red filter cut through it. We would have lingered long here but with 80 men on our heels had no choice in the matter.

Stumbled down the steep trail with our eyes seeking one last glimpse of the mountains ahead. Down a long ridge with jungle creeping out of the deep gorges on either side of us. We were level with the tops of trees whose leaves we can barely make out when we're on level ground. Down through the thickening jungle, snatching at vines and bushes so that our feet wouldn't run away with us. Out in the open again we crossed some rounded hills covered with stubby grass. Here we could look back at the mountain we'd descended looming in the gathering darkness. We kept wondering where the suspension bridge was. We were to have reached it at noon, and a bit farther on left Godi while we traveled toward Leo. Came to a tiny little village where the men wanted to stop again. But we must push on if we're to reach Leo. tomorrow. Down another hill and into a swamp. A giant tree felled along the trail made a bridge over the wettest place. We balanced ourselves all the way across without falling in and felt quite proud of ourselves—until we looked back and saw the natives doing it with heavy loads and Godi's tepoy men coming across as if it were nothing. He's such a fat lump I can't understand how they carry him through the difficult places.

When a stream confronted us we got back in our tepoys so we wouldn't get our feet wet. Ray actually took a still of me here in the last light of the day. Our new film is very fast and without a filter we may have something.

Started down such a steep trail, now in the dark, that we walked again. It hasn't rained in so long that the dust is six inches deep in the path. This helped us skid down faster and we slipped and slid along, not being able to see a thing from dust and dark, and clutching wildly at passing vines. Heard water rushing madly beneath us and had visions of tearing right down into the river. Here at last we found our suspension bridge. Fifty yards it swung across the Nsele river, looking like a great bridge of steel cables in the darkness. Great long vines hung down from jungle trees on either side of the river. From these hung the bridge and our fate as cameras and equipment went over the wobbly swaying bridge. Looking back the full moon was just coming over the mountain. Oh, for sun and time!!

Climbed the approach to the bridge, made of sticks and logs, and started gingerly across. There were vines to hang on to but there wasn't much to put our feet on. The flooring was made of crosssticks but so many had broken away that only the tough vine in the center, swung from shore to shore, was fit to step on. We had to tight-rope walk this backbone of the bridge, looking down at the rushing water beneath us. It felt just as if the bridge were rushing along—not the water—and try as I might I couldn't believe we weren't traveling sideways at a great rate.

This is the Africa we imagined and today has been so especially perfect we wonder if it was all imagined too. Perhaps we'll wake up in our tepoys, still traveling over the desolate plain.

Sat on the far shore and watched the carriers feeling their way across the bridge. The moonlight glistened on the water and provided enough light for us to see the bridge in silhouette and the surrounding jungle shining green. The vines creaked and groaned under the heavy load of men and equipment and we hoped it wouldn't break as we didn't have our cameras turned on the scene.

As we waited we decided that we wanted to sleep right on the bank of the river where we sat. If the men had to have huts let them go on to a village and come back for us tomorrow.

We cornered Godisiabois and told him about it. He talked with the men and they voted to stay with us as the next village is two hours from here. All but the cook—who griped all evening.

Set up camp by the water. The men all crackled branches in the forest behind us and in no time the night was alight with little fires. Little groups gathered around each one, ate their manioc and plaintains, and huddled together for the night. Ray rigged up the flash attachment and went around taking stills of the camp. I worked hard trying to cook him a decent meal for a change.

Leo. is two days from here so we have decided to go right on to Sanda and get a car from there to Sona Bata tomorrow night. In bed I remembered that we have no 35mm camera, film, or lights, to use at Sona Bata. They're all in Leo!! What to do now??????

Sunday, July 30 ['On the Trail'—Sanda—Sona Bata—Leopoldville]

Woke up just as the sky was beginning to brighten. The men were building up their fires to combat the early morning cold and in the surrounding jungle parrots were screeching their disapproval of so many intruders. We pulled our weary eyelids open and thought about getting up in the cold. Ray had to get up first for once so he could get my clothes. I struggled with them under the covers and the eyes of 80 curious natives. They thought it was quite a joke when I emerged fully dressed.

Packed up very quickly and while Ray chose his movie settings I helped get breakfast. Ray and I ate standing up and planning pictures and then got our own carriers ready to cross the bridge again. Took one shot while Godi was eating breakfast, in his own slow way, and then got him to shoot us. The sky was so dark that we couldn't use filters at all. Too bad we couldn't have had a bit of sun for this.

As soon as we had all the pictures we wanted we started right for Sanda. Godi still had some packing to do so we left him behind.

After crossing thee small streams in the jungle we came out into open country. Here we could see mountains on every side. The enormous one we came down yesterday began slowly fading into the horizon.

After an hour or so the men stopped to palaver over a fork in the trail. One led to Sanda the other to Leo. The men were quite set on taking the one to Leo so we sat and waited for Godi. We decided this morning to go on to Sanda, as there is no hope of reaching Leo today, and trying to phone Lutete and tell him to send our equipment on the morning train tomorrow. A phone is only a chance and so is a car. If we can't get them we'll have to skip the 35mm hospital sequence. We can't walk as there wouldn't be any time left for pictures if and when we arrived and there is no phone at Sona Bata so they can't come for us.

Godi finally caught up to us and had another palaver with our men. They were set on going to Leo and we thought for a while that we were going to be left altogether. Finally the soldiers scared them into going our way. Incidentally the soldiers carry guns but have no bullets because they might shoot someone! Godi has no bullets either so they just carry empty guns!

The men went on clucking their tongues and poking along. They are like a lot of sulky little boys. Ray and I walked, hoping that they'd step it up a bit but they just kept poking and let us get far ahead of them.

Up a mountain and into thick jungle that spread across our trail and made going difficult. It was an awful job to get the tepoys through. The jungle kept reaching out and clutching hungrily at us and we wondered sometimes if we'd get free from the strong vines and bushes. When we did struggle free showers of leaves would fall on our heads from the trees above, which seemed to be quivering with anger.

Are walking through jungle most of the time, leaves slapping and stickers scratching as we fight our way up steep trails. At the level stretches on top we would ride again.

In the jungle we climbed over fallen trees, ducked vines and branches, walked long bridges over swampy places (teetering on a tree trunk bridge) and kicked at bushes sticking out in the trail. I got dropped out of my tepoy once but miracle of miracles I haven't fallen in any streams yet. Ray's carriers have the hardest time as they have to break through the overgrown trail. They haven't even a machete and if a vine can't be broken with their hands they bite it in two!

About noon we climbed one of our steepest mountains—no trees on this one—and found the village of Kingana at the top. The men all sat around fires and ate while we waited for Godi. It was nearly an hour before he arrived and still longer before we got going again. The men are about ready to desert and all quarreling. Its a good thing we didn't go on along or we'd probably be left in a bush somewhere.

Went along a ridge high above the surrounding country. The view was breathtaking even with no sun and a gray sky. When the going is easy like this the tepoy carriers have a pipe they smoke. Ray's first man calls to a friend who lights it. After a few puffs he passes it to the man in back of him. Next Ray passes it and when his two back men are through it comes on to my tepoy. After everybody has two smokes, except my last man who is allowed to keep it longer, the first man puts his pipe away till the next time. For the next half hour long streams of spit shoot out from either side of our tepoys.

We ate en route and about 5 o'clock reached Lufuti, a lovely village of 'Bwamba' huts under tall palms. Here our men sat down and declared they wouldn't go a step farther until tomorrow morning. Godi yelled around at them with no effect and we began to get worried. We didn't know just how far he was willing to push them.

After half an hour everybody got started except my tepoy carriers. I couldn't even see them around and it took a while longer to find them. All the men in the village ran off when they saw us approaching for fear they would have to relieve some of our men. They know the state man will force them to do it so they disappear when they see him coming.

Just after we left Lufuti it began to get dark. Went down a hill into the jungle and could hardly see at all. Ray and I went first hoping we wouldn't step on a boa. Out in the open again we found the sky still lit up with afterglow but where was the moon? We wondered if we'd have to use lanterns as it got darker. But in a little while the sky, which has been cloudy all day, cleared off and the moon came sailing up behind us. The country was beginning to level off now and we went up little hills of grass and down into glades of forest. The blackness of the jungle was cut by beams of moonlight—shining white gold like spotlights. The tree trunks glistened but our feet stumbled in the darkness until the moon was higher in the sky. Then we walked through pools of lights flickering as the leaves danced before the moon. We crossed many little streams, many without bridges. One large one was bridged by a tree six feet up from the water. Walking the roundness of the tree was like walking a tight rope to me and it was so far! I had to run at the end to make the shore before I fell in. Another bridge was a tiny suspension one with a single vine for a handrail and little more for feet.

At the edge of each patch of jungle we would go out of a tunnel of darkness into the bright light of the moon. The grass shone white and as we were high on a ridge we could see it shining for miles around. The mist on the distant hills looked like snow.

When the country was level for a bit we rode in our tepoys. The men got warmed up to the spirit of the night and went hooting and singing with more noise than ever. One sang, another chanted, and a third gives a shrieking Tarzon call—regular bedlam.

We were too awed by the beauty surrounding us to even talk. I laid back in my tepoy and tried to keep a picture in my eye of all we saw. This was an experience we would carry always—even without the cameras to help.

Went through another village built on a sandy hillside that shone like snow in the moonlight. The country around seemed very desolate and we couldn't imagine Sanda being very near. Finally at 9 o'clock we climbed a hill and came unexpectedly on a palm lined avenue. And there at the end of it three arched windows were lit—civilization at last.

The civilization consisted of a Catholic mission and one lone pere. He took us in and fed us—our only meal in a long time—and we felt that he was just the nicest pere we'd ever seen or heard about.

Ray and I borrowed his car and native chauffer, packed all our stuff in the back and headed for Sona Bata. We were much nearer to Leo but the bridges were down. There was no phone and only one road open which took us a long way round to Sona Bata. We fell asleep and were jerked awake at least fifty thousand times. Then at 2 AM we reached Sona Bata and woke up Freas.

He was quite delighted at our arrival. Ray jumped in the bathtub and I had some soup and started for Leo. in the mission car with Joshua driving. The road was so bumpy that I had to brace my feet and hang on with my hands— no chance of sleeping now. We ran into and killed a striped animal, cousin of a leopard I'm told. The chauffer was tickled with the free meat and when we saw an antelope he tried to hit it too.

The scenery was magnificent about two thirds of the way to Leo. Mountains all around us and in the valleys little villages set on hillocks.

At 6:30 we reached the outskirts of Leo and met the army on its way out of town. We had to sit and wait because we just couldn't get by the mob of men, trucks, etc. The boys had all their guns, blankets and equipment, ready for anything. We wondered what was up. Finally they got by us. On to the U.M.H.

Monday, July 31 [Leopoldville]

Dashed into the U.M.H. to find Lutete in my filthy clothes, with jodphurs, jacket, and hair in a wild and dirty state. Had to say hello to a number of missionaries and then got all Ray's things ready to go back to Sona Bata. Stopped long enough for a bath then. I never knew so much dirt could come off of one person. I soaked and scrubbed from top to bottom and felt like a new person.

The Wilds with their daughter Ann arrived from Loebo this morning. They are going home with us and we should have loads of fun together. All went to the customs this afternoon. I had to get a government paper for my tusk and then we went to weigh all our ivory and ebony and declare all the other curios.

Back at the U.M.H. I had time to put our room in order before supper. I feel so funny without Ray that it doesn't feel like me. Especially at meal times.

Was really thrilled when I went down to the train to meet him. It felt as if he'd been away so long. He got his pictures all right at Sona Bata. No sun for the outside shot of the hospital though.

Had a letter from Ross saying to come home the quickest and cheapest way. He beat around about the $500, said nothing definite, but wrote twice that the Committee is very much interested in all things concerned with the Project.

Tuesday, August 1

Got up late this morning as we were so tired. Had to get all our equipment packed and labeled this morning. After dinner I worked on my expenses until 2:00 when we went to customs with Lutete. We went through a lot of fuss for the cameras and film and got them all ok-ed. Then we said we had to take them on the train with us so we had the whole thing cancelled. We'll do it all over again when we get to Matadi.

Had to pay 283 francs on our curios. Most of it was for ivory, which is very expensive to export. Shipping the freight to Matadi cost even more, 350!!

Went to see Mr. Guthrie to tell him about our trip and return his equipment. Had a very interesting discussion on languages. Guthrie is the first white man who has been able to learn any of the Bamfununga language. It is all tune and the same word may mean ten things according to the tone it is said in. He demonstrated for us but it all sounded the same to us. Saw some of Guthrie's pictures enlarged to 5 x 7. He has some real good ones.

Wednesday, August 2

This afternoon walked down town to shop and get our medical passports. We had to wait a long time for the doctor—nearly an hour for a two minute examination. Had some swell ice cream and got back to the U.M.H. just in time to use the last ray of light for a picture of Lutete and his wife.

After supper paid our bill and did all the little last odd jobs. Gave Lutete a present of 100 francs for all the help he has given us. He sure is a swell guy—about tops of all the natives we've met. Went to bed when we'd packed all the rest of our stuff. Almost the last time.

Thursday, August 3 [Leopoldville—Matadi]

Woke up at 3:30 and was so excited that I couldn't go to sleep again. Lutete called us just before 5:00 and then we got up to have breakfast and get ready to go to the train. We didn't get to the station any to soon and as we had 14 pieces of baggage with us the train began to pull out before we could get it all on. Ray had thrown some in the baggage car and some was with us—but still two pieces were missing—the Bell & Howell and our file with passports etc. in it. We looked all over the car and couldn't find them. Finally decided to telephone and have them flown on the morning plane. Someone had a bright idea then and we walked through the train looking for the missing pieces on the platforms. Sure enough we found them where someone had tossed them at the last minute.

The train was not at all crowded so the Wilds and Dr. Jones sat across from us, regardless of seat numbers, and we had a grand time. I spent the morning writing the last neccessary letters regarding customs, trip to Scotland, expense accounts, etc. Ray was cutting up and had everyone in stitches the whole trip.

Everyone was too sleepy to do much but look at the scenery after that. The Crystal mountains as we neared Matadi were lovely and we wished we'd come a day earlier in order to do a little climbing.

Mr. Berg met us and took us to the Swedish Mission where we had supper and all went to bed shortly after. The boat will sail at 6:30 in the morning and Ray and I will have to be first in the customs in order to get our film sheet oked.

Friday, August 4 ["S.S. Baudouinville": Matadi—Antwerp]

Crawled out from under our last mosquito net about four AM. We jumped into our clothes, had some coffee and cake, and went right off to the customs ahead of everyone else. We had to get all cameras and film out and the official took a long time getting it all straightened out. The customs were mobbed when we finally got away as everyone had to take all their hand baggage through. The officials were pretty lax about it though. They didn't look at anything of ours but the cameras and we even had an extra one of those that they didn't know about. We were thrilled when we saw the 'Baudouinville' all lit up and looking so shiny and new. It is much bigger too than the other boats we've been on—33,000 tons. The Wilds, a Swedish couple, and Dr. Jones are all on the starboard side with us. The cabins are beautiful.

At 6:30 the boat started away from the dock but it was fully an hour before we started down river. The swift current of the Congo created a suction between boat and dock and everytime the boat got ten feet away from the dock it was pulled back again. The rear smashed into the dock the first time but after that they put bumpers out so that we hit easily. Went down for breakfast and then took some movies as we sailed down river. Dr. Jones (J.J. or Johnny Jones took them for us. Stopped at Boma where more passengers came aboard—3 single missionaries among them. Ray and I went shopping for some shoe polish and other odds and ends we need.

After dinner we left the mouth of the Congo behind and entered the real ocean at last. Our last Congo sight was a lighthouse at the mouth of the river.

[Editor's Note: Virginia Garner's diary continues for another month, re-counting the voyage to Antwerp and subsequent adventures getting passage home, with Americans fleeing Europe on the eve of World War II. Her last entry is September 5, 1939, when the Garners arrived in Boston, just one day's sail from New York.]

Garner Equipment List

Ikoflex camera
Kalart Micromatic flash-bulb detonator
Weston exposure meter (2)
Cine Kodak Special 16 mm camera
4 ½ inch lens
1–inch lens for B&H camera (f. 3.5)
Wide-angle lens (focusing mount)
Yellow filter in universal mount
Universal filter holder
Yellow-green filter in mount
Pan-ortho #2 filter in universal mount
A filter in universal mount & holder
Magazine for Cine Special (2)
1–inch lens for Cine Special
2–inch lens for Cine Special
Camera oil, lens cleaner, chamois, tissue
Bell & Howell 16mm movie camera Model 70DA
1–inch lens for B&H (f. 1.8)
15-mm lens for B&H (f. 2.8)
Supplementary lens for B&H view finder
Herbert & Huesgen tripod
Stanrite tripod
Cine Kodak Special tripod
35 mm Bell & Howell Eyemo camera
2–inch lens for Eyemo (f. 2.5)
North East reflectors (4)
#2 Photoflood lamps (16)

105 100-ft. 16 mm rolls Eastman Panchromatic reversal film
35 100-ft. 16 mm rolls Eastman Supersensitive reversal film
One dozen half-minute flares
One dozen one-minute flares
45 100 ft. 35 mm rolls Dupont Superior Pan. negative film
150 rolls #120 Agfa Super-pan film
150 rolls #120 Agfa Fino-pan film
Changing bag
#1 super flash photo lamps (60)
Adapter for tripod
Tripods for North East reflectors (2)
Complete developing kit
Tool kit
White duck reflector cloths (2)
Oiled silk pouches (4)

Film Scenario:
"A Day in an African Village"

Title and Scene Nos.		Description
T 1		A DAY IN AN AFRICAN VILLAGE
T 2		(credit titles)
S 1	LS	Sunrise (fade in)
S 2	LS	Congo village in early morning
S 3	MS	Group of huts in village—people coming out and sitting around grass fires
S 4	SCU	Family around fire
S 5	SCU	Man by fire
T 3		THE AFRICAN BEGINS THE DAY'S WORK ON AN EMPTY STOMACH.
S 6	MS	People leaving village to begin days work
T 4		THE WORK OF MEN AND WOMEN IN THE TRADITIONAL LIFE OF AN AFRICAN VILLAGE IS DIVIDED ACCORDING TO LONG-STANDING CUSTOM.
S 7	MS	Series of shots of men burning off a field (taken at Mutoto)
T 5		THE AGRICULTURE, PRACTICED BY EVERY TRIBE, NECESSITATES CLEARING NEW PLANTATIONS EVERY FEW YEARS. A FEW WEEKS AFTER BURNING THE NEW GROWTH IS CLEARED OFF AND THE SOIL PREPARED FOR PLANTING.
S 8	MS	Men clearing off new growth
S 9	SCU	Same
S 10	MS	Men hoeing the manioc beds
S 11	SCU	Old man hoeing
T 6		ALL THE PROVISION OF FOOD FROM PLANTING TO COOKING IS DONE BY THE WOMEN.
S 12	MS	Group of women planting manioc shoots
T 7		MANIOC, THE STAPLE FOOD OF CENTRAL AFRICA, GROWS WILD IN MOST LOCALITIES BUT PLANTATIONS ARE ESTABLISHED IN ORDER TO INSURE A CONSTANT AND CONVENIENT SUPPLY.

Title and Scene Nos.		Description
S 13	MS	Group of women planting manioc
S 14	MS	Same—one woman with baby tied on back
S 15	CU	Baby sleeping on woman's back
S 16	MS	Women moving away from camera—planted manioc in foreground
T 8		'PLANTING' CONSISTS OF MERELY STICKING A TWIG OF WILD MANIOC IN THE GROUND. THE TROPICAL CLIMATE DOES THE REST.
S 17	CU	Manioc sticks planted in the ground
S 18	LS	Cultivated field of manioc—fetish in foreground
T 9		A FETISH OBTAINED FROM THE WITCH DOCTOR IS BELIEVED TO PROTECT THE CROP AND INSURE A GOOD HARVEST.
S 19	CU	Fetish
T 10		DAILY, THE WOMEN GO THROUGH THE COMPLICATED PROCESS OF PREPARING THE MANIOC FOR THEIR FAMILIES.
S 20	MS	Woman and child digging manioc roots
S 21	SCU	Woman removing roots and handing to child
S 22	MS	Woman at lake peeling manioc and putting it in water to soak
T 11		LONG AGO THE AFRICAN DISCOVERED THAT THIS POISONOUS ROOT COULD BE MADE EDIBLE AND NOURISHING BY SOAKING IN WATER.
S 23	SCU	Woman peeling manioc and throwing into water
S 24	CU	Manioc soaking
S 25	SCU	Little girl peeling and nibbling on soaked manioc
S 26	LS	Woman carrying manioc on head to village
S 27	LS	Woman arriving at hut and putting manioc on rack to dry
S 28	SCU	Woman putting manioc on rack
T 12		AFTER DRYING IN THE SUN THE ROOTS ARE CUT UP AND POUNDED INTO A FINE FLOUR.
S 29	SCU	Woman and child cutting up manioc
S 30	CU	Child cutting manioc
S 31	CU	Manioc in basket
S 32	MS	Three women pounding manioc
S 33	CU	Sticks pounding manioc into flour
S 34	SCU	Women pounding
S 35	MS	Woman sifting manioc flour—little girl tasting it
S 36	SCU	Same
S 37	CU	Sifted flour going into basket
T 13		THE FLOUR IS MIXED WITH HOT WATER TO FORM A BALL OF THICK MUSH, THE AFRICAN'S STAFF OF LIFE.
S 38	MS	Woman putting flour into pot of hot water on fire
S 39	SCU	Woman mixing mush with a stick—holding pot with feet
S 40	CU	Stick mixing mush
S 41	SCU	Woman putting finished mush into pot
S 42	CU	Rolling mush in bowl to make a ball of it
T 14		CUTTING THE FRUIT OF THE OIL PALM IS A MAN'S JOB.
S 43	MS	Man climbing palm tree
S 44	MS	Man climbing
S 45	MS	Man approaching head of palm tree
S 46	SCU	Man chopping at cluster of nuts

Title and Scene Nos.		Description
S 47	LS	Cluster of nuts falling from tree
S 48	SCU	Cluster hitting ground
S 49	CU	Cluster of palm nuts
T 15		PALM OIL EXTRACTED FROM THE NUTS IS AN IMPORTANT ITEM OF THEIR MEAGER DIET.
S 50	MS	Group extracting palm oil from nuts
S 51	SCU	Man chopping nuts from cluster
S 52	SCU	Woman separating nuts
S 53	CU	Woman throwing nuts into basket
S 54	SCU	Woman cooking nuts
S 55	CU	Putting nuts into pot on fire
S 56	CU	Woman pouring cooked nuts from pot into strainer
S 57	CU	Woman putting nuts into mortar
S 58	SCU	Pounding pulp from nuts
S 59	SCU	Woman putting pulp into water
S 60	CU	Woman stirring mixture
S 61	SCU	Skimming oil from surface of water
S 62	CU	Woman's hands skimming oil from water
T 16		THE OIL IS PURIFIED BY BOILING.
S 63	CU	Oil boiling on fire
S 64	MS	Little girl brings gourd for oil as woman removes pot from fire
S 65	CU	Pouring finished oil into small gourd
T 17		BESIDES BEING USED AS A FOOD GREAT QUANTITIES OF PALM OIL ARE SOLD COMMERCIALLY TO BE USED IN THE PRODUCTION OF SOAP.
S 66	CU	Oil pouring into gourd
S 67	LS	Station of soap company, European official and Africans
S 68	MS	Selling palm oil
S 69	CU	Same
T 18		AFRICAN CRAFTSMANSHIP IS EXCEPTIONAL FOR SO PRIMITIVE A PEOPLE BUT IS USUALLY LIMITED TO ARTICLES OF NECESSITY.
S 70	LS	Village street—men working
S 71	MS	Man weaving a mat
S 72	SCU	Hands binding edge of mat
S 73	CU	Hands binding
S 74	MS	Man making fish trap
S 75	SCU	Same
S 76	MS	Man finishing trap and showing it to boy
T 19		SPLIT JUNGLE VINES ARE MADE INTO AN EFFECTIVE SNARE FOR CATCHING FISH.
S 77	SCU	Boy putting hand into door of fish trap
S 78	MS	Series of shots of pottery making
S 79	MS	Series of shots of blacksmithing
T 20		IN THICKLY POPULATED SECTIONS GAME ANIMALS HAVE BECOME SCARCE AND SO A KILL IS JOYFULLY WELCOMED BY THE MEAT HUNGRY AFRICAN.
S 80	LS	Hunters coming across plain with animal slung on pole
S 81	CU	Animal's head
S 82	MS	Men carrying animal, singing
S 83	MS	Men arriving at village with kill—people excitedly gathering around

Title and Scene Nos.		Description
T 21		CUSTOM GOVERNS THE DIVISION OF THE MEAT. CERTAIN PORTIONS GO TO THE CHIEF AND THE HUNTER BUT ALL HAVE A SHARE.
S 84	MS	Hunters presenting chief with his portion
S 85	MS	Group receiving portions of meat in native pots
S 86	SCU	Hand putting meat in pots
T 22		IN LAKES, WHERE SCHOOLS OF FISH ARE FOUND, THE MEN USE SPEARS AS WELL AS TRAPS AND NETS.
S 87	LS	Men in dugout canoe hunting school of fish
S 88	MS	Man plunging spear into school of fish
S 89	MS	Man spearing fish
S 90	SCU	Lifting fish up and putting it in boat
S 91	CU	Fish being speared
S 92	MS	Boat moving away, man still spearing for fish
S 93	LS	Men bringing fish up from lake
S 94	MS	Men taking fish into village
T 23		LATE IN THE AFTERNOON THE AFRICAN EATS HIS ONLY MEAL.
S 95	MS	Three men sitting in front of hut—woman and child bring food in
S 96	SCU	Men washing hands
S 97	CU	Men's hands digging into shima (manioc) and rolling it into ball
S 98	CU	Hand rolling shima into ball
S 99	SCU	Men reaching for fish to eat with shima
S 100	CU	Hand taking fish
T 24		THE AFRICAN IS HOSPITABLE TO STRANGERS. A MAN WHO HAS GONE FAR FROM HIS TRIBE TO WORK FOR EUROPEANS WILL OFTEN FIND SHELTER WITH ANOTHER TRIBE ON HIS WAY HOME.
S 101	LS	Traveler, with trunk on head, nearing village
S 102	MS	Traveler approaching hut where men are eating—he sets down trunk and they greet him.
S 104	SCU	Traveler shaking hands with villagers
S 105	LS	Other villagers gathering to greet traveler
T 25		MANY YOUNG AFRICANS TODAY LEAVE THEIR HOMES TO WORK IN MINES OR TOWNS. BY THIS AND OTHER INFLUENCES THE TRADITIONAL PATTERN OF VILLAGE LIFE IS NOW BEING CHANGED.
S 106	SCU	Traveler showing zipper bag to group
S 107	CU	Same
S 108	SCU	Traveler gives bag to villager who is pleased with zipper
S 109	SCU	Bag passed on to old man who looks disapproving
S 110	CU	Old man shaking his head
T 26		WHAT A CONTRAST THIS IS TO THE DAYS WHEN MEN WALKED IN FEAR AND HAD TO AVOID ALL VILLAGES BECAUSE OF TRIBAL WARS.
S 111	LS	Traveler being shown to hut—boy bringing food
S 112	SCU	Traveler sits down to eat
S 113	CU	Traveler eating
T 27		DESPITE THE INFLUENCES OF CIVILIZATION THE AFRICAN STILL CLINGS TO MANY OF HIS OLD CUSTOMS.
S 114	MS	Wild dancing around fire at night
T 28		THE END

About Virginia
and Ray Garner

Virginia Garner (1915–2007) and her new husband, **Ray Garner** (1913–1989), embarked upon their 50-year career as documentary film makers with the Africa Motion Picture Project, producing ten short films in 1938–39. The Harmon Foundation continued to support their work for the next 18 years. Films included *How to Fly a Light Airplane*, shot at Tuskegee Institute; *The*

Mountain, featuring Virginia climbing the Grand Teton; and *Exploring the Southwest*, filmed in what is now Canyonlands National Park. Virginia's photographs appeared in *Arizona Highways* and *National Geographic*.

Virginia and Ray refined their "portraits in music" technique as they moved to color films with orchestral soundtracks, culminating in two hour-long "Ancient World" films, *Egypt* and *Greece*.

Ray directed eight specials for NBC-TV, most notably *The Way of the Cross*, *Vincent Van Gogh: A Self-Portrait*, and *The River Nile*, which won the 1962 Directors Guild Award for Outstanding Directorial Achievement. While in Israel for NBC, he and Virginia produced their own films, *Kibbutz Dafna* and *Land of the Book*.

The Garners made seven films for the Idyllwild Arts Foundation (California), beginning with *The Touches of Sweet Harmony*, shot in Scandinavia with the Youth Symphony Orchestra. Virginia taught photography at Idyllwild Arts and ran Elderhostel programs featuring their "Ancient World" films. After Ray's death in 1989, Virginia devoted herself to producing a photographic history of Idyllwild Arts.